BEREAVEMENT

BEREAVEMENT
Personal Experiences and
Clinical Reflections

Edited by
Salman Akhtar and Gurmeet S. Kanwal

KARNAC

First published in 2017 by
Karnac Books Ltd
118 Finchley Road
London NW3 5HT

Copyright © 2017 to Salman Akhtar and Gurmeet S. Kanwal for the edited collection, and to the individual authors for their contributions.

The rights of the contributors to be identified as the authors of this work have been asserted in accordance with §§ 77 and 78 of the Copyright Design and Patents Act 1988.

All rights reserved. No part of this publication may be reproduced, stored in a retrieval system, or transmitted, in any form or by any means, electronic, mechanical, photocopying, recording, or otherwise, without the prior written permission of the publisher.

British Library Cataloguing in Publication Data

A C.I.P. for this book is available from the British Library

ISBN-13: 978-1-78220-491-6

Typeset by Medlar Publishing Solutions Pvt Ltd, India

Printed in Great Britain by TJ International Ltd, Padstow, Cornwall

www.karnacbooks.com

To

the memory of a good friend and great poet

Nida Fazli (1938–2016)
                        SA

the memory of my father

Piara Singh Kanwal (1928–2015)
                        GSK

CONTENTS

ACKNOWLEDGMENTS ix

ABOUT THE EDITORS AND CONTRIBUTORS xi

INTRODUCTION xvii

PROLOGUE

CHAPTER ONE
Bereavement: the spectrum of emotional reactions 3
Salman Akhtar

SPECIFIC SITUATIONS

CHAPTER TWO
Death of mother 33
Kerry L. Malawista

CHAPTER THREE
Death of father 57
Thomas Wolman

CHAPTER FOUR
Death of sibling 83
Frederick H. Lowy

CHAPTER FIVE
Death of spouse 97
Ruth H. Livingston

CHAPTER SIX
Death of child 117
Ann G. Smolen

CHAPTER SEVEN
Death of pet 143
Christie Platt

EPILOGUE

CHAPTER EIGHT
Death: the last chapter 169
Gurmeet S. Kanwal

REFERENCES 191

INDEX 207

ACKNOWLEDGMENTS

We are deeply grateful to the distinguished colleagues who contributed to this volume. We appreciate their effort, their sacrifice of time, and their patience with our requirements, reminders, and requests for revisions. One of us (SA) wishes to thank Drs. Rajnish Mago and Stephen Schwartz for helpful comments on this project. The other (GSK) wishes to thank his wife, Bari, for putting up with a preoccupied husband, and for always being his first editor. Both of us are thankful to Jan Wright for her skillful help in preparing the manuscript of this book, and to Oliver Rathbone and Kate Pearce of Karnac Books for their unerring support of this project throughout various phases of publication.

Salman Akhtar & Gurmeet S. Kanwal

ABOUT THE EDITORS AND CONTRIBUTORS

Salman Akhtar, MD, is professor of psychiatry at Jefferson Medical College and a training and supervising analyst at the Psychoanalytic Center of Philadelphia. He has served on the editorial boards of all the three major psychoanalytic journals, namely, the *International Journal of Psychoanalysis*, the *Journal of the American Psychoanalytic Association*, and the *Psychoanalytic Quarterly*. His more than 300 publications include seventeen books—*Broken Structures* (1992), *Quest for Answers* (1995), *Inner Torment* (1999), *Immigration and Identity* (1999), *New Clinical Realms* (2003), *Objects of Our Desire* (2005), *Regarding Others* (2007), *Turning Points in Dynamic Psychotherapy* (2009), *The Damaged Core* (2009), *Comprehensive Dictionary of Psychoanalysis* (2009), *Immigration and Acculturation* (2011), *Matters of Life and Death* (2011), *The Book of Emotions* (2012), *Psychoanalytic Listening* (2013), *Good Stuff* (2013), *Sources of Suffering* (2014), and *No Holds Barred* (2016)—as well as forty-two edited or coedited volumes in psychiatry and psychoanalysis. Dr. Akhtar has delivered many prestigious addresses and lectures including, most recently, the inaugural address at the first IPA-Asia Congress in Beijing, China (2010). Dr. Akhtar is the recipient of the *Journal of the American Psychoanalytic Association*'s Best Paper of the Year Award (1995), the Margaret Mahler Literature Prize (1996), the American Society of Psychoanalytic

Physicians' Sigmund Freud Award (2000), the American College of Psychoanalysts' Laughlin Award (2003), the American Psychoanalytic Association's Edith Sabshin Award (2000), Columbia University's Robert Liebert Award for Distinguished Contributions to Applied Psychoanalysis (2004), the American Psychiatric Association's Kun Po Soo Award (2004), the Irma Bland Award for being the Outstanding Teacher of Psychiatric Residents in the country (2005), and the Nancy Roeske Award (2012). Most recently, he received the Sigourney Award (2013), which is the most prestigious honor in the field of psychoanalysis. Dr. Akhtar is an internationally sought speaker and teacher, and his books have been translated in many languages, including German, Turkish, and Romanian. His interests are wide and he has served as the film review editor for the *International Journal of Psychoanalysis*, and is currently serving as the book review editor for the *International Journal of Applied Psychoanalytic Studies*. He has published eight collections of poetry and serves as a scholar-in-residence at the Inter-Act Theatre Company in Philadelphia.

Gurmeet S. Kanwal, MD, is clinical associate professor of psychiatry at the Weill Medical College of Cornell University, New York, where he teaches and supervises residents at the Payne Whitney Psychiatric Clinic. He is supervising psychoanalyst and a member of the teaching faculty at the William Alanson White Institute of Psychiatry, Psychology and Psychoanalysis, and past president of the William Alanson White Psychoanalytic Society. He is on the editorial boards of the *International Journal of Psychoanalysis* and *Psychoanalytic Discourse*. His recent papers have appeared in *Psychoanalytic Review* and *Neuropsychoanalysis*. He has also blogged for the *Psychoanalysis 3.0/Psychology Today* website, and lectured in New Delhi, India, on interpersonal psychoanalysis. His areas of interest include culture, trauma, and the interface of neuroscience and psychoanalysis. Currently he is in full time private practice in New York City.

Ruth H. Livingston, PhD, is the coeditor-in-chief of *Contemporary Psychoanalysis*, the journal of the William Alanson White Psychoanalytic Society and the William Alanson White Institute in New York City. A graduate of Columbia University, she trained as an analyst at the White Institute. Dr. Livingston, who specializes in working with chronically and acutely medically ill patients, is the cofounder and codirector of the Living with Medical Conditions Study Group at the Institute, and has served as a member of the APA Division 39 Health Committee. She holds a certificate in bioethics and medical humanities from Montefiore Medical Center/Albert Einstein College of Medicine and Cardozo Law School/Yeshiva University. As a supervisor, she works at the White Institute, the Graduate Center of the City University of New York (CUNY), and Columbia University Teachers College where she is also an adjunct professor. Dr. Livingston's writings have appeared in *Contemporary Psychoanalysis*, *Psychotherapy*, the *Journal of Religion and Health*, in the *New York Times*, as well as in several edited books. She is currently working on a book about her experience in psychoanalytically informed treatment of the medically ill.

Frederick H. Lowy, MD, is emeritus president and vice-chancellor of Concordia University, as well as emeritus professor and former chairman of the Department of Psychiatry, University of Toronto. In addition to a fifty year career as a psychiatrist and psychoanalyst, he has been active as an academic administrator: dean of the Faculty of Medicine and founding director of the Centre for Bioethics at the University of Toronto; director of the Clarke Institute of Psychiatry; and, for twelve years, president and vice-chancellor of Concordia University in Montreal, Quebec. A medical graduate of McGill University, he trained in psychiatry at the University of Cincinnati and in psychoanalysis at the Canadian Institute of Psychoanalysis in Montreal. Also notable among his professional activities were: editorship of the *Canadian Journal of Psychiatry*, chairmanship of the Pharmaceutical Inquiry of Ontario and chief examiner in psychiatry for the Royal College of Physicians and Surgeons (the Canadian Board of Specialists). His research interests and publications have ranged from sleep and dream states through bioethics to clinical psychiatry and psychoanalysis. Now retired from clinical practice, he continues to follow the literature in these fields. Dr. Lowy has been awarded three honorary degrees and is an Officer of the Order of Canada.

Kerry L. Malawista, MSW, PhD, is a training and supervising analyst at the Contemporary Freudian Society and cochair of *New Directions in Writing* at the Washington Center for Psychoanalysis. She is a permanent faculty member at the Contemporary Freudian Society and has taught at George Washington University Psychology Doctoral Program,

Virginia Commonwealth University, and Smith College School of Social Work. She is the coauthor of *Wearing My Tutu to Analysis and Other Stories* (2011) and coeditor of *The Therapist in Mourning: From the Faraway Nearby* (2013), both with Columbia University Press. Her book, coedited with Robert Winer, *Who's Behind the Couch: The Heart and the Mind of the Psychoanalyst*, will be published by Karnac Books, 2017. She has published many scientific papers and book chapters. Her essays have appeared nationally in newspapers, magazines, and literary journals including *The New York Times*, *The Washington Post*, *Zone 3*, *Washingtonian Magazine*, *Voice*, and *The Account Magazine*. She is a regular contributor to *The Huffington Post*. She is in private practice in Potomac, MD and McLean, VA.

Christie Platt, PhD, is a psychoanalyst and clinical psychologist in Washington, DC. Her private practice encompasses a diverse population including university students, adult professionals, and veterans of both the Iraq and Afghanistan wars. Dr. Platt's writings on intersubjectivity, issues of race and ethnicity, and the arts, have been published in various publications including the *American Journal of Psychoanalysis*. A teaching analyst at the Baltimore Washington Center for Psychoanalysis, she received her doctorate from the California School of Professional Psychology in Berkeley, CA. Dr. Platt is currently writing a memoir about the year she hitchhiked 9,000 miles on her way from Cape Town, South Africa to Cairo, Egypt.

Ann G. Smolen, PhD, is a supervising and training analyst in child, adolescent, and adult psychoanalysis at the Psychoanalytic Center of Philadelphia. Dr. Smolen graduated *summa cum laude* from Bryn Mawr College and received her master's degree in social work from Bryn Mawr College School of Social Work and Social Research. She received her doctorate in philosophy from the Clinical Social Work Institute in Washington, DC. Her first profession was as a member of the New York City Ballet. Dr. Smolen has won several national awards for her clinical work, and has presented her clinical work both nationally and internationally. Dr. Smolen has published several articles including *Boys Only! No Mothers Allowed*, published in the *International Journal of Psychoanalysis* and translated into three languages. Dr. Smolen is the author of *Mothering Without a Home: Representations of Attachment Behaviors in*

Homeless Mothers and Children (Aronson, 2013). She maintains a private practice in child, adolescent, and adult psychotherapy and psychoanalysis in Ardmore, PA.

Thomas Wolman, MD, was born and raised in New York City. He attended Johns Hopkins University and the Pennsylvania State University Medical College. Subsequently he trained at the Psychoanalytic Center of Philadelphia, where he now teaches in both the psychoanalytic and psychotherapy training programs. Currently he holds the title of clinical assistant professor of psychiatry at the University of Pennsylvania School of Medicine. He has written on Winnicott, Mahler, Kohut, and Lacan, as well as on contemporary film and literary themes. He is working on a book about the character Meursault in *L'étranger*, by Albert Camus.

INTRODUCTION

This book came out of an exchange that we (S.A. and G.K.) had soon after one of us had lost an important person in his life to death. While sharing sorrow, we stumbled upon questions that intrigued us and whose answers we did not know. For instance, does the grief over losing one's mother differ from losing one's father? Do women grieve differently than men? Can children mourn? And, if so, how is their mourning different from that of adults? What other pathways, besides the "celebrated" mourning and melancholia, are available to modify the anguish of the bereaved? Is the grief over one's child's death ever resolvable? And, what does "resolution" of grief mean anyway? It was the encounter with such questions that led us to undertake putting this book together.

We enlisted six distinguished colleagues to help sort out the ambiguities in the realm of bereavement and mourning. We requested them to write about one particular loss (death of mother, father, sibling, spouse, child, and pet) and to include both their personal experience with it and their clinical understanding of it. This was no easy request. We were asking our colleagues not only to share their expertise but also their personal stories of bereavement and grief. While some of them had experiences going back many years, others were still freshly immersed in their loss. However, we knew that only with such a unique collection of essays that brings together subjective experience and the existing psychoanalytic literature could we hope to shed a fresh light on the varied nature of grief and its normative and complicated unfolding.

Now, before raising the curtain of the stage where the six poignant scenarios of grief are played out, we wish to say a few words about the confusing relationship between the three designations, namely bereavement, mourning, and grief. As we surveyed their dictionary meanings and psychoanalytic usage, we found that sometimes they are used interchangeably and at other times they are distinguished from each other. "Bereavement" seemed to be more specifically linked with death than either "mourning" or "grief," which are used in connection with losses and separations of other kinds as well. "Mourning" is used in a more generalized manner in the Kleinian and developmentally oriented analytic literature to denote the renunciation of infantile omnipotence and the shift from pleasure principle to reality principle. But "mourning" is also used in connection with death. Grief, on the other hand, is synonymous with mourning for some authors and constitutes the initial stage of mourning for others. Some authors reserve "mourning" for a process that has been successful, while others do not. And, finally, there are authors who regard bereavement, grief, and mourning as a three-step process.

Attempting to extricate ourselves from such a lexical conundrum while conceding that we might lapse into imprecision from time to time, we selected "bereavement" instead of "mourning" or "grief" for the title of our book and as the core motif for our conceptualizations. Our choice was based upon the polysyllabic somberness of the word and its phonic kinship (with prominent "b"s and "r"s) with burial and also upon its tight linkage with death. And, that's what our book is all about: death. Although, for obvious existential and clinical reasons, it explores the subjectivity of those left behind, those still living, and those suffering from pain. The hope of course is that doing so will help transform their suffering into richer and more meaningful perspectives on life.

PROLOGUE

CHAPTER ONE

Bereavement: the spectrum of emotional reactions

Salman Akhtar

Most adults encounter the death of a loved one in the course of their lives. They might lose a parent, a sibling, a spouse, a friend, or, in an event that is as searing as it is unfathomable, they might lose an offspring to death. All such losses are painful and even when their occurrence had been expected for a while, the consequent alterations in the intrapsychic economy and external life can be challenging. A chain of emotional reactions is set in motion, which is often accompanied by shifts in one's sense of personal identity and in one's relationship to others. One does recover from the laceration but is no longer the same person. This is the essence of bereavement.

The nuances of this process constitute the topic of my contribution. I will begin by delineating the affective and cognitive aspects of normal grief. Following this, I will delineate the psychosocial variables that can complicate this process. Then, I will discuss the frozen and maladaptive forms of grief, as well as other pathological responses to losing someone to death. I will also elucidate the implications of the foregoing material to the conduct of psychotherapy and psychoanalysis. And, in conclusion, I will highlight the areas that merit further scrutiny and unresolved questions that still exist in this realm.

Normal reaction to bereavement

Freud's views

Early on in his career, Freud made important observations regarding emotional reactions to the loss of a loved one. He noted, for instance (1893), that mourning can precipitate neurotic symptomatology and that "melancholia consists in mourning over the loss of the libido" (1893, p. 201). The latter remark implied that normal mourning refers to the loss of a love object and abnormal mourning refers to the loss of the self's loving quality ("libido") that goes with the lost object. Yet another early remark by Freud (1896) pertained to the self-directed reproaches that often appear after parental death and are due to unacknowledged hostility towards them.

These passing observations were elaborated by him twenty-two years later in "Mourning and Melancholia". In that seminal contribution, Freud (1917e) made the following observations about grief:

- "The mood of mourning [is] a 'painful' one" (p. 244).
- "Disturbance of self-regard is absent in mourning" (p. 245).
- "Reality testing has shown that the love object no longer exists and it proceeds to demand that all libido shall be withdrawn from its attachments to that object. This demand arouses understandable opposition" (p. 244).
- "Normally, respect for reality gains the day. Nonetheless, its orders can not be obeyed at once. They are carried out bit by bit, at a great expense of time and cathectic energy, and in the meantime the existence of the lost object is psychically prolonged" (pp. 244–245).
- "When the work of mourning is completed, the ego becomes free and uninhibited again" (p. 245).

Freud emphasized that loss of interest in daily activities on the part of a grieving individual is due to the "work of mourning," whereby "each single one of the memories and expectations in which the libido is bound to the object is brought up and hyper-cathected, and detachment of the libido is accomplished in respect of it" (p. 245). Thus, Freud laid down the foundations of how the phenomenology of grief is described in contemporary literature, regardless of whether it be "scientific" or "popular." The important features of such phenomenology are (i) affect of mental pain, (ii) idealization of the lost object, (iii) a piecemeal process, and (iv) the "freedom" of ego from the lost object (and, presumably, the capacity to find a substitute) at the end of mourning.

Freud's portrayal of mourning was superb and yet left many areas untouched. For instance, his paper (i) makes no mention of the impact of the age of the bereaved upon the mourning process, (ii) pays little attention to the gender of the bereaved, (iii) makes no distinction between the loss of mother, father, sibling, spouse, and child, (iv) does not mention the average duration of normal grief, and (v) concludes with the questionable proposal that, at the end of the mourning period, the lost object is decathected, which implies that it is forgotten or at least retains little emotional value for the bereaved.

Now, in all fairness, it should be acknowledged that eight years *before* writing "Mourning and Melancholia," Freud had explicitly declared that "a normal period of mourning would last one or two years" (1909d, p. 180). And, twelve years *after* his seminal work, he had softened the idea of object-decathexis at the end of mourning. In a letter to the Swiss psychiatrist, Ludwig Binswanger (1881–1966), whose son had died, Freud spoke of grief in the following terms:

> We know that the acute sorrow we feel after such a loss will run its course, but also that we will remain inconsolable, and will never find a substitute. No matter what may come to take its place, even should it fill that place completely, it yet remains something else. And that is how it should be. It is the only way of perpetuating a love that we do not want to abandon. (Freud, 1929, cited in Fichtner, 2003, p. 196)

Whether Freud was so moved only because the death of a son was involved or whether this statement simply reflects one of the many instances of difference between the "official" and "private" views of Freud is hard to conclude. Suffice it to say that the letter opens up the possibility that, at the end of mourning, the lost object is not "replaced" but "re-placed," that is, psychically relocated and differently invested in terms of emotions.

Subsequent contributions

Prominent among post-Freudian contributions is Lindemann's (1944) pioneering descriptive work on "acute grief" among 101 individuals who had recently faced the death of a loved one. Almost all of them reported having waves of somatic distress lasting from twenty minutes to an hour at a time; this included tightness of throat, dyspnoea, sighing, lack of muscular strength, and a sinking feeling in the pit of the stomach.[1] They had no appetite and, though their sensorium was clear, they felt unreal. Over the course of time, there often appeared the "traits of the deceased in the behaviour of the bereaved" (p. 142).

Another important contributor to the understanding of grief was Pollock (1961, 1966, 1968, 1970, 1971, 1972, 1978a), who meticulously delineated this "mourning-liberation process." He regarded mourning as "a universal adaptational series of intrapsychic operations occurring as sequential successive stages involved in the re-establishment of a new level of internal or related external equilibrium" (1978a, p. 262). Pollock divided the work of mourning into an acute stage (moving successively from shock reaction through grief reaction to separation reaction) and chronic stage (which manifested various adaptive mechanisms to integrate the experience of loss with the reality of ongoing life). He stated that the pain of the early stage reflected an automatic reaction to the love object's absence, while the pain of the chronic stage reflected the realization that there is no longer any hope that the lost object will meet the mourner's needs. Pollock emphasized that while the process is mostly unidirectional, the various stages oscillate and, at times, revert back temporarily to earlier stages as part of the back and forth transformational process. His unique contribution resides in his forging links between mourning and creativity. In his view, creative work is sometimes used in the service of mourning itself but more often it is the end-product of successful mourning.[2] Pollock (1978a) declared that:

> This end result can be a great work of art, music, sculpture, literature, poetry, philosophy or science, where the creator has the spark of genius or talent that is not related to mourning per se. Indeed the creative product may reflect the mourning process in theme, style, form, content and it may itself stand as a memorial. In the less gifted—and we have seen this in many clinical situations—a creative outcome may be manifested in a new real relationship, the ability to feel joy, satisfaction, a sense of accomplishment or newer sublimations that reflect a successful resolution of the mourning process. In some individuals, great creativity may not be the outcome of the successfully completed mourning process but may be indicative of attempts at completing the

mourning work. These creative attempts may be conceptualized as restitution, reparation, discharge or sublimation. Though they may not always be successful in terms of mourning work solutions, the intrinsic aesthetic or scientific merit of the work still may be great despite the failure of mourning completion. (p. 267)

Pollock traced the link between loss and creativity to Melanie Klein's (1929) specific observation that drawing and painting can be used to repair a psychological injury and to her overall concept of "reparation" (1940), whereby the child, becoming increasingly aware of his destructive impulses towards his love objects, attempts to restore their integrity and goodness.[3] Pollock also noted that the mourning process is regulated, in part, by the cultural and religious surround of the bereaved. He declared that mourning can have four outcomes: (i) normal resolution, (ii) arrest at one or the other phase of the process, (iii) regression to unresolved earlier stages of development, and (iv) depressive states. Pollock observed that "anniversary reactions" (a term originally coined by Hilgard in 1953) include "flare-ups" of grief and generally are a manifestation of arrested mourning.

Parkes (1972) also provided a detailed picture of normal grief in adult life. He saw the bereaved as oscillating at first between avoidance of acceptance of reality and only then moving towards pining, recollecting, and becoming nostalgic. The bereaved person's world was in chaos because in seeking what is lost, he ignores what is available and/or can be found; he feels lost at his core and finds the world meaningless. The important thing about Parkes's book-length report was that it included both clinical and nonclinical populations and drew parallels between acute grief and other forms of traumatic neuroses.

A considerably different approach was evident in Brenner's (1974) conceptualization. Scrutinizing bereavement with the characteristic lens of his theorizing, Brenner felt that the usual symptoms of grief are not primary phenomena but are defensive reactions. They are intended to ward-off "anger, hatred, and triumph, feelings which are, or would be, intolerable to the mourner" (p. 16). Brenner questioned the ubiquitous application of Freud's model and advocated viewing mourning as a compromise formation with diverse determinants and varying aims. This line of thinking was picked up by Hagman (1995a, 1995b), who differentiated bereavement from mourning; the former referred to a set of traumatic events that are psychologically elaborated and the latter referred to the resolution of the psychological attachment to the dead. Like Brenner, Hagman held the traditional stance on bereavement to be restrictive and suggested that the experience be viewed from multiple perspectives including trauma, vulnerability, unconscious meanings, object relations, defense, and adaptation.

Yet another nuance to the psychoanalytic understanding of bereavement was added by Meyers (2001), who questioned Freud's proposal that the lost object gets decathected by the ego and is given up in the process. Meyers stated:

> I disagree with the need to decathect the internalized object. This, of course, was part of Freud's old outmoded theory of the U-tube conceptualization of there being only a defined limited quantity of libido, which is invested either in the object or the self. A theory, I presume, none of us subscribe to any more since we do not believe there is a limited amount of love to go around. It is obviously quite possible to invest a new object with love and feeling while maintaining the attachment to the internal object as well. (p. 28)

Before ending this section, I must mention four other important papers: Engel's (1975) meticulous documentation of his decade-long anniversary reactions over the death of his beloved twin brother, Aberbach's (1987) fascinating proposal of mysticism and the quest for divine union becoming a creative response to loss, Foster's (1987) poignant discourse on her reaction to losing two patients successively to suicide,[4] and Leon's (1999) literary essay on how certain poems of James Tate and Sylvia Plath reflect attempts at self-restoration after the narcissistic injury owing to childhood parent loss. And, coming back full circle to Freud's (1917e) "Mourning and Melancholia," I must include the IPA-sponsored update on this monograph (Fiorini, Bokanowski, & Lewkowicz, 2007) even though only three of the nine chapters of this edited volume deal with actual bereavement; the remaining six address mourning in its broader, developmental context of the need to renounce infantile omnipotence and/or primary object ties. The chapters that do deal with bereavement are those by Pelento (2007) on the difficulty of grieving missing persons (e.g., *desaparecidos* during the terrorist regime in Argentina), Volkan (2007) on perennial mourning of large groups leading to entitlement ideologies, and Melgar (2007) on grief leading to fresh paths of creativity that are not merely the result of "working through" the loss.

Finally, there is the issue of disposing of the "things" (ranging from utensils of daily living to the accoutrements of desire and pride) possessed by the deceased. In normal grief, such inanimate objects get divided into three categories: things that are thrown away (e.g., a toothbrush), things that are given away (e.g., clothing), and things that are kept within the family and passed on as mementos and heirlooms. These last-mentioned objects are cherished and proudly displayed by the bereaved family members. Furthermore, such disbursement takes a bit of time. When either instantaneous or long-delayed, it betrays a manic effort to jump over the grief or a phobic attempt to avoid it altogether, respectively.

Factors that complicate the grieving process

The foregoing section has described the way normal grieving occurs. However, there are circumstances in which things do not go according to "schedule." Certain psychosocial variables especially tend to complicate the process of mourning and prolong the suffering of the bereaved. Such factors might exist in (i) the bereaved's premorbid personality, (ii) the bereaved's relationship with the deceased, (iii) the nature of the death, and (iv) the consequences of the death.

The bereaved's premorbid personality

The descriptions of the "work of mourning" suggest that it requires a reasonably strong ego. This raises the question whether all individuals are capable of mourning in a deep and proper way. Long ago, Klein (1940) had noted that the early failure to advance from a "paranoid" to a "depressive" position lays down the groundwork for lifelong difficulties in mourning. More recently, Greenspan (1977), in elucidating the distinction between predominantly oedipal and preoedipal character organizations, included the "capacity for genuine attachment and separation, and for the experience of sadness and mourning" (p. 385) as indicating the more advanced, oedipal organization. A corollary to this is that those with a predominantly preoedipal character organization would not be able to undertake a proper mourning when encountering a loss.

In accordance with such thinking, Sacks (1998) noted that responses to bereavement vary considerably, depending upon the "pre-loss" character organization of the bereaved and the level of his or her relationship with the deceased.

> For persons who have suffered untimely losses in the life cycle, there will always be a special poignancy to separating and individuating from their significant objects internally and, sometimes, externally. One can see how identification processes and other ego achievements might be interfered with if one cannot proceed forward and through one's loss of the object and one's relationship to it. Knowing whether the relationship to the object is more determined by a pre-Oedipal constellation or by an Oedipal one will help the clinician determine and understand the kind of anxieties and defences activated by the loss. (p. 228)

Not surprisingly, individuals with a preoedipal character organization (e.g., narcissistic, borderline, paranoid) tend to respond to object loss with denial, panic, disorganization, rage, and withdrawal instead of mournful longing and sadness.

The bereaved's relationship with the deceased

The loss of someone who was felt to be truly special by the bereaved is harder to mourn. This is because such a "special" status was due to an unusually fortunate "fit" in the relationship, the bereaved's defenses against unverbalized aggression, or a truly irreplaceable quality in the deceased. Unresolved issues existing between the bereaved and deceased also have a way of complicating grief. If one were keeping a big secret from one's father, for instance, and then loses him, the regret of not sharing it can preclude satisfactory mourning.

The death of a child is profoundly difficult to mourn. Not only is the occurrence contrary to the natural order of things (e.g., grandparents die first, then parents, then children, and so on), it is tantamount to a murder of dreams and hope for the future. Parents are left with the burden of "survivor's guilt" (Niederland, 1968) and find grieving to be a lifelong nightmare. The pain is greater when the offspring lost happens to be an adolescent. Having brought the child to the threshold of adulthood and then to lose him or her is truly devastating. The fact that parents are often at cross-purposes with their teenage children (due to separation struggles and revived oedipal conflicts) further complicates mourning such a loss.

Nature of the death

As compared to an expected demise after a gradual decline, a sudden and unexpected death of someone takes more time to adjust to. In the former instance, the ego has undertaken some "anticipatory mourning" and is not greatly shocked. In the latter instance, the rupture of the ego is brutal and more disorienting. The same is true of violent death by murder and horrible accidents. These are harder to accept, partly because they stir up the deceased's own vulnerability as well as his or her hostile feelings towards the bereaved. Similarly, suicide is difficult to mourn. The anger and guilty helplessness it produces in those left behind burdens the grieving process with additional psychological tasks.

Consequences of the death

Drastic reality change occurring as a result of someone's death can also impede mourning. The sudden death of the sole wage-earning head of a household is thus more difficult to mourn than the passing away of an elderly grandmother who contributed little tangible support to one's daily life. Family strife over the deceased's will and expected inheritance too interfere with the customary unfolding of grief. Such developments tend to thwart the much-needed mourning rituals and often cause paranoid regression in family members who use vengeance as a defense against their inner sadness.

Resulting pathological outcomes

The foregoing variables alter the course of normal grief and push the process in pathological directions. Such outcomes include the following:

Melancholia

Melancholia ("depression" in today's terminology) drew many significant observations from Freud (1917e), the most prominent among them being the following:

- In such a state, there is "a lowering of the self-regarding feelings to a degree that finds utterance in self-reproaches and self-revilings, and culminates in a delusional expectation of punishment" (p. 244).

- In melancholia, "… the patient is aware of the loss which has given rise to his melancholia, but only in the sense that he knows *whom* he has lost but not *what* he has lost in him. This would suggest that melancholia is in some way related to an object-loss which is withdrawn from consciousness, in contradiction to mourning in which there is nothing about the loss that is unconscious" (p. 245).
- "In mourning it is the world which has become poor and empty; in melancholia, it is the ego itself" (p. 246).
- "The patient represents his ego to us as worthless, incapable of any achievement and morally despicable … He is not of the opinion that change has taken place in him, but extends his self-criticism back over the past; he declares that he was never any better" (p. 246).
- "The [melancholic's] self-reproaches are reproaches against a loved object which have been shifted away from it on to the patient's own ego" (p. 248).
- "Thus the shadow of the object fell upon the ego, and the latter could henceforth be judged by a special agency, as though it were an object, the forsaken object" (p. 249).
- "Melancholia borrows some of its features from mourning, and the others from the process of regression from narcissistic object-choice to narcissism" (p. 250).
- Talking of acts of suicide during profound depression, Freud declared that "[T]he ego can kill itself only if, owing to the return of the object cathexis, it can treat itself as an object—if it is able to direct against itself the hostility which relates to an object" (p. 252).

Freud's observations regarding the apathy, anhedonia, guilty self-depreciation, and suicidal inclinations of the melancholic find a perfect match in the contemporary diagnostic criteria for depression (DSM-5, 2013, pp. 160–168). Even more impressive is his observation that melancholia often switches into mania. Freud noted that "The content of mania is no different from that of melancholia" (p. 254); in melancholia, the ego has succumbed to the object loss whereas in mania, the ego has pushed it aside and is ravenously hungry for fresh object contact.

Freud further commented that in melancholia, the feeling of loss throbs like "an open wound" (1917e, p. 253). It was, however, not till an addendum to *Inhibitions, Symptoms, and Anxiety* (Freud, 1926d, pp. 169–172) that he linked his economic explanations to object-related hypotheses regarding the origins of "mental pain,"[5] implying that the loss leading to such pain occurs at the level of ego-object non-differentiation. Weiss (1934) made this explicit by stating that:

> Pain arises when an injury—a break, so to speak, in the continuity—occurs within the ego .... Love objects become, as we know, libidinally bound to the ego, as if they were parts of it. If they are torn away from it, the ego reacts as though it had sustained mutilation. The open wound thus produced in it is just what comes to the expression as mental pain. (p. 12)

Finally, in melancholia, the identification with the lost object can also result in the bereaved taking on traits and behaviors of the deceased. An important distinction that I have noted in this context is that in normal grief, one takes on the healthier and more desirable traits of the deceased, while in depression, one takes on the morbid traits of the deceased.

Established pathological mourning

In contrast to melancholia, the syndrome of "established pathological mourning" (Volkan, 1981) is not based upon identification with the lost object. In fact, the bereaved denies the occurrence of such loss. He continues to use the present tense while speaking of the one he has lost. He feels that the news of the loved person's death would turn out to be false, that he will receive a letter or a phone call from the deceased, that he might run into the one who is supposed to have passed away, and so on. He might also develop an "obituary addiction" and manifest an unusual relationship with the deceased's grave. The compulsive reading of obituaries "... betrays not only anxiety over the death of the one they mourn, i.e. by finding no current mention of it. Conversely, the memory of the death notice as it appeared at the time of the death makes the death final—'kills' the last one" (Volkan, 1981, p. 91). The relationship of such "perennial mourners" (Volkan, 2007) to the deceased's grave also turns out to be peculiar: either there is a "grave-visiting addiction" or—more usually—the very existence of the grave is denied.[6]

Yet another feature of "established pathological mourning" is the occurrence of certain typical dreams. Volkan (1981) categorizes such dreams into three types: (i) *frozen dreams* (that lack all movement and can be like a still-shot or a slide show), (ii) *dreams of a life and death struggle* (that depict the deceased to be still living but involved in a terminal battle with life; the dreams typically end without revealing the result of this struggle), and (iii) *dreams of death as an illusion* (that show signs of life in the dead body of the loved person).

The individual with established pathological mourning not only keeps an ongoing inner contact with the dead person, he or she also maintains the illusion of external contact by means of "linking objects" (Volkan, 1972, 1981, 2007). These are physical objects associated with the deceased whose emotional significance does not fade with the passage of time. Rather, these objects acquire increasing potential for causing pain and terror. Pain results from the realization of one's loss upon seeing the physical object. Terror results from the physical object's knowing "accusation" (via projective identification, of course) that one had wished the deceased dead. Not surprisingly, such objects can neither be proudly displayed nor be summarily discarded. Their range is wide and can include:

> (1) a personal possession of the deceased, often something he used routinely or wore on his person, like a watch; (2) a gift to the mourner from the deceased before his death, such as something a husband gave his wife before perishing in an accident; (3) something the deceased used to extend his senses or bodily functions, such as a camera (an extension of seeing); (4) a realistic representation of the deceased, the simplest example being a photograph—or a symbolic representation such as an identification bracelet; (5) something at hand when the mourner first learned of the death or saw the dead body—what could be considered a "last minute object." (Volkan, 1981, p. 104)

The purpose of all such objects is to permit the pathological mourner to retain contact with the deceased, while acting as if the death has not even occurred. Metapsychologically speaking, a bereaved individual:

> ... *strives toward* healthy identification with the deceased by means of the introject. Identification has not yet occurred in the mourner, neither the total, disruptive identification with the deceased of full-blown depression, nor the enriching identification of the healthy mourner. The person in established pathological mourning thus maintains his introject of the deceased in a middle ground between healthy identification and neurotic depression. In that the introject

exists as a stage prior to normal mourning or depression, it has the potential to eventuate in either of those conditions. It cannot eventuate in "normal" mourning until the introject is no longer ambivalently perceived. In the sense that the established pathological mourner chronically maintains the introject in the hope of resolving the ambivalence, he can be said to "strive toward" healthy identification. Unlike the depressed mourner, the established pathological mourner has not surrendered all hope of resolving the ambivalence. (Volkan, 1981, pp. 113–114, italics in the original)

Other maladies

Melancholia ("depression") and "established pathological mourning" do not exhaust the list of morbid conditions associated with complicated or aborted grieving. Another outcome is evidenced in the form of complete absence of grief. Deutsch (1937) was the first to report clinical cases in which the reaction to the loss of a beloved object was a total absence of the manifestations of mourning. She proposed that this is the result of a particular dual constellation of the ego: "on the one hand, the relative inadequacy of the free and unoccupied portion of the ego, and on the other hand, a protective mechanism proceeding from the narcissistic cathexis of the ego" (p. 15). The flight from suffering, however expedient for the weak ego, is usually temporary and the need to come to grips with the painful reality of loss continues to surface throughout one's life. At times, later availability of ego-supportive figures (e.g., a loving spouse) and encounter with proxy triggers (e.g., the death of a renowned person) can mobilize the hitherto thwarted grief. An echo of Deutsch's ideas is evident in Frosch's (2014) recent paper on the narcissistic impediments to mourning.

At times, the turmoil of bereavement is masked by sundry neurotic symptoms (Anderson, 1949; Hagman, 1995a) or by resorting to alcohol or other psychoactive substances. In such instances, the presenting symptoms of the patient merely reflect maladaptive defenses against grief. Many cases of decline in the quality of the marital relationship, sudden outbreak of promiscuity and sexual perversion, and other risky behaviors that were hitherto unexpected from the patient hide insufficiently mentalized effects of bereavement. Chronic bitterness and vindictiveness—often displaced upon the dead person's physicians and caretakers—can also be manifestations of masked grief.

Implications for treatment

Having described the various pathological reactions to grief, I am prepared to make some remarks regarding therapeutic strategies in this realm. For didactic ease, my comments are divided into the following categories: (i) responding to normal grief, (ii) treating established pathological mourning, (iii) managing depression, (iv) handling the lifelong impact of childhood parental loss, and (v) tackling the occurrence of grief during an ongoing analytic treatment.

Responding to normal grief

Normal grief is not an illness. While most clinicians recognize this, Freud's (1917e) stern reminder is worthy of repeating here.

> It is well worth notice that, although mourning involves grave departure from the normal attitude to life, it never occurs to us to regard it as a pathological condition and to refer it to medical treatment. We rely on its being overcome after a certain lapse of time, and we look upon any interference with it as useless or even harmful. (pp. 243–244)

The attitude that not all human suffering is an illness must be maintained; some pains are integral to life. This does not mean that individuals in this state of normal grief might not end up at a physician's door. Often, they are nudged to seek help by well-wishers who do not appreciate the inevitability and "usefulness" of the suffering involved in grief. As a result, when someone in normal grief shows up in the clinician's office, curiosity should be directed at the nature of his support system that has led to "medicalizing" a normal process. Parallel to such investigation, the clinical approach should consist of empathic remarks, imparting of factual information regarding the nature of grief, and a relatively hands-off policy, coupled with reassurance of availability should matters become more difficult.

Treating established pathological mourning

If there is evidence that instead of ordinary grief, the bereaved has developed the syndrome of "established pathological mourning" (Volkan, 1981), active therapeutic intervention becomes necessary.

Listening to those with unresolved mourning must be respectful and empathic; loss, after all, is not a pleasant affair. The therapist should allow ample psychological space for the bereaved to elaborate their story. It is advisable to not meddle too much with sharp, intellectual comments. What the suffering of grief needs most is "witnessing" (Poland, 2000).[7] Listening patiently and making occasional, brief, and affirmative remarks that demonstrate that one understands the pain of the patient is generally sufficient. The therapist may help the patient to talk in greater detail and encourage the bringing in of the deceased's photographs for the therapist and the patient to look at together. This would facilitate the emergence of hitherto repressed memories and release pent-up emotions.

A less known technical ingredient of such "re-grief therapy" (Volkan, 1972, 1981; Volkan, Cilluffo, & Sarvay, 1975) is the use of linking objects described above. The therapist not only encourages the bereaved to talk more and more openly about his (or her) feelings of loss but also encourages him to bring his "linking objects" to the office. Encountering them, touching them, holding them, and reminiscing about them (and, through these, about one's complex feeling towards the lost person) helps to thaw the frozen grief.

Such credulous listening and affirmative stance should not, however, eclipse a certain amount of therapeutic skepticism (see in this context, Akhtar, 2013; Killingmo, 1989). In listening to someone with pathological grief, one must keep one's "third ear" (Reik, 1948) open for the verbal and nonverbal cues of a hostile attitude in the patient towards the deceased. Such hints and allusions should be gathered silently at first. In other words, the tragic motif of grief must be allowed to run its course before one begins to unmask its hostile underpinnings. One needs to wait for a considerable time before pointing out that the patient has actually been somewhat ambivalent about the deceased. It is only with the conscious recognition and acceptance of negative feelings towards the dead person that the patient can fully come to grips with his true psychic reality. This step is necessary for the proper resolution of grief.

Managing depression

Called "melancholia" by Freud, depression is yet another symptomatic constellation with which patients present to us after bereavement. Distinct from those with "established pathological mourning," depressed individuals have accepted their loss even though at the cost of psychic devastation. The ambivalence directed towards the deceased has turned, in their case, upon themselves. The libidinal vector of their ambivalence leads to self-absorption, self-pity, and the unmistakably grandiose dimension of the depressed person's nihilism (e.g., he feels *more* sick than he is, fears *greater* economic disaster than he really faces). The hostile vector of his ambivalence leads to guilty self-reproaches, a sense of worthlessness, and suicidal tendencies. His body reflects his psychic conundrum with hypochondriasis, insomnia, anorexia, and loss of sexual drive.

The syndrome definitely requires medical attention and there is considerable evidence (Cuijpers et al., 2014; Karyotaki et al., 2016) that a combination of antidepressant medication and psychotherapy is more efficacious in ameliorating such suffering than either of the two modalities alone. The addition of antipsychotic medications and even electro-convulsive therapy might become necessary if the depressive symptomatology takes on a delusional, stuporous, and life-threatening quality.

Handling the lifelong impact of childhood parental loss

Childhood parental loss often has a lifelong impact and can manifest in myriad forms. I have elsewhere delineated the guidelines for treating such adult "orphans" (Akhtar, 2011b, pp. 166–178). These include (i) providing a greater amount of "illusion" and "holding," (ii) validating the importance and the "unfairness" of such loss, (iii) discerning the defenses against the awareness of the pervasive impact of the loss, (iv) interpreting the narcissistic and sadomasochistic uses of one's status as an "orphan," (v) paying special attention to termination and post-termination phases of the treatment, and (vi) managing the countertransference experience during a piece of work that can be soul-wrenching at times. In my earlier contribution, I have elucidated these guidelines in detail and provided clinical illustrations to explicate their use. Their listing here is to whet the reader's appetite and to encourage him or her to look up my detailed discussion of technique with such patients (see also Settlage, 2001).

Tackling the occurrence of grief during an ongoing analytic treatment

Although patients in analytic treatment often suffer important losses *during* the course of their treatment, literature on the consequent technical challenges is meager. A shining exception is Schlesinger's (2001) paper aptly titled "Technical problems in analysing the mourning patient." Two longish excerpts from this remarkable paper should suffice, I think, to convey Schlesinger's message.

> Mourning recurs in waves, and as will all emotions, episodes rise to a peak and then dissipate. This basic quality should not be confused with intermittent "resistance" against recognizing loss or against mourning. The distinction may be subtle at times, but it is an essential one. It would be better, technically, to err on the side of assuming normality, for to interpret the subsidence of an episode of sadness wrongly as resistance is like to induce guilt in the patient for not being sincerely sorrowful. It can also be considered "normal" for the patient to attempt to mitigate the pain and to dose the mourning; not all such instances of defense require interpretation. Sometimes, an empathic observation such as, "It's hard when waves of sadness come over you," can provide support both for the patient allowing himself to feel the pain and for his reluctance to do so. An element of resistance may be present, of course, but without any implication of pathology and without obligating the analyst to "do something about it." (p. 122)

Schlesinger observes that in such treatments, countertransference-based urges to "help" can be hard to bear.

> Some clinicians have difficulty tolerating the seeming passivity of remaining in a posture of witnessing; they feel impelled to intervene, to "do something." More common, perhaps, is the wish to spare our loved ones, including our patients and ourselves, pain of any kind, and in particular, prolonged pain, and we may feel impelled to alleviate our distress by intervening to ameliorate their suffering. It takes great discipline to allow a patient (or a loved one) to experience the processes of grieving and mourning fully and to appreciate, and help them appreciate, the importance of doing so. The tendency to interpret inappropriately at such times, or even to offer unneeded support, perhaps better called by its right name, "meddling," may be almost irresistible for the analyst who has also become attached to his patient and for whom empathy has drifted too close to identification. (p. 124)

Schlesinger warns against the temptation to "pathologize" the patient's suffering or to somehow hasten its course. And, he acknowledges that the patient might invite such mistreatment by blaming himself for "carrying on" unnecessarily and for "too long." The analyst must recognize and interpret such masochistic seduction while encouraging the patient to take his time and to be prepared for the waxing and waning of his grief.

Some inoptimally addressed realms

Three areas still remain unaddressed. These include (i) children's capacity to mourn, (ii) gender differences in the capacity and experience of mourning, and (iii) cultural variables in shaping the process and outcome of grief. Brief comments on these now follow.

Children's capacity to mourn

Outstanding contributions to this important area of concern have been made by Bowlby (1960, 1961), Wolfenstein (1969, 1973), and E. Furman (1974). Bowlby (1960, 1961) observed the suffering of a large number of children orphaned (or traumatically separated from their parents) during World War II, and based upon this experience identified three phases of mourning: protest, despair, and detachment. He surmised these phases to reflect anxiety, sadness, and retreat, respectively. The phase of protest consisted of crying loudly, shaking one's bed, looking eagerly towards any sight or sound which might turn out to be the missing parent. This phase lasted for as long as a week and sometimes longer. Sooner or later, despair set in and was followed by detachment. Bowlby described this sequence in the following poignant passage:

> The longing for mother's return does not diminish, but the hope of its being realized fades. Ultimately, the restless noisy demands cease; the child becomes apathetic and withdrawn, a despair broken only perhaps by an intermittent and monotonous wail. He is in a state of unutterable misery. (1960, p. 15)

Anna Freud (Freud & Burlingham, 1944), Spitz (1946), and, much later, Nagera (1970) recognized that such reactions were grief-related but did not accord them the full status of intrapsychic mourning. Bowlby disagreed with this view. He held that the children he had observed demonstrated the reality of grief and of a sustained mourning process. The phenomenological and dynamic features typically associated with mourning (e.g., pain, denial, seeking consolation, unaccountable oscillation of feelings, despair, resignation) were all evident in the case of children, just as these were in adults. Bowlby did allow, however, for the possibility that childhood parental loss might fester and lead to pathological formations in adulthood. Later on, writing in collaboration with Parkes (Bowlby & Parkes, 1970), he modified his scheme to include four phases: (i) psychic numbness and denial, lasting for several hours to a week or so, (ii) intense yearning for the last figure, lasting from weeks to months, (iii) disintegration, greater anguish, and structural regression, and (iv) reorganization and recovery to a greater or lesser degree. However, in all other aspects, his ideas remained consistent with his earlier proposals.

Wolfenstein (1969, 1973) noted that under favorable circumstances, the child who has lost a parent does achieve some detachment from the latter in a way which is different from adult mourning.

> A child cannot tolerate the protracted painful remembering and giving up of a lost object that occur in adult mourning, during which it is not yet possible to seek or want a substitute. If a child is able to accomplish some decathexis of the lost parent, it is more likely to be in the presence of a suitable substitute who serves as a recipient of detached libido and a source of satisfaction of needs. (1973, p. 452)

Wolfenstein also presented literary and artistic examples of how the image of a parent lost in childhood persists over time and reveals the "dual aspect of near and far, present and absent, lost and inalienable, and living and dead" (1973, p. 434).

Even more direct and, frankly, hard to read because of its heartbreaking contents, is E. Furman's (1974) monograph, *A Child's Parent Dies*. Her book is rich in clinical material and reports in detail on ten children who needed therapeutic help soon after one of their parents died. Furman underscored that the child must have reached a stage of development where the object loss does not disorganize those ego functions needed for mourning, namely perception, memory, and object constancy. Obviously the older the child, the greater the ease with which mourning can be completed. Furman held that the infant and even a toddler is incapable of distinguishing between death and other causes of parental unavailability. However, from age three onwards, some comprehension of death is possible, provided the child is helped in this by empathic adults. The younger the child, the greater the assistance needed from the parent. Hoffman, Johnson, Foster, and Wright's (2010) recent research on a child's ability to grasp the three essential features of death (universality, nonfunctionality, and irreversibility) is highly pertinent in this context. Essentially, it confirmed Nagy's (1948) early findings that (i) children from three to five deny death to be a regular and final process, (ii) children between five and nine years personify death, and (iii) children after nine years recognize death as an inevitable part of the life process (see also Parens, 2010, in this regard).

A profoundly important aspect of Furman's book is its delineation of humane ways to treat a child whose parent has died. Her approach is based upon two assumptions, (i) a child must not be shielded from the reality of death, and (ii) a bereaved child must be allowed and helped to cry and mourn as fully as possible in order to prevent the loss (and its associated affects) getting repressed and distorting the memory of the trauma and of the dead parent.[8]

Furman also noted the effects of childhood parental loss upon the subsequent personality development. She observed that many of the "very good" children were simply quiescent and suffered an outbreak of symptoms later in life which was seemingly unrelated to their earlier loss. Often the entry of a substitute parent revealed the true lack of the child's developmental progress.

Settlage (2001) carried this line of thinking further. He focused upon the repression and non-assimilation of aggression in the functioning and structure of the core self and object representation consequent upon childhood parental loss. This leads to excessive dependency on external sources of soothing and acclaim, turning of aggression towards the self, depletion of assertive potential, inordinate separation anxiety, a childlike stance in life, and an exaggerated fear of death.

Concurring with E. Furman (1974) and Settlage (2001) and extending their "developmental line" to full adulthood, I (Akhtar, 2001, 2011b) delineated the multifaceted and lifelong impact of childhood parental loss. I grouped the manifestations of this "syndrome" into the following seven categories: (i) continued intrapsychic relationship with the dead parent, (ii) mental pain and defenses against it, (iii) narcissistic imbalance, (iv) disturbances in the development of aggressive drive,

(v) problems in the realms of love and sexuality, (vi) disturbances in the subjective experience of time, and (vii) contradictory attitudes towards one's own mortality. While I refer the reader interested in the details of these proposals to my earlier essay, there is one point I do want to emphasize. This pertains to the adult's continued intrapsychic relationship with the dead parent he or she lost in childhood. Freud (1927e) had long ago made this observation in the treatment of men who had lost their fathers at ages two and ten. He noted that each of them:

> ... had failed to take cognizance of the death of his beloved father—had "scotomized" it—and yet neither of them had developed a psychosis. Thus a piece of reality which was undoubtedly important had been disavowed by the ego ... I also began to suspect that similar occurrences in childhood are by no means rare ... It turned out that the two young men had no more "scotomized" their father's death than a fetishist does the castration of women. It was only one current in their mental life that had not recognized their father's death; there was another current which took full account of that fact. The attitude which fitted in with the wish and the attitude which fitted in with reality existed side by side. (p. 155)

Pollock (1961) observed approximately similar phenomena in three adult patients who had lost a parent before the age of six. He noted that:

> Throughout the years there had been a retention of the deceased parent in the form of a fantasy figure who was in heaven; to whom the patient could talk and tell whatever he or she wishes; who never verbally or actively responded to the patient; and who was always all-seeing and omnipresent. (p. 350)

Cournos (2001) came very close to this in describing her lifelong reactions to the loss of her father at age three and her mother at age eleven. She noted that she "... could certainly recite the fact that my mother was dead and never returning. This belief existed side by side with the fantasy of remaining in an on-going relationship with her" (p. 141). Echoing E. Furman (1974), she emphasized that a child has a limited choice in seeking a substitute parental figure and, thus, finds an adaptive value in maintaining a living image of the deceased parent. The findings of the

Harvard Childhood Bereavement Study (Silverman & Worden, 1993) confirm this. The investigation was based upon contacting families seen by funeral directors in the Boston, Massachusetts, area where a patient had died leaving behind a child between the ages of six and seventeen. Approximately half of the eligible families agreed to participate in the study; this included 125 children whose average age was twelve. When interviewed, 81 percent felt that the deceased parent was watching over them and 57 percent reported speaking to him or her. The parent might appear to "spiritually" accompany the child, and later, the adult everywhere. Such "accompaniment" is evident in the bereaved adult's fantasy, creativity, parapraxes, and especially in his or her dream life. In my earlier essay (Akhtar, 2011b, pp. 147–180), I have provided several illustrations of this.

Gender differences

One prominent question pertains to the impact of gender upon mourning. I do not think we know whether men and women differ in their capacities to mourn and, even if differences exist in this regard, do such differences cut across all sorts of losses or show a certain specificity? Some light on the former quandary is shed by Altman's (1977) observation that women have a greater sense of commitment in love relations. He traced this deeper capacity to an earlier event in the girl's development, namely the shifting of her love from mother to father.

> This renunciation prepares her for renunciation in the future in a way that the boy is unable to match. The steadfastness of commitment is, in this view, the renunciation of alternative possibilities, and the future woman has already made it in childhood. The boy has not, can not, and will not. (p. 48)

On the one hand, this observation leaves us wondering if it can be extrapolated to issues of mourning in general and bereavement in particular. On the other hand, we can not overlook the heterosexual bias in the developmental model being proposed here and therefore are compelled to be cautious about generalizing from it.

About the second quandary (i.e., do women and men grieve some losses better than each other) too, we know little. In my admittedly limited experience, girls tend to be more adversely affected by the loss of the mother than boys. The loss of mother deprives them not only of the primary love object and symbiotic partner but of a role model and scaffold for the elaboration of their core gender identity into an era and culture specific gender role. The same applies to the boy's losing a father during childhood. Moreover, for both genders, such loss occurring at ages four to five or at fourteen to fifteen years is perhaps more difficult owing to the oedipal conflicts at the former age and their hormone-based revivification at the later age.

We also have some evidence that adult women respond differently to their mother's than their father's death. According to Meyers (2001), the woman "deals with the death of the father as to the loss of an 'other,' beloved or otherwise, while she deals with the loss of the mother as a loss of part of her self" (p. 20). The former loss occurs primarily on a dynamic front, the latter on a structural basis. As a result, greater shifts in identity and caretaking attitudes are accompanied by the loss of their mother in women. Meyers allowed for specific differences in individual women in the manifestations of mourning their mothers, depending upon their personal dynamics and relationship with their mothers. However, she firmly held that:

> They have in common an internal change, the sense of loss of part of the self that was partially a "mother within" or an open-ended connection with the external mother in her continued need-fulfilling function as described. This may be dealt with by filling in loss in the greater self by identification, a kind of "becoming" mother. This may manifest itself in a variety of ways from temporary assumption of activities that mother used to be involved in, to more permanent attitudinal changes and sense of self. (p. 20)

Masur (2001) expressed reservations about Meyers's views and responded with the following rejoinder:

> [Is it] reasonable to say, as an alternative to Dr Meyers' hypotheses, that in a *subset* of adult women who have not experienced early object loss per se and who have also not been able to separate optimally from their mothers that identification with mother at the time of her death might both be adaptive and defensive? That is, that while "becoming mother" might be the best resolution possible for them following mother's death, it may also represent a

defense against experiencing both the reality of their loss and the painful feelings associated with that loss. And flowing from this, is it reasonable to then say that for the larger population of more optimally separated women, mourning is still the rule? But what is lost for the women who identify rather than mourn? It can be suggested that while identification may be, as stated, the best adaptation possible for them at this time, they forfeit an experiencing of their true and passionate feelings both about their mothers and the loss of their mothers as well as a sense of themselves as independent, authentic, and unique individuals. (p. 42, italics in the original)

All these observations are thought-provoking. However, they do not exhaust the possibilities of gender-based differences in mourning and bereavement. More data is needed.

The role of culture

Another important variable pertains to the role played by culture-at-large in facilitating or improving the grieving process. To be sure, how different cultures view death in general plays a role here (Akhtar, 2010; Etezady, 2010; Guzder, 2010; Moradi, 2010; Nagpal, 2011). Individuals belonging to cultures that regard death as "apart" from life might find mourning more difficult (owing to the narcissistic injury associated with the idea of death) than those from cultures which regard death as "a part" of life, hence expectable and acceptable. However, it is also true that all religions provide rituals surrounding death, including those involving the disposition of the dead body, the communal "witnessing" of grief, the periodic return to the trauma of loss, the "totemic feast" (Freud, 1912–1913) by which the bereaved arguably incorporates his lost love object, and so on. And then, there are poetry, songs, fiction, and memoirs of grief that readily become the literary and musical "containers" (Bion, 1963) of what still remains unexpressed in the human struggle to mourn and let go.

The realm of cultural facilitation of mourning is rich and extends to monuments, naming of streets, faces on postage stamps, and national holidays in honor of great heroes. One also wonders about the effect this new cyberworld of ours and its constant connectedness[9] has on the bereavement process? Hartman's (2012) recent proposal that the burden of individual loss is increasingly mitigated by mourning's fresh twin, cybermourning, is worthy of consideration in this regard. In his view, as society moves from a reality based on the acceptance of loss and limits to one of infinite access and renders the object usable by millions of people, the need for mourning becomes eclipsed.

There are still other questions in this realm. For instance, how do the innovative methods of body disposal (e.g., turning the deceased into a diamond) alter the course of grief?[10] And, do societies with "stiff upper lips" permit as full mourning as do the Latin American or Middle Eastern cultures? Or, on a more plebeian level, does burial perpetuate grief and does cremation more fully conclude it? The temptation is to not allow such external markers their due and to focus upon what goes on inside the bereaved's mind, but such dichotomy is false since the internal world is at least in part dependent upon "stimulus nutriment" (Rapaport, 1960) from the external reality. And, of course, the relationship between culture and mourning goes beyond the grief of one individual; it involves the traumas of society-at-large and can often take myriad forms over the course of life, with profound consequences of a sociopolitical nature (Volkan, 2007).

Conclusion

In this contribution, I have offered a broad overview of the psychoanalytic understanding of normal and pathological forms of bereavement. Taking Freud's (1917e) seminal essay on the topic as a starting point, I have described the phenomenology and metapsychology of grief. However, I have not restricted myself to his views and have included the notions conceptualized by subsequent analytic contributors, especially Bowlby, Deutsch, Pollock, and Volkan, among others. As a result, my discourse has produced an enriched portrait of post-loss depressive syndromes in all their complexity and nuance. I have followed this up with brief remarks pertaining to the technical implications of the ideas fleshed out in terms of phenomenology and psychodynamics. I have also attempted to address any unresolved issues pertaining to the impact of age, gender, and culture upon mourning.

Allow me now to conclude with mentioning the need for anticipatory mourning over one's own mortality. Shneidman (2008) has written meaningfully about it and delineated the concept of "good-enough death" and how one can plan for it in advance. I too have discussed this in great detail in my book, *Matters of Life and Death* (Akhtar, 2011a).

The fact is that just the way a mature individual has to allow himself or herself to undergo the pain that accompanies the normal process of grief over someone else's death, he or she has to bear the healthy sadness at the thought of the coming end of his or her own life. Wheelis's (1966) wise, if ironical, reminder applies to all of us.

> A fire becomes, not less, but more truly a fire as it burns faster. It's the being consumed that pushes back the darkness, illumines whatever there is of good in our days and nights. If it weren't brief, it wouldn't be precious. Let me say it flatly: we are lucky we die and anyone who pushes away the awareness of death lives but half a life. Pity him. (p. 68)

Notes

1. The sole psychoanalytic paper on "sinking feeling" (Hitchcock, 1984) suggests that it reflects the acceptance of a repudiated piece of reality and that "[T]his event, while manifested at any libidinal level of organization, has separation as a common denominator" (p. 328).
2. In the history of our own discipline, there are many illustrations of such an outcome of mourning. The most prominent of these is Freud's (1900a) *The Interpretation of Dreams*, which he said "revealed itself to me as a piece of my self-analysis, as my reaction to my father's death" (cited in Jones, 1953, p. 324).
3. Klein (1940) distinguished three types of reparation, namely (i) *manic*, which reverses the parent–child relationship and is hence contemptuous, (ii) *obsessional*, which seeks to undo the imagined destruction of the love object by imagined acts of undoing, and (iii) *creative*, which is genuinely concerned with the welfare of the love object.
4. A recent book by Adelman and Malawista (2013) explores in detail the complex emotions that are aroused in therapists by the death of a patient.
5. See Akhtar (2000) for a thorough review of literature on the topic of mental pain.
6. The development-facilitating use of visiting graves (Akhtar & Smolar, 1998) stands in sharp contrast to such pathological reactions.
7. A particularly painful situation involves the death of an ex-spouse, the separation from whom has not been internally resolved.

8. In the emphasis upon children's reaction to death, one must not overlook that mourning at the other end of the life span, that is, during old age, might have its own variations. Little data exists in this realm, though it is my impression that the elderly react with less emotional disturbance to the loss of loved ones.
9. *The End of Absence*, a recent book by Harris (2015), constitutes a powerful commentary on how the contemporary cyber-connectedness has robbed people of the throbbing experience of missing others.
10. Roach (2003) deals extensively with all sorts of curious ways in which the dead bodies are now disposed in her book, *Stiff: The Curious Lives of Human Cadavers*.

SPECIFIC SITUATIONS

CHAPTER TWO

Death of mother

Kerry L. Malawista

For psychoanalysts, mourning has been an area of interest and study since Freud's seminal paper, "Mourning and Melancholia." Later, with the work of Anna Freud, Melanie Klein, and John Bowlby, the question of how one mourns expanded to children. This chapter explores how a child mourns the death of a mother—someone who is essential to one's identity—and arrives at a place where mother is remembered with love, but without the daily ache of her loss. In other words, what facilitates a child's healthy mourning? I reflect on these questions by examining three vignettes from my experience of my mother's death. Memoir, like psychotherapy, entails an emotional journey, a reimagining of the past, and a search to understand the self. While this is the story of one family's loss, like a single case study, it highlights the dynamics we may see in children after the sudden death of a parent.

Excerpt I

"Crash"

"Rum, pum, pum …"
"Again, and one and two and …"

Miss Dorothy bellowed in her raspy, smoky voice as the flute promenaded us through what felt like the millionth round of *The Nutcracker*. She was either too old or too ditzy to know better than to perform *The Nutcracker* for an end of the year show. In May! I can still feel the floor vibrating as her cane tapped out the beat on the dull, worn-out wood flooring of the old Ridgefield firehouse, a compact brown brick building just up the street from our elementary school. I remember glancing at my sister, Carol, and rolling my eyes as we whirled across the floor, signaling, "When will this class ever end?".

Back then, I so much wanted to be a ballerina, like Ellen, the popular girl from my fourth grade class. What I didn't want was a poke from cranky Miss Dorothy. I thought she was too old for that tight purple leotard that made her look all lumpy. Her hair was stiff with hairspray and had me wondering how she slept on it at night. I glanced at the clock—just five more minutes—and twirled across the floor one last time. When Miss Dorothy tapped her cane to end class, Carol and I headed up the creaky stairs, out into the afternoon light, a too-early summer heat hitting our faces. Up the hill we trudged, Carol and I, lugging our tutus and our blue-plaid book bags. As we crossed Abbott Avenue, a dark blue Plymouth pulled up beside us. I stared at the car, not sure who was waving at us. I moved closer to get a better look, Carol right at my heels. To my surprise, Mr. Charlie, who lived across the street from us, rolled down the passenger window. Just then the sky turned gray. A storm was approaching, one that often follows a sunny, hot day.

"Hi, girls. Your dad asked me to pick you up from ballet. Sorry I'm late."

Carol and I piled into the back seat of his car just as the first drops of rain began to fall. We glanced over at each other, wondering why my dad had sent him, but we weren't the type to question a grown-up. As the car turned onto our street, we saw Mrs. Nancy, his wife, peering out her living room window. She waved us inside, like she had been expecting us. I looked at Mr. Charlie, still wearing his dark sunglasses despite the rain, who said, "Yeah, why don't you come on in for a snack." With an uncertain look between us, Carol and I followed him inside. Something wasn't quite right, but I had no words to go with the feeling. I remember our surprise at seeing my older sister, Kathy, already sitting on Mrs. Nancy's couch. Carol and I walked over to join her. We sat and we sat, watching the clock tick, tick, tick. No one told us why we were sitting there. Mr. Charlie and Mrs. Nancy seemed to have completely forgotten our snack.

"Hey, come look," Kathy said as she pulled me over to the window for the third time. "See, there is Uncle Jim. Why is he here?" By now, there were at least four or five cars parked in front of our house. "Something is wrong. Why won't they tell us?" she kept repeating.

Sitting there next to Kathy, I was also wondering why so many people were showing up at our house. I couldn't quite see their faces, but I could make out the familiar droop of Uncle Jim's shoulders. In the kitchen, I could make out Mr. Charlie's low voice, as he murmured into the phone. Finally, he came into the living room and said he would walk us home. I thought, "We only live across the street, why is he walking us home?".

The three of us followed him across our eerily quiet cul-de-sac, up the ten stairs and into our front door. As we crossed the threshold, I immediately noticed my grandparents and a blur of other faces in the living room. The sight of all these red swollen eyes confused me. Definitely not our usual "Chicken Delight Thursday" night.

I eyed the room for my mother, quickly heading to the kitchen to ask what was going on. Instead, at the kitchen table I saw Rhoda and Lester. That was odd. Why were our old neighbors here, the ones who had moved away the year before? Everything was slightly out of place, like a looking-glass world. Karen, sitting on Rhoda's lap, hopped off and ran to me, wrapping her tiny arms around my leg. I hoisted her up onto my hip.

I asked again, "Where's Mom?".

Lester shifted uneasily in his chair.

"Your dad is waiting for you," Rhoda said gently as she shepherded us down the hall to the bedroom I shared with Kathy, the one with the matching green bedspreads and curtains my mother had sewn. The shades were drawn, the room dark, except for a thin slat of light creeping in from the bottom of the closed shades. Gradually my eyes adjusted to the darkness and I searched for what was familiar. I saw my father sitting on the edge of Kathy's bed, his head hanging down. He seemed small, yet too large for the room. His shirt hung loose on his shoulders. Seeing him slumped over like that confirmed that something was very wrong. Afraid to look straight at him, I scanned the room. Our dolls with the secret space for our pajamas that Auntie Joyce gave us were right where they always were, on our beds. The Beatles poster still hung on the far wall. My favorite white lamp with the fringe was still where it always was, right next to my bed.

"Girls …" he began, but his voice stuck in his throat.

He started again, gently laying his hand on Carol's leg, where she sat to his right. Karen had climbed up next to him. Kathy and I stood right in front of him, not looking at each other. Clearly, he had been crying. I'd never seen him cry before.

"Girls, I have very sad news."

My knees felt weak. I glanced away, trying to land my eyes anywhere else but on my father's face. When I peeked back I saw he had taken off his glasses and was wiping his eyes. I thought about how I had never seen him without his glasses, that his eyes looked different, smaller, and somehow weaker. There was not a sound from the rest of the house. I felt like a firefly, trapped in a jar, looking for a way out. Wasn't anyone going to stop this from going further?

"There has been a terrible accident." Slowly, he choked out the rest of the words. "Mom's gone." His words hung in the air.

"What do you mean she's gone?" I understood, but hoped I hadn't.

My father reached his hand out to me. I held it, but I also didn't want to be touched. I was afraid I would come to pieces, start crying and never stop. Then, I thought I needed to keep from crying to protect my little sisters.

Barely audible, he said, "She died."

Kathy said, "No! No!" I'm not sure who asked, "What happened?"

"We are not sure yet, but she was in a car accident." He may have said more. I can't recall all his words—a wall had gone up between my ears and my mind.

"But, where's Bobby?" I asked. I knew my two-year-old brother was always with my mom.

"He's in the hospital. He's very, very hurt."

My mind kept jumping around, never landing on any clear thoughts. I couldn't make my brain understand. How could my mother have been here this morning, making us our breakfast and now be gone, never to return?

Freckle-faced four-year-old Karen immediately turned to me and asked, "When will Mommy be home? I want Mommy."

Karen repeated that question over and over and over again for months to come. Each time it ripped through me, as I had to repeat those awful words: "She's not coming home. She died."

Back in that room with my father, I knew I needed to get away. I had to be by myself. I scurried out of the room and grabbed Sammie, our recently acquired and not-so-well-trained Samoyed puppy. Walking outside with her, my eyes were momentarily surprised and blinded by the bright light that shone through the trees. The sky had somehow cleared itself of clouds. Some birds chirped above.

I sat Sammie down under the crab apple tree, shedding the last of its pink blossoms. Dad had given it to Mom for their tenth anniversary. Branches from a nearby bush grabbed at me like claws. In that moment, Sammie was all I had, and I desperately needed her. Never an easy dog to control, today was no different. Suddenly she spied a squirrel in the branches above. She yanked and she jumped, leaving scratch marks up and down my legs. Her pulling away gave me an even lonelier feeling. Frustrated, I thought she should somehow know. She should understand that today, of all days, she should be good for me!

I kept saying to her, "Sammie, stop! Don't you know what just happened?" I told her over and over again that Mom died. "Don't you understand?" I pleaded with her. "Mommy died."

But I could not get her to understand or to calm down.

Reflections on "Crash"

For many years, child therapists have debated whether young children have the developmental ability to grieve the loss of a parent, with some child therapists (E. Furman, 1974, 1986; R. Furman, 1964) maintaining that mourning is possible in childhood, and others (e.g., Wolfenstein, 1966) believing it is not possible until late adolescence. These differences in opinion may be rooted in two factors. *First* is the interchangeable use of the terms grief and mourning. Grief is seen in all humans, as well as other mammals, when there is appreciation of a significant loss. It is a biologically chaotic and overwhelming raw state that can include shock, numbness, weeping, longing, irritability, anger, and trouble sleeping and eating. John Bowlby (1960) observed this capacity for grief in children as young as six months of age. In this way, all children grieve. Mourning, in contrast, is a more complicated ongoing process that is set in motion after a loss, requiring a higher level of abstract thinking to truly comprehend death. The question then arises: at what age does a child have the cognitive ability for abstractions and an understanding of the finality of life? The age many researchers pinpoint varies from between six and nine years old (Smilansky, 1987).

The *second* reason for this disagreement may be derived from Freud's (1917e) notion of *adult* mourning. He saw mourning as the "bit-by-bit," painful and slow struggle to accept a death, which includes a gradual withdrawal from the loved one and a willingness to find comfort and relationship elsewhere. Freud writes, "With the work of mourning complete, the ego becomes free and uninhibited again" (p. 245). If we think of mourning as this "bit-by-bit" withdrawal of the attachment to a parent and the acceptance of the reality of the loss, then mourning is not possible for a child—maybe not completely possible for anyone when losing someone essential to one's identity. How can a child de-attach from a mother who is basically an extension of him- or herself, indispensable to every aspect of a child's daily life? How can a child lose a necessary part of the self?

When a parent dies before a child reaches adulthood, the world is irrevocably changed in the most fundamental and devastating of ways. As Rita Frankiel (1994) writes, the child's "need for nourishing interaction and care ... is so central to the survival of young children that the withdrawal necessary for adult mourning is simply not possible" (p. 328). Winnicott (1960b) reminds us that there is no baby without a mother and no mother without a baby. While he was describing infancy and the slow developmental process of separation, this is actually a process that unfolds throughout the course of childhood and adolescence. There can never be a complete withdrawal of attachment. After the death of a parent, it may be more like the author John Irving (1989) describes in his novel, *A Prayer for Owen Meany*. He writes:

> When someone you love dies, and you're not expecting it, you don't lose her all at once; you lose her in pieces over a long time—the way the mail stops coming, and her scent fades from the pillows and even from the clothes in her closet and drawers. Gradually, you accumulate the parts of her that are gone. Just when the day comes—when there's a particular missing part that overwhelms you with the feeling that she's gone, forever—there comes another day, and another specifically missing part. (p. 139)

Irving is describing the protracted and painful, ongoing process of a boy mourning his mother, a continual losing and re-finding of the "missing part," gradually recognizing what is lost in the world. To this I would add the necessary and corresponding re-discovering and re-finding aspects of the dead parent within the self.

In this way, mourning is a process, not an outcome, and the course it takes will look very different for children than for adults. Children lack the ability to tolerate or sustain the inconsolable pain that would threaten to overwhelm them. The capacity to bear such a devastating loss emerges over the course of maturation, as children begin to make sense of the world and their own experience. For this reason, right after learning of a significant death, it is not surprising to see children eager for a quick return to "normal" life, resuming their regular activities at school and with friends. Some may not even shed a tear, appearing as if they feel nothing. Of course, the truth is that nothing will feel "normal" for a very long time, try as they might to hold on to life-as-they-knew-it. This explains why many therapists and writers, witnessing this lack of emotion, have described children as unable to mourn. Robert Furman (1968) noted that when adults are exposed to the poignancy and pain of a child's mourning, "... they prefer for their own sake to deny its existence" (p. 374) and instead see the child as not in mourning.

Older adolescents, capable of higher abstract reasoning, may begin to show what appears to be adult-like mourning. Yet, they too, will struggle in ways particular to their stage of development. For example, an adolescent girl, already grappling with issues around female identity, might feel at a loss without a mother to know what it means to be a mature woman. In addition, separating from one's parents often involves anger—rejecting their values, refusing their support, or other forms of rebellion—in order to establish a separate identity. A parent's death makes the process more complicated. For example, if there had been friction or conflict in the relationship, the teen will not have had the chance to repair the rift or to resolve guilty and angry feelings.

Initial reactions to loss

When young children sense that something is amiss, they often experience a kind of ominous foreboding—a tingling sense that something is out of the ordinary—yet they lack the experience to fully understand or anticipate what is to come. In the first excerpt, I showed my older sister Kathy and I hard at work, trying to absorb and integrate the reality of our mother's death—putting together the disparate pieces of the puzzle. Often, when something troubling or painful is on the horizon, children are left out of the loop in a benign attempt to shield them. Adults instinctively want to protect children from sorrowful experiences and the feelings that may accompany the event. However, for children, being held in a state of suspended curiosity can, at times, be even more terrifying and disorganizing than hearing the news from a trusted adult, even if the news is sad or devastating. When something is both out of the ordinary and unexplained, a child may draw the wrong conclusion or even imagine things to be far worse than they actually are. Yet in that moment, my siblings and I were about to experience one of the worst things a child can face.

For most children, the moment of being told a parent has died is etched in their memory, yet at the same time it is often denied. As I watched my father ready himself to speak, I was trying to stop time, fervently seeking to distance myself from the entire scene. For me, scanning the room for familiar objects, tethering myself to what was expectable and known, was my attempt to dissociate myself from the words my father spoke; turning my attention to what *was* still present and familiar in my home as a way to fend off the surge of anxiety at what *was* clearly missing, moving back and forth between recognition that our world had been irrevocably changed to a state of protective denial. Salman Akhtar (2011b) describes this as a "… split in the ego … One part knows that the parent is dead. The other part holds on to the internal representation of the parent, intrapsychically 'behaving' as if he or she were fully alive" (p. 151).

This type of dissociation or disavowal is a way to protect the self from overwhelming pain, a way to cope with and stave off an unfathomable reality. In an earlier paper, Linda Kanefield and I wrote, "[D]isavowal protects the mourner from overwhelming pain. In this way the individual may acknowledge the reality of the death but not yet completely integrate the meaning and acceptance of the loss until the truth can be tolerated fully" (Malawista & Kanefield, 2013, p. 20). It is a way "to protect the psyche by having an alternate way of experiencing, a way of staving off an unbearable reality" (p. 21).

In other words, children—and of course, adults too—protect themselves by allowing their attention to wander away to a safe place. As with any emotional defense, it is useful to think of it as occurring along a spectrum. At one end, it can be a subtle attempt to distract oneself, progressing along a continuum, to a feeling that one is standing outside oneself, looking on, as if the experience was happening to someone else. At the other end of the spectrum, it can manifest as a more severe breach of reality, or psychosis. In this way, the individual may outwardly acknowledge the reality of the death but not yet completely integrate the meaning and acceptance of the loss until the truth can be tolerated fully. As a nine year old, I had the cognitive ability to understand and verbally acknowledge the reality of death. Nonetheless, I didn't yet have access to the deeper meaning of the loss.

Another way children attempt to control the overwhelming feelings is to take on some of the tasks and roles of the deceased parent, identifying with the dead parent as a way to keep them close. Freud (1921c) wrote, "Identification is known to psycho-analysis as the earliest expression of an emotional tie with another person" (p. 105). After a loss, the expression of this tie becomes even more compelling and necessary. Upon hearing the news that my mother had died, my first instinct was to look after my siblings, just as my mother would have. By looking after my younger siblings and trying to locate my brother, I was unwittingly invoking my mother's maternal instinct, striving to bring her back into the room with me. I was doing what children commonly do to cope with loss, that is, taking on some of the tasks of the parent who died, in this way identifying with the dead parent as a way to keep her close. In that moment, the child need not miss the dead parent—she *becomes* the parent.

This reaction can also be understood as a manic defense, a common reaction employed when a child loses a parent. Akhtar (2001), referencing Melanie Klein, describes how the three components of the manic defense—omnipotence, denial, and idealization—are all "attempts to deny the ego's 'perilous dependence on its love objects'" (p. 103). Some children may move to a precocious level of development, feeling they no longer need the missing parent, denying and leaping over the significance of the loss by becoming busy and productive. In contrast to a latency age child who comprehends death, from the moment my youngest sister heard the news, we see her inability to comprehend the meaning of death. Still too young developmentally to integrate and absorb this devastating and unimaginable news, she needed to hear that my mother had died again and again. In fact, it is not uncommon to hear young children speak of the parent in the present tense long after she or he is gone. When a preschool child loses a parent, we may see a number of behaviors that indicate the child is in distress—unruly and aggressive behavior, a regression to bed-wetting, clinging to the remaining parent, or the type of persistent, repetitive questioning we see in Karen. Bowlby (1961) pointed out how even children as young as one year old will repeatedly search for their deceased parent in the last place they knew that parent to be. One man, who came to therapy following the sudden death of his wife, related the heartbreak of witnessing his two-year-old daughter roaming the house, looking under the beds, in the closet, for wherever her mother might be hiding. This game also served a secondary function of bringing the mother's presence back into the room by initiating a game that they had played together, "hide-and-seek."

Another common initial response to such shattering news is withdrawal. One eight-year-old girl, who entered treatment following the death of her mother from cancer, told me that for several days after her mother died, she sat alone in her backyard clubhouse, not wanting to see or speak to anyone. "I wanted them to all just go away. I didn't want to see all these strange people in my house, looking at me like that." Similarly, when the painful reality threatened to overwhelm me, I sought refuge away from my family and comfort with our dog. Even though I knew Sammie couldn't understand, I was using her as a way to rehearse the reality, bolstering my ability to integrate and absorb my now-transformed world.

Excerpt II

"What if I fell in?"

The first days after Mom died were all hazy. I was trying to make sense of something that didn't make any sense. Mostly I tried, as did everyone else in the family, not to talk about her. I also took on my mom's approach to life's troubles: you look for the best in a situation. And these first days after her death, I did my utmost to find whatever that might be. First, I tried to convince myself that things could be worse. Like, my brother could have also died in the car accident. Or my mother could have been pregnant and that would have meant two deaths.

"I mean, a nuclear bomb could have blown up the whole planet," I informed my almost-twelve-year-old sister, Kathy. "That would be worse."

"Or a meteor might have hit us and destroyed all of Earth," I added. "Or a tornado could have swept our house away, like happened in *The Wizard of Oz*."

"You're an idiot," she retorted and walked away.

The next day, I came up with, "We could be on a rocket ship stuck floating in space."

See, I thought, *there were lots of things worse than Mom dying.*

Next, I set my mind on what could be "the silver lining," something my mother also taught me. I thought I found it: I would get to ride in a limousine. I had always wanted to ride in one, and now, here was my chance. I imagined a driver, wearing a black cap and black suit, bowing to me as he opened the car door, inviting me into the limo. "Thank you, James," I say. There I would sit, like Eloise in the Plaza, upon fur-covered seats. But as quickly as the fantasy appeared, so did the burning shame. How terrible I was to even think about wanting to ride in a limo, especially when my mother would be riding in a casket in the car ahead of me.

Despite feeling ashamed, the secret longing remained. I didn't dare speak my wish aloud. Everyone would know how selfish and terrible I was. Even so, I tried to find little ways to ask my father if there would be a limo for the service, hoping no one would glean my real wish.

"So, Dad, how do we get to the funeral?" I asked.

"What? Oh, don't worry about it, Stringbean. I will figure it all out."

But I didn't believe he had it all figured out. He was too busy running back and forth to the hospital to see Bobby and trying to take care of all the phone calls and visitors. He walked around as if in a trance, doing his best to get everything done, telling all the relatives at our house that he was okay, but I could see he had on the same clothes from the day before.

As things turned out, there were no limos at my mother's funeral. I'm not even sure whose car I rode in to the service. All I saw as we stood waiting outside the church was the white coffin being carried from the hearse towards the familiar large stone church. I couldn't get my mind around the idea that my mom was in that box. I tried to imagine what she looked like in there. I had never seen a dead body. My dad said she looked like she was asleep. We kids hadn't gone to the wake that was held two nights before the funeral. I couldn't understand why they called it "a wake" if she looked like she was asleep. While Kathy was angry she didn't get to go to the wake, I wasn't sure I wanted to. My dad didn't let us go, saying we wouldn't want to be there. I wanted to go along with whatever he wanted. I, like most children, wanted to protect my father from any further duress. I was not about to question his judgment about attending the mysterious "a-wake."

But then when I saw the casket, I worried: "What if she wasn't really dead in there? What if they made a mistake and she was trying to get out?" That gave me the worst feelings inside. I inched closer to the casket so I could hear if she was awake. I didn't hear anything. Back in the church, the bells chimed. Every pew was filled, with neighbors, teachers, even kids from school. It was as if our whole town was at her funeral. I searched each of the rows as we passed in procession towards the front pew. A roomful of mothers, but none of them was mine.

From the church, we headed directly to Madonna Cemetery in Fort Lee. We drove slowly through row after row of gravestones, finally stopping at an open site. I saw workmen standing off to the side, a pile of dirt heaped high nearby, shovels in hand at the ready. All of us kids were ushered over to the gaping hole in the ground. I saw them carry my mother's coffin out of the hearse over to the tarp nearby.

When they lowered the coffin down into the chasm, I thought it would never stop. The hole looked so deep. Someone handed me a red rose, directing me to walk over and throw it into the hole. I was afraid to get too close. What if I fell in?

Reflections on "What if I fell in?"

For a child who loses a parent, there is a continual sense of disequilibrium, an ongoing feeling that the world is not the safe place it had been just days earlier—calamities may strike at any moment—a nuclear bomb, a meteor, a tornado. When a parent dies, most children are left with the ongoing wish, whether conscious or unconscious, of re-finding the lost parent. This fantasy that the parent is still alive, or is somewhere watching over them is a universal one and often remains for years after—maybe a lifetime—even when a child or adolescent tells you they know their parent is dead and can recall all of the details of how the parent died. Edith Jacobson (1965) introduced the notion of reunion fantasies in adult patients who imagined a magical reunion with a parent who died when they were young. Silverman and Worden (1993), interviewing 125 children between the ages of six and seventeen (average age: twelve years old) four months after their parent died, found that 57 percent reported speaking to the deceased parent, and 43 percent of these, mostly younger, felt that they got an answer. Eighty-one percent imagined the parent was watching over them, a nearly universal fantasy. After one year, most children still experienced their parent as alive in their minds. Imagining the lost parent as a presence watching over the child is a nearly universal fantasy.

In therapy, we often see adults who come to us with some present-day difficulty, seemingly unrelated to having lost their parent in childhood. In the first meeting or two, they likely have no difficulty articulating the facts surrounding their parent's death. Yet, as the work deepens, we find ourselves revisiting that early loss, with some patients discovering an unconscious fantasy that the parent is still alive. With further exploration, we learn the many ways this unconscious fantasy has influenced the course of their life and may indeed be tied to their current difficulties. So while it may appear on the outside that our adult patients have grieved the absent parent, they may not have truly accepted or integrated the loss internally.

Linda Kanefield and I (2013) suggested that adults have the same difficulty as children in accepting and integrating the reality of death, albeit through an adult lens. We distinguished between the conscious recognition of the external loss of someone from the internal acceptance of the loss, arguing that even in "normal" mourning, the bereaved may continue to maintain the fantasy that a loved one is still present. We referred to this period—where the lost loved one is not alive, but not yet accepted as gone—as the "middle distance." It is a "psychological way station where the bereaved struggles to accept the reality that a loved one no longer exists and then finds a way to integrate the loss and form a new cohesive self-narrative" (p. 18).

Joan Didion, in her 2005 memoir, *The Year of Magical Thinking*, beautifully captures her ongoing fantasy and conviction that in spite of the finality of her husband's death, he might still return to her. While at nine, I had the abstract reasoning to understand that my mother was truly dead, never to return, we see the equally powerful fantasy that she could still be alive in the casket. Likewise, pre-latency children reside in an egocentric world of magical thinking, where thoughts lead to actions. This is commonly seen in the fantasy that the parent left them because they were unlovable or because of something they did or did not do. In these fantasies, the parent is still living in some faraway place and will one day return to them. For example, one forty-year-old woman, Jane, recalled the morning at the breakfast table when her father scolded her for hitting her younger sister. Later that same day, the building her father worked in collapsed, killing him and leaving five-year-old Jane bereft, with the unconscious conviction that her father's death was the result of her having hit her sister. Secretly, she was burdened by this fantasy, never uttering the pain and guilt she suffered for this imagined thought and action until she began therapy.

We can envision that any of my siblings, or I, had at one time or another wished our mother dead or injured. This wish and fear is so common that we hear it in the familiar children's rhyme, *"Step on the crack and break your mother's back."* While I am not directly aware of my siblings harboring some unconscious responsibility for our mother's death, this would not be an unexpected response. And just as bad behavior can cause harm, so too a child might think good behavior can bring about the parent's return. This was also true for my patient Jane. In her treatment, she came to understand that she had needed to be the "perfect" teen through her adolescence, both to keep her surviving mother safe, but also with the hope and fantasy that if she was very, very good her father might return. She remained the little girl, always left waiting, wondering when her father would come home.

Following the death of a parent, almost all young children are left with some worry about their surviving parent—whether they will be able to take care of them—fearing they may collapse under the strain. This may be particularly true when a mother dies and the father had not previously handled much of the day-to-day care. To help maintain my conviction that my father could indeed take care of five children on his own, I took pains to protect him from any further duress. For example, when Kathy vocalized wanting to go to the wake, I was unable to express my desire to go or disagree with his decision. Many children who lose a parent will inhibit their anger. This may be because the parent they are angry at is not there to be angry towards. Others may deny or be unwilling to fully absorb their surviving parent's grief or they may inhibit their aggression for fear that it was their anger that had killed the parent, and fear losing the remaining parent. Akhtar (2001) makes the important point that analysts should not interpret the lack of anger in adult patients who have lost a parent in childhood as "defensive but empathize with the horrid fact that the patient feels no right to feel angry at all" (p. 102). We can understand such efforts to cope—protecting the surviving parent, maintaining a deep connection to siblings, and the compliance/need to be perfect—as a wish to make reparation for normal childhood wishes, desires, and pleasures that, if not for the traumatic loss, would be quietly folded into the child's development.

Another common response to catastrophic loss may be silence, not only from family members but also from the greater community—school, friends, and neighbors. Often, these well-intentioned adults feel tongue-tied, not knowing how to respond to a death, or what would be helpful to the child. They may wish to spare the child the pain of revisiting sad events, thinking that changing the subject, saying nothing, or distracting a child is the gentler approach. However, children have a powerful need to verbalize their feelings. It helps them gain mastery of their experience, integrate their feelings, create a narrative, and organize what may be a confusing and even terrifying experience. Silence may also reflect a more general denial of the reality of the impact on a child of losing a parent.

The psychoanalyst, Francine Cournos (2001), described her own family's experience after her father's death and their desire to protect one another from pain. She writes, "Throughout this entire series of events, my mother and I maintained a pact of silence. As a child, I believed this protected us, and that we would simply fall apart and stop functioning if we discussed our experiences with illness and death, however obvious their impact on our lives" (p. 137). Older children and adolescents may also be praised for being "so strong" and "keeping it together," relieving family members from the burden of having to worry about how the children are faring.

Mourning is also made difficult by the fact that as children mature, their memories, knowledge, and relationship to the deceased parent often remain sealed off at the age they were when the death occurred. There are no new memories or experiences to update the relationship. When parents die prematurely, they can remain idealized, frozen in time, forever the all-loving parent of early childhood, rather than a full and rich picture of who they actually were. We see this when celebrities or important figures die young—whether James Dean, John Kennedy, Marilyn Monroe, or Heath Ledger—they remain forever idealized. And here, too, as with Elvis, we often hear the fantasy that they are actually still alive.

In this excerpt, we see how quickly a child's protective defenses arise, such as the common strategy of rationalization, like my coming up with worse case scenarios than a mother dying.

My next approach was to console myself with the promise of something special and exciting—riding in a limo—revealing the age-appropriate, self-centeredness of a latency age child. Yet, naturally, this excitement was short-lived. My longing and pleasure at riding in a fancy car collided with the awareness that the limo's sole purpose was to carry us all to my mother's funeral. In this way, such shameful childhood wishes and desires can become dangerous or inhibited in the aftermath of parental loss. Another type of shame response we may see after a parent's death is a pervasive feeling of being different than other kids, deficient in some fundamental way. For others, there may be envy of friends whose families are still intact and unspoiled. Billy, a nine-year-old boy whom I treated after the death of his mother, told me how furious he became if anyone publically mentioned his mother's death. He related hating the feeling of being different than the other kids. For him, as for many children, the loss of his mother meant he was personally lacking in something essential that all the other children appeared to have. Some children will even go so far as to conceal the loss of the parent, speaking of the deceased in the present tense, as if still alive. Several children seen in therapy related feeling shame for taking pleasure in the attention they received after the death. When I have put this into words, normalizing the experience, several expressed their shock and relief that anyone else could have felt this way—perhaps they were not as bad as they imagined.

Excerpt III

"Whirly-bird Queen"

My first clear memory during those first weeks was playing in our backyard with my neighborhood friend, Scott Russo. If I were the Whirly-bird Queen of our backyard, I would say Scott was the Whirly-bird King. Just like me, he couldn't get enough of that ride. Even though our Whirly-bird was frayed a bit at the edges from constant use, and one of the metal bars had dislodged from the center and swung unhinged from one of the seats, we all still loved the Whirly-bird best. To make it spin, you pushed your legs at the same time as you pulled your arms back and forth against the person sitting across from you. I loved spinning as fast as I could, my hair whipping and twisting across my face. We all clamored to be the first to get on; I was usually first, and the last to get off.

That day, we were spinning that Whirly-bird for all it was worth. Then suddenly everything stopped. I noticed the look on my friend's face, his eyes registering the cut even before I felt the pain. The bar from the center of the platform—the pole on which it spun—had detached and somehow hit the exact point where my hand was pumping, slicing my index finger with a swift, deep gash. I watched frozen as drops of blood dripped down my finger and landed on the white cement, spreading slowly outward, forming a jagged halo. My head was already spinning, but now I was lightheaded and felt like I might faint. I jumped off and started to run inside, stopping short on the basement stairs with the sudden and shocking realization that my mother was no longer waiting inside for me. No Mom who would know what to do. No Mom to take care of my cut. My mind was a jumble. What do I do now? Where do I go? My dad was still at work. I knew it was a bad cut. I needed a grown-up. Just as I started to panic, I recalled a new neighbor had moved in across the street a week earlier. I had heard the mom was a nurse. I took my chances and headed across the street. I rang the bell. A woman with dark hair, big twinkly blue eyes, creamy skin, a round face, and—like my mother—a few extra baby-pounds, promptly opened the door.

"Hello ... oh my! What happened to you?" Her voice was warm and curly. She smelled like babies, a mix of Johnson & Johnson powder and Desitin diaper rash cream. I thought I even saw a juice stain spread cross her shoulder. I was smitten. I followed her upstairs and into the kitchen, when she turned to ask my name. "Kerry," I squeaked. She said I could call her Georgia. With a practiced glance and barely a hesitation Georgia inspected my cut. "Well," she said, as she wrapped my hand in a kitchen towel, "let's get that fixed up for you."

As she walked me over to the sink to wash it off, I saw her kids, Holly and Jason, spread out around the kitchen table. Two-year-old Jonathan was sitting in a high chair eating Cheerios. All the while, with gentle expert hands, Georgia kept checking my still-bleeding finger. After several looks, she said, "You know, I think we should get you to the hospital for a few stitches."

My heart began to pound. Hospital! Images flashed through my mind of my brother, his tiny two-year-old body near death in his hospital bed. His face was puffy and a bandage lay across his head and the lower part of his jaw. Tubes were coming out of each arm.

I panicked. There was no getting me to a hospital. I pleaded with her not to make me go. Seeing my terror, and probably already knowing about the sad state of affairs across the street—five kids who just lost their mother—I'm sure she couldn't bear to put me through another trauma. Hesitantly, she acquiesced. "Well, maybe we can make a good butterfly bandage that will hold it together." Butterfly bandage! My knees and elbows had seen plenty of Band-Aids, but never a butterfly. As she pulled the bandage out of the box, I thought it really did look like a butterfly, thin in the center and spread out wide on both ends. Georgia showed me how the center part stretched over the cut and the outside wings pulled tight so that the cut stayed together and could heal. As she finished bandaging my finger, she asked me how old I was. When I told her nine and a half, she said she would have guessed at least ten or eleven, adding, "You're pretty smart for your age." A warm feeling bubbled up inside of me.

Georgia rechecked the bandage, reassuring me that the bleeding had finally stopped. I was not going to have to go to the hospital after all. She'd known just what to do. I tried to hide the few tears that suddenly sprang into my eyes. "How about some cookies?" Georgia asked, as she pulled the familiar bag of Oreos out of the cabinet. Oreos! I suddenly realized I hadn't had one since my mom died. Georgia gave me a squeeze as she walked to the sink, and told me to wait with her until my dad arrived home—she wanted to make sure that I didn't need a tetanus shot. She didn't need to ask twice. What she had is just what I wanted—cookies and hugs. I stayed behind with Georgia and Jonathan. I imagined we were two moms getting together for an afternoon chat, just like my mom used to do with her neighbor friends. I turned up the next day, and most days after that. Georgia always answered the door with a big smile, looking like I was just the person she was waiting to see.

Reflections on "Whirly-bird Queen"

In this final excerpt, we witness my overwhelming panic, my mind a jumble, unsure where to go or what to do when the assaulting reality that my mother was truly gone came crashing through my defenses. Not surprisingly, it occurred at a moment of injury, a time when a child ordinarily turns to her mother for comfort and aid. Latency-age children and adolescents fear experiencing such powerful feelings and worry that they will be inconsolable and unable to carry on in their day-to-day lives. Like adults, they anticipate they will "fall to pieces," unable to regain a sense of control, wondering how will they ever survive this catastrophe. I am sure I felt afraid that if I let go, I would be inconsolable without the person I needed to comfort me.

Consolation and recovery depend on maintaining and building connections to the living. Naturally this leads to the wish to re-find the lost parent in fantasy or a bond with a new surrogate parent, a stable loving figure allowing the child to feel it is safe to love again, without the fear of loss. Erna Furman (1981) has written, "When an adult is ready to reinvest his love, he can actively seek a new person. The child cannot do that, particularly when he wants a new parent" (p. 172). I would argue children do actively seek other maternal figures. Here, I mustered my resources and sought connection with someone like my mother, a nurse. A maternal presence was not only yearned for, but was required. While a positive sign of resiliency, we can also understand my quick thinking as another way to protect myself from the acute awareness of my mother's absence—to not miss what I couldn't have. At the same time, there was the pleasure in finding someone who reminded me of my mother.

As adolescence approaches, a "new mother" may also be wished for in order to relieve the child of unconscious guilt, especially when the child feared she had been an oedipal victor. If a stepparent is brought into the family, the initial hope and longing for a "new" mother will usually bring a more complicated reality. The stepparent may quickly disappoint, not living up to the idealized parent of fantasy, making her the target of anger that cannot be directed at the idealized parent who left them. If no stepparent arrives, the surviving parent may find himself the object of the child's anger. Later, in this scene, we see me once again take on my mother's role, chatting with a neighbor friend, as a way to both hold on to my mother and not to miss her. Of course, this was a process that started long before she died. Georgia provided some of the direct comfort I hungered for, a way to help ease the pain and loss of my mother.

Going forward

My intention in revisiting my childhood loss has been to highlight some of the ways children respond to a parent's death. Of course, how each child manages such a traumatic event is affected by many factors, including the age of the child when the parent dies, was it sudden or following a long illness?, his or her inborn resilience, temperament, and overall health, the quality of the relationship with the deceased parent, the support network that surrounds the child, and the stability of the remaining parent. E. Furman (1981) writes, "Some may be better able to cope with this tragedy than others; for all, it becomes a lifelong burden" (p. 172). Akhtar (2011b) has provided a summary of the many ways a child might react to the psychological impact of a parent dying, including: "... (i) continued intrapsychic relationship with the dead parent(s), (ii) mental pain and defenses against it, (iii) narcissistic imbalance, (iv) disturbances in the development of aggressive drive, (v) problems in the realm of love and sexuality, (vi) disturbances in the subjective experience of time, and (vii) problematic attitudes towards one's own mortality" (p. 150). While this is a thorough list of possible outcomes, and, of course, the death of a mother leaves its imprint, we need to keep in mind that our understanding is gathered from a clinical population that has sought treatment. As Akhtar later added, "This list needs softening ... a reminder that the outcome of such calamity is far from uniform" (p. 163).

While as analysts, we are trained to find what is problematic, it is important to keep in mind a child's resiliency in the face of trauma and what may promote healthy and adaptive ways of coping and what facilitates a child's thriving after a significant death. What allows a child to mourn after the loss of someone essential to his or her identity? Fundamentally, healing is built upon what Winnicott (1960a) referred to as a good "holding environment." A surviving caretaker's ability to tolerate the child's sad and painful feelings, letting the child know it is okay to cry, be angry, or just silent. Children need permission from the grown-ups around them to mourn. In my own family, we were fortunate to have a father who was maternal, warm, devoted, and empathic. A father who, particularly for his generation, had been unusually involved in parenting prior to my mother's death. Who quickly reestablished a familiar routine—a return to "normal life"—that meant getting our life back on track: school and friends. Another aspect of healthy mourning, and an often overlooked but crucial one, is the surviving parent's belief that the child can weather the trauma and succeed. To not see the child as a victim, or as an "exception," entitled to a special status based on loss.

The literature speaks to how significant loss leads to rage, hate, despair, and depression. Akhtar (2011a) touches on this idea when he writes, "... it is the emergence of mental pain, with its characteristic admixture of hurt, disbelief, bitterness, and anger that forms the greatest threat to their ego stability" (p. 153). As clinicians we, of course, listen for and interpret the rage and hurt at the abandonment, the possible guilt at continued happiness, or a whole myriad of responses the child might have. But viewed alone these feelings are a recipe for continued pain and instability. What must not be left out of the equation is how gratitude and love modifies hate. In Kleinian terms, for resilience and health to triumph, love and attachment need to surpass hate and destruction. The surviving parent, and clinician when involved, must help the child, over time, allow love to neutralize destructive aggression.

When both love and hate can be borne towards the dead parent, the capacity to make reparation is then possible. These ideas link to Freud's (1917e) theory that melancholia develops when hate interferes with the identification to the deceased. If the internal mother, or parent who dies, remains persecutory, a hated, abandoning figure, she can never be mourned. In this way, healing necessitates the taking in of the good love object through the process of identification and internalization—allowing the lost parent to live on in the child. For this to occur, the child must connect and maintain an ongoing internal relationship with the loving aspects of the lost parent and the healthy identification and internalization of that parent. If the basis for identification is to keep a close tie to a loved one, it makes sense that this would be a crucial aspect of mourning. Melanie Klein (1957) points out that when we see identification after a loss, the individual is not doing this for the first time, rather he or she is "reinstating" the object, which must be built on a foundation of a good loving bond before the loss. Meaning that if the earlier relationship with the deceased parent was inadequate or compromised, mourning will likely be compromised.

This taking in of a psychic presence is a slow process, one that needs to continue on into adulthood. This does not mean a taking in of the mother in concrete ways, such as her clothing style or occupation, but in new and imaginative ways, allowing for the individual's unique, authentic self to develop—not remaining attached to the internalized version of an all idealized or all frustrating childhood mother. And of course, like any other mental activity, identification with the dead parent can in and of itself be used defensively, never allowing for the grief that mourning requires.

Treatment

A final question to address is whether children are in need of therapy after the death of a parent. While I have seen many children and adolescents after the loss of a parent—on occasion even been contacted on the day the parent died—we should not assume treatment is required. While the wish "to do something" is understandable, prematurely seeking treatment to head off a possible future problem is not necessarily helpful or always effective. When done precipitously, treatment may even interfere with grieving, instead offering a quick fix, as if therapy could prophylactically protect the child from pain. While I let the parent know I appreciate such attention and the sensitive recognition that special care is needed, I suggest we meet without the child, encouraging the parent to allow the child time to absorb the news and to wait and see how he or she is adjusting. My initial work with the parent is providing support and education on what the child might be experiencing and in essence, modeling the ways to provide the assistance the child needs—helping the parent to help the child. Encouraging the parent to follow the child's lead, helping the child to express feelings, and pointing out that the parent should not be surprised if the child shows no reaction at all. I highlight that it is important to hold in mind that the child can survive this and to not assume a pathological response, speaking to the strengths the parent has already shared with me about the child. I remind parents that a healthy adaptation to loss occurs in the context of a warm, empathic, and secure home and family life, that the child will thrive best if the surviving parent is available and not so overwhelmed by his or her own grief (Parens, 2001). At the same time, I point out indications that mourning is not proceeding well, such as changes in school performance, a withdrawal from friends and social life, truancy, stealing, or symptoms such as depression. Children who prior to the death had particular psychological or developmental vulnerabilities, will, of course, likely suffer with greater symptoms and pathology after a death. When therapy is called for, it can provide the support a child needs to gradually accept the death, tolerate the painful affects that have been warded off, and gradually develop new and resilient ways of coping.

Conclusion

In the end, grief and mourning do not have a quick time frame. Children who experience such a crushing loss will re-experience the grief throughout their life, whether it is a moment of seeing a warm exchange between a parent and child, or at significant life events such as a graduation, marriage, and birth of a child. With each new transition, the loss of the parent returns and is reworked, again and again. As Edna Furman (1981) said, "A parent who is well known and loved will forever be missed to some extent with each new developmental step" (p. 172). After some time, one may turn sorrow into something meaningful, sublimating grief into devoted parenthood, professional success, and creative endeavors.

CHAPTER THREE

Death of father

Thomas Wolman

At the age of six, my best friend died of a brain tumor. It was during the summer and it happened suddenly. One minute we were playing together on a sunlit beach, the next minute he was gone. I remember being told the news in a matter-of-fact manner and then not a word. My parents never discussed it, at least in my hearing. I got the impression that this event was not to be talked about. I must have thought—and here I am extrapolating—that death was an event so acutely embarrassing or shameful that nobody wanted to talk about it. I knew about shame because I felt ashamed of my inability to throw and catch a ball with any dexterity. Interestingly, this problem with my body image was a trait I shared with Richard, my friend. His death seemed to be a natural evolution of this physical flaw, which had simply morphed and metastasized into a horrific "thing."

Over the succeeding weeks and months, this "thing" gradually took hold of me, and wouldn't let me go. I became increasingly fearful of dying and this fear was at its worst at the hour of sleep. I was trying to be a good boy and not talk about it, but one night I broke down and called my father in the middle of the night. I confessed to him that I was afraid of dying like my friend Richard. And I will always remember what my father said to me. He said: "This will never happen to you."

Upon hearing these words, I was immediately reassured and was able to go back to sleep. Indeed, these words appeared to resolve the matter, as if nothing more needed to be said.

I bring up this childhood memory because it was my first experience of death and that death is irrevocably associated with my father. For me, his intervention was important not just for the powerful reassurance it offered, but because it broke the silence surrounding my friend's death, and which I associated with my mother. It was sufficient that my father had spoken and in speaking had decided the matter like a king who merely has to say something in order to "make it so." In effect, my father's words substituted for the "thing" that had invaded my mind like a tumor and literally forced it "outside" where I could keep my distance from it for the rest of my life. Thus, the father's symbolic intervention brings death into the conversation. No doubt, I heard the unconscious message hidden by the negation, "never" as: "This *will* happen to you and to me as well."

Father loss and the primal horde

You could say that my father's reassuring words established the *possibility* of his death at some time in the distant future. However, we know intellectually that death is more than a "possibility": it is an imperative—in fact, the only absolute imperative of human existence. With this in mind, let us take a brief detour into Freud's (1912–1913) myth of the primal horde, in which the murder and death of the father was unthinkable until it actually happened. In another paper (Wolman, 2015), I spoke of the primal father's quest for unquenchable life at all costs, an attitude I called *primal greed*. Here I want to examine the sons' reaction to their father's death in Freud's myth. With this foray, I aim to highlight the challenges and impasses the sons must endure in the wake of this loss.

In Freud's telling, the brothers band together in order to defeat and kill the father. But we need to keep in mind that this remarkable event occurred before the establishment of any kind of social order. Can we, then, say that the act was premeditated? I do not think so. Such planning would have required the group to assign tasks to its members and to reconcile opposing views on how to proceed. They did not infer that their superior numbers would carry the day. And, in the absence of moral restrictions they did not know they were committing a crime, much less a murder. One rather gets the impression that the horde slew the father while in the grip of overwhelming hate and rage. The brothers came together unthinkingly as a "flash mob." They must have been shocked by their own audacity.

This same internal thrust drove them to cut the father up into bits and then devour him. Freud (1912–1913) proposes that they killed and devoured the father in a single act. Eating the father was not their considered response to having killed him. The act of devouring may have been the origin of the totem meal but the latter is a distant derivative of the former. At the time of the original "meal," the brothers would have had no more knowledge of why they were consuming the father than of why they killed him in the first place.

But no sooner had they killed and devoured the father, than they were overcome by remorse. Freud (1923b) makes an immediate connection between this remorse and a sense of guilt. But guilt actually comes later as a result of what Freud calls "deferred obedience." We must think of the remorse as a second emotional state, second only to their hatred, but equally overpowering. For each member, remorse is felt directly, much like a physical blow to the gut. As Freud explains it, the sons were unaware of their love and affection toward the father, and thus the stunning realization that they have killed him acts like the rending or tearing apart of a vital organ. In this regard, their affects are not unlike those described by Melanie Klein (1940) in the "depressive position."

In the wake of their terrible deed, the sons are left on their own to confront these divisive feeling states and the consequences of what they have done. It takes the group a period of time to accept the impossible position they find themselves in. They realize that given the relatively even distribution of power among them, no single member can emerge as winner in a "war of all against all." That is to say, a life or death conflict with one's rival is unresolvable by the exercise of power alone. Moreover, just as they grasp the impossibility of possessing all the women, it begins to dawn on them that killing the father has left them in a state of lingering dissatisfaction. We must consider that the killing is an act of bloodlust in which it is impossible to distinguish the sexual and aggressive components, the act of killing from the glutinous devouring. Still, they are not fully satisfied because none among them actually takes the father's place. The father's impossibly complete satisfaction in copulating with all the women will be forever unattainable. Moreover, their homosexual inclination—an undercurrent in their peer relationships—can never reach the apex of taking the place of the women in sexual encounters with the father. For just as they envy the father his power, they envy the women who participate in the father's orgiastic sexuality.

There is yet another impossibility faced by the sons and easily missed in Freud's (1912–1913) highly condensed account. He writes that the killing of the father "can in no real sense be undone" (p. 144). No matter what they do to "revoke" the act, to expiate their sin, or to retroactively insert a taboo against killing, they simply cannot turn back the clock. The reality of the deed resists every effort to soften or blunt its effects. Freud admits that acts of expiation and "deferred obedience" can achieve psychological effects, but they do not free the sons from their basic predicament. Even the entire range of man's formidable capacity for symbolism will prove inadequate to negate the actuality of their monstrous deed. For our purposes, the role of the mythical crime is there to remind us that the loss of the father can never be fully repaired or atoned for. Hence, every time a son or daughter confronts the loss of the father, he or she must contend with something in that loss that defies or resists efforts at reconciliation.

Freud is quite clear, however, about the inaugural act which ultimately frees the sons from the "tumult" of warring emotions: the incest taboo. They put this taboo into effect by publicly resigning and renouncing their claim on the women. In taking this step, the sons make a basic assumption that incest in any shape or form is ruled out in advance. They treat it as a fundamental axiom, such as "parallel lines never meet," which defines an area of the impossible. For this reason, the incest taboo applies universally and without exception, for even one exception would render incest "possible." Psychically, the renouncing of the women amounts to accepting that the impossible *is* actually impossible. That is what it fundamentally is. They cannot take the father's place, they cannot possess all his women, and they cannot undo what they have done. Thus, the act of renunciation/resignation is as much an act of recognition as it is a prohibition. And as such it stands as a commitment, an oath, and a declaration of identity. In stating what you are not, you say what you are. Thus in excluding incest, the sons pave the way for *names* which identify each subject in an exogamous network of relationships.

The transformations brought about by the earliest prohibitions conform to a tripartite structure. We can call the initial phase primordial, prehistorical, or "primal." At this stage, the sons behave as a true "horde" in which each member's internal world resembles the "fog of war." We can see this phase as a succession of powerful and transfixing emotional states: rage, envy, greed, and in reaction, remorse. Or, we can think of the killing as a single "happening" whose single thrust includes and encompasses the simultaneous killing, dismemberment, and devouring of the father. Additionally, we can see the entire prodromal phase as one of orgiastic sexuality run amok. In this sense, the killing satisfies the group's bloodlust, and the devouring their oral greed. We can even postulate an event never mentioned by Freud: a bacchanalian orgy held to celebrate the killing. In this "proto-festival," the sons participate in an orgy with the women during which much food and drink is consumed, the father's head serving as the centerpiece of the banquet table.

Such a fanciful idea is not so improbable. The sons kill the father in a paroxysm of bloodlust fueled by years of sexual frustration. And really, after killing the father, there is nothing to stop them from immediately taking possession of the women. True, no single man would control all the women, but as a group they could "share" the women just as they later would share the totem meal in token of the spoils of victory. We can further imagine the "orgy" of remorse that might occur in the aftermath of the bacchanalia. This might include cries of horror, tearing one's hair out, rending one's garments, and prostrating oneself on the ground. The men would beat each other with switches and exhibit their wounds in public display. There might be a rash of suicides and self-immolations. And in all these manifestations, the identifying feature is the lack of modulation, restraint, or limits.

The second or middle phase is the incest taboo itself. In our interpretation, the act of renunciation comes after the reality of incest and murder. It therefore stands halfway between that *reality* and its later symbolic substitute. Yet it is not fully symbolic because it creates the possibility for laws which have not yet been formulated. And it still carries about it the aura of the "real" since—like the impossibility of one man possessing all the women simultaneously—it cannot be questioned, mitigated, or gainsaid. That is to say, it is the original law, and as such, it cannot be compared to any subsequent law. As an original, it shares a common element with the original and *nonpareil* crime it is meant to oppose.

We can best illustrate the third phase through several examples of the triadic formula: prehistory—transitional form—symbolic networks.

The transformation of the horde proceeds along parallel lines. If we focus on the group's evolution we get: group cohesion based on homosexual ties—exogamy—social organization. Regarding the "first festival" we get: bacchanal—totem meal—communion and other religious rites. Since the totem meal commemorates the murder, it implies a turning point in the meaning of history: prehistory—the founding historical act (the totem meal or alternatively, enactment of the incest taboo)—history as "commemoration." The original prohibition begins with: father's real powers and the sons' revulsion against killing a revered object—prohibition, "No!"—proscriptive laws. The positive aspect of law unfolds as follows: real filial attachment—selection and naming of totem (one of the "names of the father")—covenant with the father, and later pacts and contracts. Finally, we can speak of a period of unfettered primitive emotion and rampant sexuality—first principle of restraint and re-channeling—partial loss of sexual satisfaction conceived as loss of a "vital organ" (castration).

These somewhat abstract formulas apply to the universal task of mourning the loss of one's father. Take, for example, the distinction between "killing" and "murder." We may assume that the sons were originally unaware that killing the father was a "crime." Only after the fact—in the time of what Freud calls "deferred obedience"—can they acknowledge the act as "murder." And the ambiguities of this distinction linger to this day. In the Torah, for example, the commandment, "You shall not kill!" is interpreted by commentators as an injunction against murder, not against instances of justified killing (as in the case of self-defense, warfare, or execution for capital crimes). It is nevertheless interesting that most of us remember the commandment simply as "Thou shalt not kill." In our minds, the sweeping universality of this imperative—its complete lack of any exceptions—is what makes it "compelling." And, as psychoanalysts, we know that a person who has killed somebody in the heat of battle or as a justified act of self-defense will likely feel guilt. In the unconscious, there is no distinction—subtle or otherwise—between "killing" and "murder." It is as though every homicide bears the trace of the primal father and everyone wears the biblical "mark of Cain."

In this example, the mind cannot separate the original "killing" from the "murder" it will become after the fact. In another instance, the opposite pertains, and two attitudes that are obviously connected remain separate. We can see this partition standing between "love" and "honor." Freud tells us that, in the myth, the sons retain feelings of love, admiration, and affection for the father that were brushed aside until after the killing. But the sons do not "honor" the father until after the totem is established. Then "honor" is bestowed in symbolic gestures and acts of praise and gratitude. Think of the phrase "pay one's respects." This almost always refers to a formal act such as attending a funeral, and the word "pay" implies a symbolic debt to the honoree.

In the Torah, the fifth commandment states: Honor thy father and mother. Significantly, this command remains in force even when the father or mother is deficient, negligent, or abusive. It is therefore not necessary that one love the parent in question. Thus, two attitudes thought of as connected are here set apart. Such a division makes sense in the context of the myth because "honoring" the totem commemorates both the original murder, as well as the efforts to expiate and atone for it. Indeed, the very act of honoring the father surrogate inevitably brings to mind the crime that made it necessary in the first place.

Honor thy father

My father, although a non-observant Jew, was thoroughly permeated with the strict morality of the Torah, especially the Decalogue. He learned these precepts from his mother, who was always quoting biblical wisdom, and from a *cheder* (school). In the 1920s, *cheders* prepared boys for their bar mitzvahs by the rote learning of Hebrew passages.

As an adolescent, I remember my father reminding me to "Honor thy father and mother." He did not speak about any of the other commandments. He reminded me at a time when I was rebelling against his authority. He reminded me at exactly the time when I was feeling rebellious and hateful. He was also reminding himself. When I was in my late teens, he was in the middle of an ongoing feud with his own parents. He had always been extremely close with his brilliant and overbearing mother, but now that love had turned into hate, the way good milk sours. He coped with his hate and the ensuing guilt by rigidly and formally "honoring" his parents in the teeth of his loathing for them and everything they represented for him. Consequently, he never renounced them or cursed them. He maintained his weekly visits to them religiously. And most shockingly, this man who was used to ordering people around, never openly defied his mother or told her off with angry words.

As you can imagine, the commandment to honor your father and mother stuck in my mind as well, all the more so because I felt scorn when I first heard it as a teenager. Later, I came to know its effects in my emotional attachment to the mourner's *kaddish*, a prayer said at every Jewish funeral. During the saying of *kaddish* during my father's burial, I openly cried. After the funeral, I would sometimes think: "All I want when I die is for the assembled mourners to say *kaddish* over me." There must have been something about the prayer which freed me to express my grief. I have thought long and hard about the powerful effects of the *kaddish*. In addition to its poetic, incantatory language, commentators point to one surprising observation: It never once mentions grief, mourning, or the somber burial of the dead. Instead, it does one thing over and over: It praises the name (names) of God. Two characteristic lines describe God as "blessed and praised, glorified and exalted, extolled and honored, adored and lauded." In other words, the praise is poured on wholeheartedly, generously, and without restraint.

And as listeners and psychoanalysts, we can hear two *leitmotifs*. On the one hand, we hear the excess of praise. Such a panegyric seems unwarranted by the event in question. It is almost unseemly in its exuberance. We have to ask the question whether the prayer aims to counter the mourner's doubts about God's intentions or even his existence. Does it not also counter the grieving survivor's temptation to "curse God and die," as recommended by Job's wife from the Bible? There, the latter phrase means to "renounce" God. Thus, the prayer may function to bolster and support the name of God.

Note, however, that the prayer exhorts us to praise *His name and only His name*. We must keep in mind that the Torah makes a distinction between the name of God and God's immutable reality. We can praise his name while remaining profoundly befuddled by his ineffable being. Thus the prayer harks back to the sons' commemoration of the primal father in which the totem—the name or names of the father—substitutes for the ineradicable actuality of his original tyranny and murder. On the other hand, the prayer sets up a dramatic counterpoint between the moving words of exaltation and the void at its very heart. I mean the void created by non-mention of the obvious loss faced by the speakers of the prayer. In part, this absence reflects and magnifies the initial response of mourners of any important loss: being at a loss for words. In any funeral these days, it is common to tell the bereaved honestly that one "doesn't know what to say" or that one is at a loss for words.

Another phrase is: "There are no words." That is, even if one *had* words, there are no specific words nor are there *enough* words in the entire language to encompass or express, much less to repair, this loss.

For myself, the poignant quality of the prayer—the element that unlocked the flow of tears—stems from the contrast between the superfluity of words and the starkness of the void around which they circulate. By pointedly not mentioning the loss, the prayer in effect amplifies its reality *as loss*—that what has been lost cannot be regained. And yet the prayer heroically combats this real loss by reinforcing the ties to tradition—the symbolic links between the past and future. The very fact this prayer has been said for a thousand years so testifies. The prayer says: You may have lost your father but you need never lose his legacy—his paternity. You may have lost your father but you can always speak his name—a name that invokes him in your mind. And it is this continuing relationship with the father's word—with everything he stands for in your mind—that forms his true legacy. Indeed it is only thanks to the viability of this relationship that I was able to shed tears.

Freud and the loss of the father

We know that Freud emphasized the role of the father in the Oedipus complex to such an extent that it fell to his heirs to rediscover the obvious role of the mother. Freud described the loss of his father as the most "poignant" of a man's life. In his monumental study of Freud's self-analysis, Anzieu (1975) characterizes *The Interpretation of Dreams* (Freud, 1900a) as a dutiful son's creative working-over of his father's demise. Yet while emphasizing the father complex, Freud wrote little about the ordeal of *losing the father*. However, there is one place in his work where the father complex and the problem of mourning reunite: the case history of the Rat Man (1909d).

Very early in the treatment of the Rat Man, Freud's patient observes that his obsessive symptoms worsened after his father's death. Freud makes a connection between the patient's neurosis and his unresolved sorrow at this loss. Indeed, he goes so far as to say that his "sorrow had, as it were, found a pathological expression in his illness" (p. 186). This connection emerges in the fourth session on the couch, when the Rat Man recounts the story of his father's death nine years earlier. He remarks that this loss had "tormented me from the very first" (p. 175). In the previous sessions he had described the rat torture. On a simplistic and preliminary level, we can view his rat obsession as a form of self-torture over his father's death. At first, however, the reproach had not tormented him. Instead, he promoted the father into a living phantom, which he might at any moment encounter again. Only after eighteen months did the "recollection of his neglect" (p. 175) recur to him.

Freud's use of the word "neglect" is interesting in light of his investigation of the source of the Rat Man's pathological guilt. As we know, Freud made a direct connection between this guilt and death wishes against the father. But perhaps this ultimate source of guilt sidesteps more concrete actions on the patient's part, ones for which he might reproach himself. Freud tells us in this regard that the patient emotionally disavowed the fact of his father's death, while accepting it intellectually. But in disavowing the fact, he may have failed to bury the father with the honors he deserved. We get a hint of this possibility at the moment when his self-reproaches acquire real "teeth": the occasion when he pays a condolence-call on the family of a relative. In offering condolence, we say something of the order of: "I'm so sorry for your loss." In so doing, we acknowledge the loss and declare that it cannot be gainsaid or contradicted. Our words of consolation offer a first step toward reconciliation. But the Rat Man might have said to himself: "Because I repudiate my father's death, I am unable to provide consolation to myself or my family. And I shall therefore find no consolation—shall indeed remain inconsolable—for the pain of losing my father."

In the conundrum then faced, the patient cannot provide the father a proper burial if he refuses to fully accept the finality of his death. If we take this "neglect" to its most extreme degree, it means allowing the father to decay and rot, uncovered, on the ground. This is what happens when you literally refuse to bury somebody (as in the case of Antigone's brother, Polynices, in Sophocles' play). And it is quite possible the patient did entertain this fantasy because once, while visiting the father's grave, he thought he saw a rat emerging from the ground. In his private fantasy, he assumed it had been having a meal on the body. Such a desecration represents—besides its many other meanings—a transgression against the dead. The symbolic safeguards accorded the body such as the coffin, shroud, and tomb are not in place. Moreover, the dead father as a symbolic entity, whether we view him as "paternity," "fatherhood," "legacy," or "inheritance," is cast aside in favor of the real father in his present state of advanced decomposition.

Freud attempts to address these issues of burial in remarks to his patient on the funereal statuettes crowding his office. He notes that their "burial had been their preservation" (p. 176). He makes a distinction between processes of "wearing away" occurring in the light of day, versus the unchangeableness of the tomb. He then goes on to expand the metaphor into a discussion of the conscious versus the unconscious, which takes doctor and patient somewhat far afield. However, Freud no doubt jars something loose in the patient's unconscious.

In my view, Freud is playing upon the ambiguous meaning of "preservation." This word means keeping something alive by petrifying and immobilizing it in its state of deadness. In his fevered imagination, the patient might have wanted to "preserve" the father by holding him in a state of "suspended animation" in which he is neither fully alive nor completely dead. He can neither let him die completely nor live fully. His image remains permanently intact at the cost of immutability and inertia. In his fantasy, the patient has fabricated a "monument" (statuette) to his father's death and "buried" it so deep within his mind and behind so many layers of swathing and protection that nothing can get to it. This crypt protects it from being psychically "worn away." In effect, the father's name is withdrawn from circulation within a field of symbolic associations, the psychic equivalent of "seeing the light of day."

Freud returns to the patient's favorite fantasy "that his father was still alive and might at any moment reappear" late in the case history. He describes a curious piece of behavior, which appears to reenact this fantasy: the patient interrupts his work between midnight and one in the morning, and opens the door as if the father is standing there. Then he returns to the hall, takes out his penis, and looks at it in a mirror. Freud notes that the hour between twelve and one is "the hour when ghosts are abroad" (a possible allusion to *Hamlet*). He speculates on the simultaneous compliance (the patient is hard at work) and defiance (he is about to masturbate) in the act. But given the importance of his need to keep the father alive, the two parts of the enactment may be related. The father's ghost may be analogous to the patient's image of himself in the mirror. Looking at his penis in the mirror, our patient might simply be verifying that he is "intact," just as he wants to ensure that his father is "preserved." In his identification with his father, he, too, is a kind of wandering ghost, neither quite dead nor alive. And if Freud is correct that his unclothed penis refers to masturbation, then perhaps it reveals his unwillingness to father children (his lady is revealed to be infertile) and his unreadiness to commit himself to fatherhood, in the full sense. If the father is not officially dead there is no need to accept the covenant with the dead father.

So far, we have focused on the imaginary aspect of the patient's disavowal: his preservation—in fantasy—of the father's image or "phantom." But the counterpart to this imaginary scenario is the Rat Man's symbolic negation of the father's name. In practice, this entails his *refusal to pay a debt*. His obsessive need to pay back Lt. A. merely sidesteps the issue. The entire mass of his labyrinthine and incomprehensible thinking renders obscure the identity of the person he is indebted to, and makes a mockery of the whole enterprise of paying off the debt. Part of that effort to deride his legitimate debt is the creation of absurd *vows* (of which the command to pay Lt. A. and only Lt. A. is one). One, of course, thinks of wedding vows, but also the vow to remember and pay homage to the dead.

We know—thanks to the case history—that unpaid debts comprise a critical segment of the patient's prehistory. Long ago, the father made a choice to marry a rich girl whose family offered him a comfortable job in preference to a poor girl he was also attracted to. Now the Rat Man in his youthful idealism may have thought that his father "sold out." But regardless of his feelings, the point is that his father made a choice, one that he stuck by and never recanted. Let us not forget that the patient owed his very existence to this choice.

Yet, the father's history reveals an even more consequential debt. As a young noncommissioned officer, the father had gambled away a small company fund for which he was responsible. An unnamed friend helped him out of this jam by advancing him the money. Later, the father intended to pay back the friend but could not trace him. The father was left with an unpaid debt that could never be discharged.

But this debt differs from the first in one respect: it involves more than just the literal payment of money. For the friend also saved the patient's father from scandal: in other words, he prevented his name and reputation from being besmirched; he preserved his status in society—the loss of which could have resulted in his eclipse from the symbolic network. Who knows whether such a black mark might have disqualified him later in the eyes of his prospective wife's family? Thus from one point of view, he owes *everything* to this friend.

If we then move ahead in time to the onset of the Rat Man's neurosis, we find that the patient cannot bring himself to assume his father's debt. On one level, this might involve his trying to locate the heirs of his father's friend and offering to reimburse them the original debt. But in attempting to repay this ancient debt, one is recognizing a debt to the father: that he will pay the father's unpaid debts. He owes his father this duty. But recognizing this debt is essentially an acceptance of the father's legacy *whatever that legacy consists of*.

When you assume the father's legacy, you submit yourself to the symbolic law associated with the father. That law cuts you off from the lost object of your desire (originally the mother), restricts your access to other forbidden objects, reduces the intensity of your sexual satisfaction, and exacts "payment" for the satisfactions it does permit. That payment Freud subsumes under the "malaise of civilization." It is an ongoing payment that only ceases with your death. Thus it is the symbolic equivalent of the Rat Man assuming a debt he can never repay. In other words, assuming the father's "name" means relinquishing the father as a living man. The minute you place yourself in a line of "names" that go backward and forward in time you are in effect a "dead man." The moment you take up the father's "place," you see that in occupying that place you too shall die. In fact, the father's place in the line of succession—another word for his "name"—represents a kind of *memento mori*—the imperative that you must die.

The Rat Man wants to put off this realization and its corollary—the acceptance of his father's death—for as long as possible. His temporary solution is, according to Freud, a "flight into illness." Falling ill, he finds he cannot commit himself to any important course of action. He cannot marry, he cannot work, and he cannot have children. For this man who so values the significance of words, the act of submitting himself to his "word of honor" entails not merely the loss of freedom, but self-eclipse. It is as though his "word" might take over his place in the world, making him superfluous. Yet in the way just implied, his neurosis renders him "dead" insofar as he cannot fully engage himself in life. At this impasse before his father's grave, his symptoms—in their real and perpetual suffering—offer the only solution available: a "living memorial" to his loss.

Contemporary views on father loss

Akhtar and Smolar (1998) in their paper, "Visiting the father's grave," examine their patients' response to father loss, and the role visiting his grave plays in advancing or finishing the work of mourning. Using a developmental framework, they note when the loss actually occurred and also when the loss of the father emerged in treatment. Naturally, the loss of the father during early childhood—as in case #1—creates its own complications. While we know some children are capable of mourning at such a young age, there is the likelihood such mourning will be incomplete. Yet the mother's dedication to the father's memory and her keeping a scrapbook of mementos helped the patient maintain a connection. However, her secretiveness about the scrapbook and her reluctance to lend it to her son suggests she may not have talked to him directly about the father on many occasions.

Nevertheless, visiting the father's grave in the context of psychoanalytic work helped the patient move forward with the task of mourning. His discovery of the mother's scrapbook was significant in that it provided a series of symbolic reference points guiding the patient through the "revisiting" and the resumption of the psychical working-over necessary to come to terms with the loss. The scrapbook contained words and sayings of the father as well as words said about him by people who knew him. And the photographs naturally fell into the role of belated linking objects.

In his mourning work, we see a revival of the idealized father, which in this case was necessary to reconstitute and support the ego-ideal. Because of the timing of the loss before the Oedipus complex was fully engaged, the patient needed to reconstitute the father in his mind as a love object. Thus part of his task was to work through the loss of the "real" father and reestablish his attachment to him, or to undo the repression of those attachments. In this regard, I think it was important that the patient wanted to reenact an imaginary moment when he said goodbye to his father. A child of three may not have been able to do this at the time. But later, he may feel left out of the process, as if it had happened without his being able to have a say in it.

In case #2, the issues were perhaps less complex since the loss of the father occurred in adulthood. Nevertheless, there was the same repression of grief and the incomplete working through of typical oedipal issues such as competitiveness. In this case, the ambivalence toward the father was already conscious. The patient did, however, rediscover the depth of his love for his father. In remembering his father, two things stand out: the father's gift to him of a book about sexuality and his "inheritance" of the latter's golf clubs. These objects functioned as symbolic mementos of the oedipal covenant with the father.

Both objects implied an endorsement of the son's manhood despite the competitiveness in the relationship.

For both cases, visiting the father's grave allowed ceremonial renewals of the pact with the father, both within and without the analysis. These enactments included declarations of love and of leave-taking, endorsements of manliness, and the request of the father's blessing for a marriage. And in remembering their fathers, the men simultaneously "memorialized" and "eulogized" them.

In a series of papers, Calvin Colarusso (1997, 1998, 1999) frames the adult's attitude toward his own death and that of his parents in the context of adulthood developmental tasks. In young adults, he outlines the reorientation toward physical aging, choice of a spouse, having children, aging and death of parents, solidification of peer relations, and attitudes toward work and mentorship. If there is a theme that runs through Colarusso's work, it is the growing psychical awareness of death and attendant loss. In the decision to marry for example, he stresses the words "until death do us part," binding the couple "in the most demanding terms." Perhaps his strongest views are reserved for the death of a parent, which often occurs in this time period. Facing the death of a parent, the young adult can no longer sustain the illusion of immortality based upon what Calorusso calls "identification with Father and Mother Time." In his view, infantile narcissism becomes less able to ward off the dawning realization that, at some point in the future, the child will follow in the parent's footsteps. Here I would merely add that "lessen" does not mean "obliterate" as he seems to imply: Throughout life, the increasing awareness of personal death must contend with its disavowal, which never disappears so long as the ego reigns.

It is during midlife, typically, when one fully realizes the fixed limit placed on the life span. Colarusso writes of a "developmental line of the passage of time and death awareness." Although not failing to note the possibilities for growth, creativity, and psychic enrichment at this stage, he paints the prospect in stark colors: with the death of both parents, "... suddenly, there is no one between oneself and the grave." Indeed, the loneliness and isolation of the individual confronting death becomes a primary psychic challenge in late life. However, the arduousness of this task is assuaged to an extent by personal engagement in maintaining the body image, preparing for death, accepting the death of loved ones, conducting a life review, maintaining sexual interests and activities, and modifying relationships with children and grandchildren.

The relationship with grandchildren and the connection between fatherhood and grandfather-hood proposed by Colarusso is directly applicable here. He enumerates three developmental functions for grandfather-hood: (1) grandchildren can serve as a "narcissistic buffer" against the traumas of old age and the nearness of death; (2) they promote and, to an extent, realize the wishful fantasy of "genetic immortality," and (3) they serve as a "denial of imperfections and unrealized potential" via identification with desired qualities and their "unbounded future."

These gifts, in my view, create a link or "tie" between being a father and being a grandfather. All three of the functions erect imaginary protections against death. Such protections are necessary in the same way that the ego is necessary: no one can face reality without some amelioration. But the grandchild brings benefits that go beyond the imaginary. As a "real" object in his grandfather's life, he adds the element of the unpredictable and provides a focus for continuing engagement with life. And on the level of the symbolic, grandfather-hood places the older adult on the line of predecessors and successors extending into the past and future. True, such an idea promulgates the fantasy of immortality but, at the same time, it gives us a *symbol* for immortality in place of the real thing. The grandfather is thus faced with a continuing dilemma: as the aged father and grandfather, he rises to the status of a *living embodiment of fatherhood*. Yet, that very status continually reminds him of his imminent death. Thus while he may not be able to "imagine" the death of his grandchildren, he can acknowledge that only their *lineage* transcends death.

Is it necessary to point out that psychoanalysis offers multiple opportunities for supplementing the work of mourning? In each of the cases mentioned in these papers—starting from the Rat Man—there is a mutual interplay between the work of mourning and "working through" in psychoanalysis.

One overlap between the two processes lies in the area of *names*. A young adult patient I had in analysis contemplated naming his furniture company in honor of his father. Interestingly, he himself—upon coming of age—had changed his own last name by one letter. This change was the equivalent of going from "Stein" to "Steen." In this single stroke, he altered his connection not only to his father, but to his Jewish roots. However, the missing letter persisted unabated in his unconscious. Consciously, he announced: "I am not my father!" Unconsciously, he added *sub rosa*: "But I am still my father's son."

The life and death of my father

As I write these words, I am remembering and "commemorating" my father. And, in bringing his name—Wolman—back into circulation, I am—symbolically—extending the family name into the future. Lest this aim seem too grandiose, I am also reopening feelings and attitudes toward my parents that I thought I had "laid to rest." For me, this loss was indeed the most "poignant" of my life. In the twenty-one years since my father's death, I have thought long and hard about the meanings of this event, and that process of self-analysis is still ongoing. In this contribution, for purposes of privacy, practicality, and brevity, I will confine myself to the key issues of debt, covenant, gratitude, and reconciliation. These problems helped to circumscribe the work of mourning for myself and for all the grieving sons discussed so far.

Let me begin with the moment—always critical—when I learned the news of my father's death. My father had been suffering from a chronic illness and I knew his end was near. Nevertheless, the phone call from my mother caught me off guard. She was suddenly wailing in my ear: "He's dead! He's dead! Come here! Come here!" In the depths of her grief, my mother was incapable of acting like a parent. She could not prepare me for what was coming nor could she express any awareness that this loss was happening to me as well. The "nakedness" of my mother's neediness and her self-absorption felt overpowering. Later, this episode brought home to me something my father had always done for me and for which I am indebted to him. He always served as buffer between my mother and me; he was always ready to intervene when my mother's labile moods and unpredictable reactions got the better of me. His presence was a guarantee that I would be protected.

To understand this dynamic, the reader needs to know where I stood in my oedipal configuration. In my family, I viewed my mother as another sibling vying for my father's attention, along with my younger brother. In most circumstances, I did not perceive my mother as a maternal presence. Frequently, for example, my mother would scold me for doing something that annoyed her but which I viewed as an injustice. I was at that time an extremely compliant, not to say, docile child. My problem was that I had no way of knowing what I was doing wrong because my mother never told me. My father, however, would rebalance the scales, almost always taking my side.

In the summers, our family rented a house near the beach. This was the setting for my relationship with Richard A.—the boy who died in my sixth year. During that summer or the one previous, I was often alone with my mother while my father was at work. A powerful "screen memory" (Freud, 1899a) of this time consists of my being in a "dark place" inside the house, where the windows did not let in much light. I fantasized that my father would rescue me by coming home and taking me to the zoo. Basically, I felt that I did not evoke much interest or excitement in my mother, unless I should become ill or have an accident (the latter of which I managed to make happen on several occasions that summer). I saw my father as the antidote for my depressed mental state. Going to the zoo represented for me an escape from crushing boredom, yes, but also the kindling of desire in myself. Through my father, I revived my interest in the world because he was interested in me.

But it was more extreme than that. I knew my mother preferred me when I did nothing to "interrupt" her. I speculate that in my fantasy, she wanted me to be immobile, inert, and in a word, "dead." In fact, I used to test this idea by "having accidents," such as falling and cutting my chin, falling with a glass in my hand, etc. My aim was to see if my mother would be upset at the prospect of my dying. And she was. The one thing that got her attention was when my existence was threatened. This was how I knew she was my mother.

So not only did I owe my father for his buffering role but also for my feeling alive and engaged with the world. I needed him to be both mother and father to me and, surprisingly, he pulled this juggling act off quite well throughout my childhood. When I started a new school in the seventh grade, for example, he helped me with my homework. Sometimes—to my shame—he actually *did* my homework for me. This was his maternal side. But he was also available as father. In the second grade, for example, my long pants did not have the newfangled zipper in the fly. I was forced to pull down my pants while standing up to urinate in the boys' room. One time, standing there with buttocks bared, another boy touched me there and I heard giggling behind me. I told my father what happened and he took action: he bought me a pair of pants with a zipper.

I should say that from age five to fourteen, I basked in my father's protective love. In a series of letters I wrote to him on his birthday, I pledged to him my undying gratitude. These letters seemed embarrassing to my adult self for their sycophancy but they were absolutely sincere. It was only later during my adolescence that this precarious equilibrium started to break down. I began to see my father's love as suffocating, controlling, and inhibiting. I felt a powerful urge to defy him and I did so in many instances. I saw his generosity as a way of controlling me. He gave freely to me of his largesse, but he expected absolute loyalty in return. Moreover, there was *no sharing* of power and responsibility with my father. His support was conditional on my remaining in a subordinate position. He fostered dependency in me and I played right into it. One time in my late teens, we were playing tennis together, and he could not stop telling me what to do at every turn. He was acting like a hovering mother hen and a demanding master sergeant at the same time. In place of my former compliance and gratitude, I now felt only defiance and resentment. In an act of protest, I walked off the court.

In my youth, I was especially perplexed by my father's attitude toward money. As a child I received an allowance but in general, I could ask for whatever I needed. My father made no demands on me to earn my own money. His attitude was: I have it so you don't have to worry. Even when I was much older, he used to say to me, "Don't worry, when I'm gone, you'll be a rich man." Of course, as a teen, I had not the slightest idea of what it was like to *not* have money. I always saw him as having a virtually unlimited supply of it. Indeed, his wealth was something in which he took great personal pride. And he didn't mind showing it off. One time, on a trip to Paris during my late teens, he took the whole family out for a meal at a prestigious French restaurant. But when he saw the prices on the menu, he almost gasped. Suddenly, he was asking us to only order an appetizer for our dinner. I knew he could afford the meal, so I just didn't "get" his behaving as if he had insufficient funds.

It was only much later, after I had become financially self-supporting and the father of two children, that I came to understand the central role of money in my father's life and therefore in *my* life. Money lay at the heart of my father's career path, his marriage to my mother, and the broader history of our family. In fact, a willingness to talk about money with me enabled him to reconnect with his own history, and therefore with mine as well. These understandings evolved over a series of conversations we had not long before his death.

The first thing he wanted me to understand was the pact he made early on with his own father regarding money and career. When the depression hit, my father's father lost his livelihood in the fur business founded by his wife's family. He asked my father to forego his aspirations to do something in the performing arts in favor of something that would earn a good income. They considered all the professions, but in 1933, there was just one that was fully open to Jews in America: accounting. My father resolved to become an accountant (as did my grandfather at a later date), primarily in order to make money. For both my grandfather and my father, this was a matter of family survival since my father soon became the breadwinner for the whole family.

My father explained to me for the first time that when the Great Depression set in, nobody in my grandparents' family would lend them money—most especially some that still had it. It became commonplace for people to renounce their debts because if they didn't, they would end up with nothing. But my grandfather was scrupulous to a fault about repaying his debts and this left him at a disadvantage. Nevertheless, he was able to secure a loan for $10,000, on which the family subsisted for over ten years (this accords with the average income of the time of $1,000 per year). My father resented both the extended family's neglect and his own father's unrealistic attitude.

My father's "burden" and the bitterness of his obligations surround the buying of his first automobile. While serving as a US treasury agent in Texas, he bought himself his first car for about $200. Included in the cost were free driving lessons so one could obtain a license. My father was at the time in his early twenties. But when he told them about the car, his parents railed against his rash decision for literally taking food out of their mouths. My father dutifully sent his parents most of his paycheck. Thus a purchase, which today would count as an expected rite of passage for a young adult, he had to fight tooth and nail for. And he fought this fight against his own conscience throughout his life, whenever he consciously rejected his parent's values and the world they stood for.

My grandparents were even more aghast when my father decided to marry a girl who, in their eyes, had no Jewish upbringing. Until shortly before his engagement to my mother, he had been seeing a woman whom they probably would have accepted. My father's choice was based upon the same practical and, some would say, material considerations as his choice of career. He initially had the idea that my mother's family had money, in part due to their more lavish lifestyle. This turned out not to be the case. But even so, they represented for my father a degree of sophistication and a network of influential people that could not fail to help his future career. Hence, in a single stroke, he opted for material considerations and broke with family tradition (and here I do not mean to imply that these were the only factors in his choice).

So, on the one hand, I now realized what my father sacrificed so that I could have a comfortable life. As psychoanalysts, we recognize the multiple meanings of money (Blanton, 1976; Carrington, 2015; Freud, 1908b; Krueger, 1986). We know for example, that an aura of shame and sexual "dirtiness" may follow it. But, we also know that not so well-kept secret: that you must have money in order to enjoy the fruits of twenty-first-century America. So, if my father overvalued money, so be it; because for him, money was his source of satisfaction, the basis of his prestige, and his legacy to his family. And I, along with other children of Depression-era parents, now take that lesson to heart. We no longer take for granted that what we have is guaranteed. Yet for some of the same reasons, we have inherited our father's fear of poverty.

In these discussions and in my later reflections, I acknowledged my debts to him. These debts included: money, love, protection, and emotional availability when I needed it. And he, for the first time—at least as I saw it—acknowledged his debt to me for providing him with grandchildren and by earning the professional respect of my peers. One of my father's fantasies was to found a powerful and influential dynasty that would extend indefinitely into the future, granting him a kind of immortality. So, in my efforts to advance the family name, I may simply be helping him (and me) to fulfill that wish.

However, at two different forks in the road, I took a detour in order to preserve my father's legacy. The first involves my father's mother. My grandmother—a formidable woman—served as the repository of family lore and tradition. When I was sixteen, she wanted to have a close relationship with me, and as part of this relationship she asked—or rather demanded—that I write her a letter once a week, telling her about my life. At the time, I viewed her request as intrusive and predatory. I could not understand what she wanted from me. So, I went to my father and complained. He did not confront his mother on the issue—interestingly he never was able to confront her—but he did give me permission to break off my relationship with her.

In retrospect, I saw myself as a pawn in the ongoing struggle between my father and his mother. He had transferred his emotional investment onto his new family at her expense. I now believe that at one level, she was seeking through me to reestablish the links to the past. These are exactly the links that my father was intent upon smashing. I therefore inadvertently participated in his unconscious "excommunication" of my grandmother. But, since my father's death I have found myself remembering conversations I had with my grandmother before the break—conversations in which she tried to tell me the detailed history of her family and how it intertwined with the fate of the Jews. I seek now to repair those links. I did it by making sure that my children and grandchildren have access to their traditions even if in the end they opt not to follow them. And I do it by honoring my debt to my grandmother in the "letters" I am writing now.

And in a more minor but certainly affectionate manner, I try to meet my father on the path he took *away* from his forebears. Throughout his life, my father was a fanatical tennis player. You will note that it was on the tennis court where I had a fateful confrontation with him and walked off the court. This protest extended well into my life during which I chose to forego tennis entirely. Yes, I was deeply engaged in other pursuits, but I viewed tennis as my father's game. But for my father, tennis wasn't just a game. Since the 1930s when he took it up, it was a time-honored pathway into mainstream American life. On the tennis court, my father could be accepted as a social equal and could mingle with people he considered "upper class."

After my father's death, I started playing tennis again and could once again enjoy the sport and the social interaction it brought. And, it didn't hurt that my late analyst also played, as did my earliest analytic mentor. Indeed, tennis is almost the official game of psychoanalytic society. When playing, I imagine my father on the sidelines urging me on or even telling me what I am doing wrong, for I no longer fear his criticisms. I can hear him exulting in the game and in the fact that my children play and hopefully my grandchildren will also.

In the year leading up to my father's death, there was one event so fraught with psychical significance, it seems to project my father's legacy to me in stark relief. The two of us were emerging from a taxicab on a rainy morning in New York City. My father rammed his head into the top of the cab's doorframe with enormous vehemence, slashing open a large wound in his scalp. His head bleeding profusely, we got back in the cab and hurtled to the nearest hospital ER, where he needed in the order of 100 stitches to close the laceration. Oh, and did I forget to mention that it was Yom Kippur—the Jewish day of atonement? This was one of those moments where—as a psychoanalyst—I knew that the unconscious had spoken. This was clearly no accident. I had witnessed first-hand the uncanny *intentionality* of my father's action. And in retrospect, I think it was clearly meant for me to see and witness. It was as if my father were transferring a lifetime's worth of guilt on to my "head."

As I am writing these words, I associate to a folk song with the title "He Had a Long Chain On." A good man comes up to the afflicted old man with the "long chain" and "offers to set him free." The old man replies, not unkindly, "I guess we had best let it be." Much could be said about this "bungled action," and I invite the reader to bring his and her own associations into play. I just want to make one point leading into the conclusion of this chapter: the fact that my father's culpability was unresolvable in his lifetime and may prove impossible to fully resolve.

Concluding remarks

I hope that this discourse has established that there is a kernel of reality in the dead father, which is immutable and unmovable. It goes back to the sons of the primal father who can never erase or undo the stark reality of the primal crime. Although there is some element of thing-like resistance in all lost objects, it is most characteristic of the father because of his role as impediment and barrier. We have seen that this role is not just prohibitive: it is also protective.

This "real" element in the father exists regardless of the particular oedipal configuration at work. Thus, we see it in the sons' response to the "impossibilities" of the primal father. We also see it in the Rat Man's friendly and non-authoritarian father. Indeed, his neurosis seems all the more severe in proportion to his love for his "real" father. Recognizing his loss would have butted him against the farthest limit of human life: death, and he preferred to keep that particular "encounter" at arm's length. My father's "accident" on Yom Kippur delivered the message: There will be no "at(one)ment" for you.

On a less abstract level, the unresolved "reality" of the father actualizes the child's need for *separation* from his Oedipus complex. This separation is never neat and tidy. My father, for example, would have lauded me for writing this chapter, because it would increase my prestige, and ultimately my earning potential. In today's lingo, he would be interested in how it could be "monetized." The idea of other motives for engaging in meaningful work, while not unimaginable, would remain slightly alien to him. And, there is just no way to fully bridge this gap. In fact, the point is that this gap should not and cannot ever be closed. It is necessary to acknowledge that gap in order to separate. It ultimately becomes part of the "covenant": you are my father, and I am your son and we are not the same. In the end, the son must walk away while, of course, carrying on the father's legacy to a certain extent.

Before concluding this discourse, I would like to add two other points. The first pertains to losing the father in childhood versus during adulthood. The second applies to gender differences in the psychical impact of father loss.

The loss of the father in childhood may produce impediments in the laying down of psychic structure. Here, much depends on timing. The loss of the father before the so-called resolution of the Oedipus complex can retard or weaken the establishment of the ego ideal. Such an outcome could attenuate or even jeopardize the child's relationship with the internalized father figure. However, this effect will be mitigated by specific factors in the child's history such as the presence of father-surrogates and the mother's diligent preservation of the father's words and mementos. On the other hand, such efforts depend on whether a secure affective bond with the father has been fully established. Thus later attempts at repair may require the reconstruction of such a bond or the recovery of its early stages from repression.

Obviously, the loss of the father in adulthood need not threaten the father's psychical representation or that of the internalized "parental couple." But father loss in adulthood can certainly revive oedipal conflicts especially those that were only partially resolved. Structurally, father loss in adulthood thrusts the son (and possibly the daughter) into the role of usurper, thus raising the unconscious specter of murder. In mourning the father in adulthood, the grieving sons and daughters must confront their own unresolved ambivalence, of course. But they must also come to accept what I call—for want of a better phrase—the dead father's tenacious resistance to being reconciled.

As regards gender differences in the processing of father loss, a full accounting of the topic would require a paper of its own. Nevertheless, let me propose three possible differences, which may elicit further exploration. The first posits that the loss of the father may precipitate a thrust toward independence and self-reliance in the girl. Such a move would counter the temptation to sink back within the orbit of the all-encompassing mother. Second, grieving daughters may initiate a search for a father-substitute in their adult partners, whereas the boys would seek further identification or counter-identification with him. A grieving daughter might also seek "compensation" for the loss of her father in conceiving and giving birth to a son. And third, the loss of the father could have destabilizing effects on the girls' *Idealich*, in contrast to the *Ichideal* (Freud, 1914c). That is to say, the girl often has no trouble maintaining and preserving within herself the paternal values; but the devastating loss of the father may damage her ability to see herself as "special" in his eyes.

I now want to end with an extrapolation of Freud. As psychoanalysts, only one or two links separate us from Freud. My link to Freud was revealed to me in this moment from my training analysis: when talking one day about the pioneer analyst, Karl Abraham, I pronounced his last name with a long "a" sound, as in "honest Abe." My analyst corrected me, speaking his name with the proper German short "a." That was in effect my introduction to Freud and the pioneer generation of analysts who preceded me.

As psychoanalysts, we are inextricably linked to our founder. Whether we take pride in our faithfulness or in our daring leaps forward, Freud is always there in the background. We cannot let him go. Not one of us feels indifferent to him. It is always personal. How many of us own little statuettes of him, or in my case, a funny little Freud doll, like his funerary objects? Some of this fixation stems from impediments to mourning brought on by the dual traumas of mass immigration, WWII, and the Holocaust. In the wake of such incomplete mourning, I am reminded of a postmodernist novel by Donald Barthelme (2014), titled *The Dead Father*. It depicts the sons pulling their father's corpse behind them on their journey. As a community, we are still torn over how to preserve his legacy. But the question remains: is it even possible to fully integrate Freud's legacy and to finally permit him to "rest in peace?".

CHAPTER FOUR

Death of sibling

Frederick H. Lowy

Bereavement through the death of a sibling shares the features associated with grief and mourning that follow all significant losses. There is a large general literature that discusses these as well as a rich professional/academic literature, from Freud (1917e) through Kubler-Ross (1969) to Volkan (1981) and other contemporary writers. Yet the death of a sibling, whether in childhood or adulthood, frequently also exhibits features that differ. This chapter will focus on these differences which often are not acknowledged or even recognized. The psychoanalytic, psychiatric, and clinical psychological literatures contain fewer specific references to sibling loss than might be expected; the death of a sibling, after all, is by no means rare at any time and becomes more common as one ages. As a number of authors have pointed out, no other major loss is so neglected, although in recent years there have been efforts to fill the gap (for example, Akhtar & Kramer, 1999; Edwards, 2010; J. Mitchell, 2003). By contrast, the impact of the loss of one's parent or one's child has been the subject of very many published case reports, considerable formal research, and much theoretical consideration. Fanos (1996), among others, has pointed out that "When a child dies, siblings experience a unique loss of their own with little societal recognition of the impact" (p. xi).

In this chapter, sibling death in childhood and adulthood will be considered as well as the special case of the death of a twin. Finally, on a very personal note, I will reminisce about the death of my only sibling, my younger sister, five years ago.

Nuances of sibling relationship

First, it will be useful to reflect again on the special significance of siblings. Although it is the child's parental relationships that, for good reason, are considered most important among environmental and experiential contributions to the development of the psyche, sibling relationships also play a major part. A child's relationship with a sibling includes a wide range of experiences. Not having any sibling prevents a child from sharing in material and emotional provisions offered by the parents but also leaves him lonely and excessively dependent on parents. Having siblings offers a child an opportunity to share secrets, cooperate in ego-building endeavors, elaborate daydreams, and socialize beyond the parental orbit. However, the relationship can also become a fertile soil for envy, jealousy, and resentment. Striking degrees of love and hate can develop. More often, ambivalence prevails and the relationship receives many chances to transform itself throughout childhood, adolescence, and adult life.

The importance of sibling rivalry was recognized early on in psychoanalysis (Freud, 1900a, 1910d, 1917e) but the overall tendency was to view sibling attachments largely as displacements from parental objects. A number of later investigators (Ainslie, 1997; Neubauer, 1983; Provence & Solnit, 1983; Volkan, Ast, & Greer, 1997) raised doubts about this assumption and noted that sibling relationships "tend to be more vital to development than is often suggested" (Parens, 1988, p. 32). These bonds can influence evolving character traits and exert lifelong impact on object choices.

Mitchell, in her 2003 book, *Siblings*, attributes the early inattention to sibling relationship to Freud's almost exclusive focus on oedipal relations. While not abandoning the vertical child-to-parent dynamics, Mitchell adds the horizontal sibling-to-sibling contribution to an individual's subjective formation. Indeed, Sharpe and Rosenblatt (1994) point out that "Sibling triangles exist independent of parent–child triangles … and may exert definitive effects on the individual's identifications, adult object choices, and patterns of relating" (p. 491).

As is frequently the case, it was clinical observation that led these authors to this conclusion: "The most striking common theme in all of our cases exhibiting unresolved oedipal sibling conflicts is the patient's experience of a guilt ridden oedipal victory or a crushing oedipal defeat ... in relation to the perception of a parent's preference of one sibling over another or over the spouse" (p. 1980).

This is well illustrated in the widely known film, *Ordinary People* (1980; directed by Robert Redford). A younger son feels guilty about the death of his rival, the older favored son, in a boating accident. It was an accidental death, the older brother being the one not strong enough to hold on to the boat. Psychotherapy helped the survivor accept that having been stronger was not a valid cause for the guilt that he felt. Often, as in this film, the parents, caught up in their own grief, forgot that the surviving sibling was traumatized as well.

The neglect of sibling relationships has emerged as an important issue in some therapeutic failures. For example, Szalita (1968) conducted second analyses with thirty-seven patients and found that inattention to an important sibling relationship was a factor in dissatisfaction with the previous analysis and the previous analyst. This should not be surprising. The sibling bond is influenced by a host of issues including parental behaviors, birth order and the nature of the sibling relationship itself. Akhtar and Kramer (1999) have provided a comprehensive survey of such variables and I take the liberty of quoting a summarization of them by Akhtar (2009) below.

> (1) Absence of parents often intensifies the sibling relationship; (2) loving relation between parents solidifies sibling relationship; (3) parental favoritism can poison sibling relationship; (4) the presence of adopted siblings poses special challenges for both the adopted siblings and their "biological" counterparts; (5) the relationship between twins is more complex and highly vulnerable to the parental attitudes towards them; (6) having opposite sex siblings can deprive a child of some play activities but can also be utilized as a second theater to work through oedipal fantasies by displacement; (7) the "developmental distance" (Solnit, 1983) between siblings is often more important than the count of calendar months. However, an age difference of less than two years can complicate the older child's separation-individuation and an age difference of more than five years can cause marked indifference or resentment in the older

sibling; and (8) the presence of a positively (e.g., via extraordinary beauty or talent) or negatively (e.g., via congenital defect or serious illness) "special" sibling can lead to other siblings' needs being overlooked" (p. 18).

Sibling rivalry can be intense and in the extreme circumstance can lead to serious violence. This is seen in several animal species and of course, over millennia, in humans; murder of a sibling by another sibling is depicted in ancient literature: the Judeo-Christian Bible (e.g., Cain killed Abel out of jealousy for God's perceived greater love); in mythology (e.g., Romulus killed Remus over the priority in choosing the location of Rome); in literature (e.g., Claudius killed his brother, Hamlet's father, to become king of Denmark and to take his wife); and in the psychiatric literature (see, for example Bourget and Gagné, 2006). Examples from modern literature and film abound. In William Faulkner's (1936) *Absalom, Absalom*, Henry Sulpen kills his half-brother Charles Bon; in Thomas Harris's (1999) *Hannibal*, Margot murders her abusive brother Mason; in John Cheever's (1999) *Goodbye, My Brother*, a near fratricide occurs. Successful film fratricides include Michael Corleone's of Fredo in *Godfather Part II* (1974, directed by Francis Ford Coppola), and Scar's of Mufasa in *The Lion King* (1994, directed by Roger Allers).

Good or bad, loving or hostile, constructive or destructive, the sibling relationship retains the potential to offer the growing child an arena for practicing ego skills, a chamber of shared secrets, a conduit for role-modeling, and a safe haven from the complexities of the ongoing dialogue with the parental objects. It is therefore not surprising that loss of a sibling is a grievous one and mobilizes deep and painful mourning. The shades of such affective turmoil, however, vary according to the nature of the relationship that existed between the siblings and the age at which this loss occurs.

Sibling loss in childhood

It should not be surprising that the effects of sibling loss in childhood are often severe. Siblings interact from birth or the time of the birth of the second and subsequent children in a family. Sibling relations are often close and often conflicted. They may take the form of a close bond, an alliance vis-à-vis the parents and the world beyond the family. Just as often this alliance is fragile and reversible, threatened by more insistent rivalry for parental affection and external recognition. Two examples from psychoanalytic history are of interest in this context. Sigmund Freud (1856–1939) and Harry Guntrip (1901–1975) both lost younger brothers early in their childhood although their reactions to this trauma differed, as observed by Rudnytsky (1988). Guntrip was three and a half years old when his brother Percy died. Turmoil in the family followed: Guntrip's father blamed his mother for Percy's death because she had refused to breastfeed the infant. Guntrip became seriously ill and was sent to live with a maternal aunt. He then suffered total amnesia for these events and was not able to mourn the loss of his brother. At the ages of twenty-six and thirty-seven, separation from a brother figure triggered bouts of illness again. It was not until Guntrip's analyses with W. R. D. Fairbairn and D. W. Winnicott that he was able to deal with his absence of grief about Percy's death and his removal from home. It was only after he learned of Winnicott's death in 1971 that his amnesia finally lifted.

Freud was only eighteen months old when his seven month old brother Julius died. His biographer, Peter Gay (1988) notes that Freud admitted to Wilhelm Fliess that he had welcomed Julius's death with "malevolent wishes and genuine childish jealousy" (p. 11). This letter to Fliess in 1897 and a later letter to Ferenczi in 1912 contain Freud's only known written references to Julius. Clearly, as Freud experienced guilt about wish fulfilment in the death of his little rival, he also may have had "childish jealousy" toward his sisters whose birth rapidly followed Julius's death. Indeed, Freud's conduct toward his sisters in 1938, when at eighty-two he left Vienna for London, has been a subject of speculation. Through the intervention of powerful friends (Princess Marie Bonaparte, Ernest Jones, and American Ambassadors William Bullitt and Hugh Wilson) Freud was allowed to leave Nazi Vienna with six companions. Exit permits were obtained for his daughter Anna, his sister-in-law Martha, his maids as well as his surgeon, Dr. Hans Pichler, and his physician, Dr. Josephine Stross. Apparently no attempt was made to obtain exit visas for his sisters. Peter Gay (1988) wrote that "It was fortunate that Freud died never knowing how his sisters would end" (p. 629). In fact, four died in Nazi concentration camps: Adelfina in Theresienstadt; Mitzi, Pauline, and Rosa in Treblinka. The Macedonian writer, Goce Smilevski (2012), stressed in a best-selling novel that Freud did not attempt to procure exit visas for any of his four sisters. Indeed, Ernest Jones (quoted in Rudnytsky, 1988) speculated that Freud's survivor guilt in relation to Julius's death was reawakened throughout his career and that he was in effect "wrecked by success" (Freud, 1916a) by the fulfilment of unconscious death wishes against Julius.

It is increasingly recognized now that sibling relations play a significant role in their personality formation, indeed, in their very sense of self and identity. As Pollock (1962, 1978b) pointed out, the process of bereavement when a sibling dies may differ markedly from that of the loss of a parent or a spouse. Crehan (2004) pointed to the increased likelihood of a pathological grief reaction that she attributes to incapacity to sustain mourning and, if the surviving child is young enough, to an inability to understand what death is. Sharpe and Rosenblatt (1994) also, usefully, call attention to the need to understand sibling rivalry in the context of the child's developmental level:

> We distinguish preoedipal dyadic sibling rivalry, in which the sibling is experienced relatively unambivalently as an unwelcome intruder, from the more advanced oedipal rivalry, wherein the rival is ambivalently loved and hated with resultant internal conflict and guilt. (p. 494)

When a sibling dies in childhood, either suddenly or after a chronic illness, the impact on the surviving brothers or sisters, immediate and long term, is invariably significant and at times catastrophic. The grief and mourning of the parents over the dead child can involve a degree of withdrawal from the surviving children forcing them to attempt to cope with their own loss unsupported. This results in a double loss for them. Pathological grief reactions, survivor guilt, guilt about rivalrous death wishes, symptoms associated with the post-traumatic stress syndrome (especially in the case of sudden unexpected death) are among the many phenomena that bring survivors to treatment. What is known about the survivors clinically derives from the few reported formal studies and the many individual case reports in the professional literature. Notable among the research reports are those by Cain, Fast, and Erickson (1964) and Joanna Fanos (1996). Albert Cain and colleagues studied the reaction to sibling loss in fifty-eight children in psychiatric treatment. In half the sample strong feelings of guilt persisted for five years or longer. Symptoms included depressive withdrawal, wishes to have died instead of the sibling, excessive risk taking, and punishment seeking behavior. In some cases there was the pervasive fear of impending death. While cautioning that their findings were from a psychiatric clinic population rather than a random sample of the general population, the authors identified identity formation distortions and the pathogenic effect of parental withdrawal following the death. The complex pathological distortion involved in children's disturbed reaction to the death of a sibling include such areas as affect, cognition, belief systems, superego functioning, and object relations. The distortions are not merely intrapsychic, they are inevitably intertwined with and partially products of the dynamics and structure of the family. They include not only profound immediate reactions, the least of which often are physical and psychological symptoms, but tendencies toward enduring symptom formation and distortions of character structure.

Fanos interviewed seventy-five adults who had lost a sibling earlier in life (mainly in childhood and adolescence) due to cystic fibrosis. She documented the family disruption, distortion of sibling relationships, the ordeal of the eventual death of the chronically ill sibling, and the roles of the health professionals. Feelings of guilt in sibling survivors seem to have been omnipresent. Significant findings were reported when sibling death during adolescence was examined (Fanos & Nickerson, 1991). These included the surviving sibling(s)'s questioning of previously strong religious beliefs, difficulty in accepting that the lost sibling was truly dead, experiencing an upsurge in nightmares, and hypochondriacal symptoms. There was also extensive concern about the health of parents, other siblings, and friends resulting in clinging behaviors in some and in others the opposite, withdrawal from important objects to protect against the pain of possible further bereavement.

It is important to note, however, that positive outcomes of sibling loss also occur including deeper appreciation of life and of caring for loved family members, as well as development of resilience and adaptability in the face of later stressful experiences. Martinson and Campos (1991), following up adults who as adolescents lost a sibling through cancer, reported that almost 50 percent retained "a positive legacy of the experiences." Oltjenbruns (1991) also studied bereaved adolescents and found that almost all (96 percent) had developed strengthened emotional bonds with others. A positive outcome for both survivors of sibling death and society at large occurs when, in the attempt to adapt to the loss and as symbolic reparation, they structure their careers accordingly. An example is Dr. Christian Barnard's development of the artificial heart, a procedure that could have saved his younger brother's life.

Mention should also be made of the phenomenon of the "replacement child" (Cain & Cain, 1964; Volkan, Ast, & Greer, 1997). This refers, in pure form, to a new child conceived and reared to replace the lost child in a desperate attempt by the bereaved parents to manage their grief. For the other children, often still in mourning themselves, the replacement child may be experienced as a new rival who has also robbed them of parental attention. Much of the literature on the replacement child syndrome focuses on parents, often Holocaust survivors, whose previous families have perished and who now hurry to replace them (see for example, Anisfeld & Richards, 2000; Berman, 1978).

Loss of an adult sibling

On December 22, 1988, twenty-six-year-old Ken Dornstein lost his older brother David when a bomb on Pan Am Flight 103 exploded over Lockerbie, Scotland. David had been Ken's mentor, protector, and idol. Ken could not stop thinking about the loss of David so he devoted his life over the next twenty years to discovering the truth about the bombing and to identifying the bombers. The need to maintain contact with the lost sibling is not always as dramatic or as long-standing as depicted in this gripping story told in a recent *New Yorker* article (Keefe, 2015). Yet, it reflects the profound impact on the surviving sibling often produced by the death of a brother or sister in adulthood. For many it is a defining life moment; the educator and author, Jill Ker Conway (1989), wrote about the death of her older brother: "He had been like the sun in my universe and most aspirations in my daily life had centered on gaining his approval ... I would always be trying to live out his life for him" (p. 116). Another example: long after his death at age nine, Jack Kerouac's older brother Gerard monopolized Kerouac's thoughts to the point that he "became a sainted ghost in the family" (Kerouac, 1963, p. 14). That lost siblings can "loom larger than life" in families even more than living children was pointed out by Kieffer (2008).

In addition to the popular literature, the clinical experience of grief counselors, psychotherapists, and psychoanalysts has informed the professional literature. The clinical picture that emerges on examination and in treatment of the bereaved survivor differs widely depending upon the personality, the nature of the lost relationship, the family attitudes and responses to the death, and also the circumstances of the death. Variants of note are death by suicide or other violence, including the heroic death of a sibling in the military or police or as a firefighter.

For some surviving siblings the loss is relatively unconflicted and simply unambiguously sad. A companion, a partner, a friend is gone and not only his or her future is lost but also the future role that she or he would have played in the life of the survivor. Of course, for other survivors the loss also exacerbates guilt and anxiety as a conflicted relationship comes to an end. Where there had been repressed hostility, there is now guilt about the fulfilment of unconscious death wishes which in primitive magical thinking unconsciously make the survivor responsible for the death. Sometimes the death is experienced as a loss not only of a close companion of many years at the conscious level but also the conflicted unconscious loss of a love object, the long-repressed incestuous urges now fueling symptoms that bring the surviving sibling to treatment.

The loss of a twin

The case of twins deserves special comment. "Twins", wrote Dorothy Burlingham (1952), "exhibit the closest tie between individuals" (p. 2). Closely interacting in utero and thereafter, usually throughout childhood and often much of their adulthood, they form tight bonds. They sense each other's moods, fears, and joys; they are attuned to each other's intentions and can accurately predict each other's behavior, all to a greater degree than other siblings (Ainslie, 1997). Yet, the close twin bonds are by no means uncomplicated; their rivalry begins in the womb and is intense during infancy, mostly for maternal attention and care. Later they begin to share, often to the point of insisting that each must get exactly what the other gets. Twins have been objects of high interest, at times of veneration, from the dawn of recorded history. They figure prominently in the theology of many societies and appear frequently in literature and drama. They have intrigued philosophers and scientists and have been subjects of experimentation since the studies of Francis Galton in the late nineteenth century. The possibility of careful comparison of identical twins, fraternal twins, and other siblings has made them ideal research subjects of geneticists and psychologists interested in the "nature vs nurture" issue, sorting out the various contributions of genetics, epigenetics, environment, and learning to human identity formation, personality structure, and lifelong behavior. Of special interest in this regard are the several Minnesota twin studies. These involve long-term follow-up and study of pairs of twins who illustrate the varying contributions of genetic and environmental/experiential influences on behaviors, psychological development, and mental and physical health. Notable are the studies of monozygotic (identical) twins separated at birth and brought up in different environments by different families (Bouchard, Lykken, McGue, Segal, & Tellegen, 1990; Segal, 2012). These twins exhibit remarkable similarities including attitudes, personality traits, and psychopathology despite having had no contact with each other for years prior to the study. Since the pioneering study of Burlingham (1952), psychoanalysts too have been active investigators bringing to bear psychoanalytic methods and theory to the twin bond. They have elucidated the intrapsychic dialectic between the wish for individualization and independence versus the equally strong wish for interdependence, at times to the point of fusion, to mitigate the fear of separation from each other. (See, for example, Ackerman, 1975; Lewin, 2014).

George L. Engel, professor of medicine and psychiatry who established the biopsychosocial approach to illness, was a twin. His brother Frank, also a professor of medicine, died unexpectedly of a heart attack at age forty-nine. Twelve years later George published a landmark paper (Engel, 1975) in which he reported and analyzed a decade of his dreams and memories centered upon the loss of his twin and the earlier death of his father at fifty-eight, also of a myocardial infarction. He used this self-analysis as a springboard to discuss the psychology of twins, the nemesis of anniversary reactions with their unconscious sense of time and mortality/immortality, as well as the giving up-given up complex. Engel had kept written records of his traumatic dreams and associations and used them to reconstruct the dynamics of his extremely close and rivalrous relationship with his identical twin. Connecting these dreams, memories, and parapraxes to his own symptoms he demonstrated the power of the anniversary dates of the deaths of his brother and father to influence his unconscious fears and somatic symptoms.

Notable in Engel's paper is his discussion of the psychology of twins, inspired by his personal experience and a review of the psychoanalytic literature on the subject. While separation/individuation from the primary caregiver (usually the mother) is a developmental challenge for all children, for twins this challenge is extended to involve the other twin. "Indeed," notes Engel, "the intimacy and intensity of the interaction between the twins may actually accelerate the separation from mother, only to be replaced by a prolonged symbiosis between the twins, whose separation and individuation from each other may be consequently long delayed" (p. 31). Attachment to each other, at times almost to the point of fusion, positively intensifies inter-twin relations and solidifies the separate identity of the twin unit. While this unit confers many advantages to each twin, including a narcissistic sense of omnipotence, it comes at the price of identity diffusion and delay in individuation. Because of their intense interaction, twins must develop their own psychosocial systems of controlling aggression between them as well as the accompanying libidinal impulses.

Engel commented on the grief that follows the death of a twin, identifying three features that influence the response: "the enduring diffusion of the ego boundaries between self and object representations, the narcissistic gains of twinship, and the delicate balance of the defences against aggression" (p. 33).

In view of the intensity of the twin bond it is not surprising that the impact of the loss of a twin can be devastating to the remaining "Lone Twin" (Woodward, 2010). The lone twin feels as though he or she has lost a major part of the self. Survivor guilt feelings are magnified as well as foreboding that the survivor now has to live for two or could die from a similar illness or in a similar way.

Some personal reflections

My sister died on the 12th day of January 2011 after a long and ultimately unsuccessful battle with recalcitrant encephalitis. Excellent medical care in Dundee and Manchester could only prolong but not master the antibiotic resistant infection that devastated her immune system. That is not how Henny's life should have ended!

My vibrant, outgoing, willful, frenetically energetic sister had carried her own family over major obstacles while successfully playing demanding and very public roles in Britain. She seemed indestructible and now, on the last visit my wife and I paid to her bedside, she was hopelessly frail, barely capable of eating and of talking, clearly aware that she would never see us again. And we, for our part, were sadly also aware that the Henny before us was already far distant from the Henny we had known. When we returned to England shortly thereafter for the funeral it was only left for her survivors, her children and ourselves, to honor her wishes regarding the scattering of her ashes.

94 BEREAVEMENT

Henny and I had been very close as children though not without a measure of sibling rivalry. Less than three years apart, we shared most experiences as we were born into and grew in a tightly knit family in Austria and then, of necessity, Portugal. We lived in Burgenland, southeast of Vienna, where my father was a merchant managing a large general store established there by his grandfather. My mother, a language teacher, was born in Vienna. Assimilated into Austrian life, they were both ill-prepared for the Nazi takeover of their country, their business, and personal assets. My father, especially, had been skeptical about reports from Germany of Nazi atrocities since Hitler became chancellor in 1933. Now, after a brief imprisonment and confiscation of assets, my parents sadly recognized that their world had changed forever. Henny and I were largely shielded from the turmoil of those days. The family remained together which made us as children feel secure. We were with our parents and they prepared us as best they could for the challenges ahead.

In 1938 the first challenge for Jews in Austria—after March 12, part of Germany—was to leave the country. This was not an easy task then and, of course, it became virtually impossible later with dire consequences for those who could not get out. In 1938 there were special exit taxes for Jews to pay, exit visas to obtain, repeated visits to offices and police stations, and then long lines at consulates of countries that might be prepared to accept them. There were not many. Our family managed to get to Italy and then to Portugal, a country that became a haven for many refugees. Henny and I quickly adapted to life and school in Lisbon. We had our parents and grandparents who made us feel secure. However, after the German military occupation of Vichy France in 1942, bringing the Nazis to the border of Spain, there was concern in Lisbon that they might go on to occupy the Iberian Peninsula. Some Jewish parents, including ours, were able to send their children to the United States where they but not the parents were admitted as refugees. We huddled together as child refugees separated from our parents. I was the big ten-year-old brother, specifically charged by our parents to protect and take care of Henny as we boarded the ship carrying children from war-torn Europe to America. Henny and I became closer and we remained close as we adjusted to yet another new country, new language, new schools, and foster parents. More secure as the American culture became our culture, we developed different circles of friends and, as most late latency mixed-gender siblings do, continued to separate and individuate.

Henny continued to look up to me as we successively reached adolescence and young adulthood. I now recall with great regret that

I was not sufficiently generous with my help and attention when she wanted to be included in my circle of friends, much more interesting to her than her boy classmates who seemed to her so immature by comparison. I, sadly, often shooed her away, not wanting my "kid sister" to intrude. Later, as we lived very different adult lives, often on different continents, my admiration for her whirlwind, fast-paced, mercurial activity was mixed with sadness and frustration. Henny's first marriage was difficult and eventually failed, leaving four children who depended heavily upon her all the while she struggled to build a career of her own on her own. I often blamed myself, irrationally, for having been the one who inadvertently introduced her to her charming but narcissistic and cyclothymic first husband. Her second marriage to an English artist was much more successful but, sadly, it ended after ten years when he died of pancreatic cancer.

Throughout our adult decades—Henny was seventy-six when she died—my sister and I maintained regular contact and saw each other whenever possible. I have good reason to believe that she continued to admire me and to praise me to her friends—which invariably left me feeling uncomfortable. Often I also felt guilty, again irrationally, because my life had been easier and smoother and more conventionally successful than hers. And, in her last few years she declined fast with all the tribulations and indignities that attend serious illness in a twenty-first-century tertiary care hospital—repeated tests, new therapies, sleep broken by well-meaning nurses programmed to monitor around the clock the bodily signs that increasingly became irrelevant. Finally, my wife and I watched my dear sister taking matters into her own hands by pushing away proffered food and drink and insisting that intravenous infusions be stopped.

What did I feel, the surviving sibling? Most of the emotions and a few of the symptoms described in the literature: certainly loss and sadness; the emptiness of bereavement; empathy and sympathy with her children and grandchildren whose loss, in many ways, was far greater than mine. Of course, also survivor guilt! I was now the last remaining member of our family of origin, blessed with a loving wife, children, and grandchildren, and memories of a satisfying career. Now Henny, who had been there for me, witness to the major events of my life both sad and joyful, was no longer there. Despite the strong and available social supports in my life, as the remaining survivor, I experienced brief but painful moments of feeling alone without her. These moments, inevitably, were accompanied by even briefer flashes of irrational anger—"Why did she have to get herself sick when her own family and I still needed her?"

Fortunately, I had none of the major symptoms so often associated with painful loss—the recurrent dreams, flashbacks, panic attacks, and depression often seen in the post-traumatic stress disordered survivors. What does remain with me is the lingering regret that I could not spend more time with her, did not sufficiently encourage her to share her difficulties, and did not take a more active role in her life to alleviate her burdens and enjoy her optimism and successes. Of course, she never asked me to do any of these things. She was proudly her own person and I miss her.

What differentiates my mourning for Henny from the grief reactions I experienced at the death of my parents is hard to put in words. However, to be sure, the circumstances were different. My parents' deaths were not unexpected, my father's at age eighty-three after years of cardiac and renal disease and my mother at ninety-nine after a full, healthy life. I mourned the loss in each case but these were normally expectable deaths and I had my sister with me for our parents' funerals and to share mourning over their deaths. By contrast, I felt that my sister, still very vibrant until the infection in her seventies, died unjustifiably early. Despite my medical background and my awareness of antibiotic resistant organisms, I felt angry that I had (unfairly) lost my dear sister. And, of course, she was not there to mourn with me. However, my sorrow was shared with her children and their families as well as with my wife and our children.

Conclusion

Siblings are major contributors to a child's psychological development with implications for identity formation, elaboration of character structure, and sometimes psychopathology. The loss of a sibling is therefore a major challenge to the ego's capacity for mourning and adaptation. Bereaved siblings must deal with a panoply of conflicted feelings and often have to do so without the support of their grieving parents. They mourn the loss of a close confidant and soulmate but also sometimes struggle with guilt over jealous rivalry and unconscious death wishes. The professional literature, having relatively neglected sibling loss until recently, now contains reports of some formal studies and many informative case histories. This contribution is a modest addition to this contemporary trend.

CHAPTER FIVE

Death of spouse*

Ruth H. Livingston

"Stay, stay awhile." An incantation, or so it seems to me, and haunting when Marion Coutts keens it in *The Iceberg* (2014, p. 269), the evocative memoir of her husband's death from a brain tumor. Reading these words strikes my marrow: I'm stunned ... because a year and a half ago I, too, said them—exactly as she did.

I knew, and didn't know—or didn't *want* to know—that my husband was dying. Here we are in the ICU. He says, "You have to let me go." But we are talking! Holding each other! I say: "I know that, and I will, but not yet. Stay, stay awhile." Later, I understand this is for me, not for him. And there comes a day when he cannot stay. I let him go. I tell him I love him, and I let him go.

This is a chapter about the death of a life partner, and it is difficult to write, harder than the essays I wrote after my parents died some ten years ago. Prepared or not prepared for the event, there is no standard, no map, no template: the living go on, somehow, inexplicably. We go on. We do not know how we do it; we just know it's the only choice we have.

---

*This chapter is dedicated to my husband, Robert H. Livingston, who died January 4, 2015. I am grateful to the widow/widower friends and patients who contributed immensely to this chapter.

So we do. Reader, you should be aware that this is a biased report. I write here mostly of my experience[1] and add what I have learned from patients, friends, and writers[2] who have also lost their partners. For the most part, all of these accounts arise from strong—although of course not perfect—relationships, and this is the lens through which I write. We are mourning and this will continue. Often we are sad, and that too will continue. We are not necessarily depressed. We feel blessed to have the relationships we did. Some of us have been more paralyzed than others. Some have created new object relationships. Some of us continue to idealize our relationships with our gone partners, which might keep us from the much-heralded Western culture's edict to "move on." And, finally, so much, of course, hinges on the quality of the relationship, the length, the very tenor of the two people in it, and how they lived together and loved. Lucky me that I loved and felt so loved.

I am in year two since Bob's passing. Passing—a strange word for death as if the event is barely a whisper, when it feels like an avalanche. It is still nearly impossible to believe, to process, and words are often inadequate. My journey to learn who I am without Bob has seen moments of grief, guilty elation, tenderness, rage, even eroticism, and other emotions that I can barely allow myself to feel. Yet I will try to capture some of these for you.

Stay, stay awhile

There are sudden deaths and ones we know are coming. These have different shadings and texture. But what is universal, I believe, is that the death doesn't happen just to the one who physically dies, but to the partner and to the "third," (Benjamin, 2004)—the union itself. It is "our" death, not "his" or "hers": the death and transformation of a sometimes long life of togetherness, a storehouse filled with experiences, joys, sorrows, sacrifices—the death of a "shared history" (Notman, 2014, p. 70). Leavy (2011) describes the experience thus:

> The feeling of one's individual selfhood has been blended with the self of the other by the seemingly interminable dialogue, spoken and unspoken between them. I *am* she or he: we reflect on another, know ourselves in response to one another. The *I* who addresses the other exists as such *with* the other. (p. 700, italics in the original)

Death of a spouse is the demolition of an edifice where what's left standing is the rubble: a fragile hint of a scaffold telling us who we are and who we were in and before the relationship, and who we will be now that one person is physically gone and the other is in the world, living one's worldly life. Coutts (2014) says it best: "I have lost the second consciousness that powers mine. Lost my sounding board, my echo, my check, my stop and finisher. I am down to one" (p. 266). There is a sense of fragmentation and a realization of one's own fleeting immortality. It is a monumental event, and it is totally surreal.

Early days

Numbness. What just happened? As Notman (2014) writes, there is "a moment before and a moment after" (p. 68). "I still recall the physical feeling of a punch in the stomach and still recall curling up in a ball in the chair," says one friend. My "moment": I am in the ICU, and suddenly the monitor beeps. Curtains are pulled. Nurses tiptoe around the bed. I holler, as if he can hear me, "I love you!" I drape my body over his. I watch as life leaves this vibrant, complicated, and wonderful person, my love. Then, I sit (not alone for friends are there, but alone) for a long time. When it's time to leave (and there is a time), I kiss him, his skin cold, and tell him again. I collect his belongings. Then, back to the space we built and shared for nearly thirty years. I'm making the obligatory phone calls as if slogging through quicksand. Offers of help with this task do not appeal to me. It's my job. Sometimes in those calls, I'm longing to be taken care of, but find myself having to take care.

In the days that follow, home is bustling. Friends check in, bring food, flowers. It's so full of Bob here, I cannot see the gifts. What I see are closets jammed with crisply ironed shirts he's not worn for fifteen years and those he has; jeans with holes and some in perfect condition. I see his carpenter suspenders, eyeglasses, lip salve, and aftershave. Then the quirky things: countless measuring tapes, pencils and pens, extension cords, slides from trips before our marriage, photos of women, now in their seventies, whom I don't even know but he did way back when. Odd collections of his favorite number (four), and every telephone he ever bought. Idiosyncratic wiring of electrical gadgets that bewilder me when I go to use them. Thirty years of tax returns.

I begin the process of dismantling, of dissembling the material, the detritus of life. It's a grievous task. This will continue for many months, extending into this second year, as layers and layers of Bob's life are sorted into piles labeled "toss," "file," "donate," "give to friends," "save." The "tossed" go into large garbage bags, and I'm nauseous as I discard them. The "save" pile is daunting; why am I saving? To mark his life? To keep a part of him? Sometimes the "save" is dictated by Bob himself. Who do I think I am, making these decisions so cavalierly? In the end, I have no less Bob than I had before. Because it is not the material things that keep him around, of course: it's him.

A friend tells me that the day after her husband died suddenly, she maintained the same routine she had for years: "I made sure nothing about my day was different," she says. "But of course, nothing was the same, nor will it ever be." As for me, I schedule a series of "gatherings," my own kind of shiva,[3] for friends, family so as to feel as if one foot, at least, is reaching out to connect to others. These are well attended and give me a sense of agency. With each, I have an eerie feeling: "Finally, I'm grown-up. I can have a 'party' without Bob." We were a team of entertainers. There is also some glee in this thought: Why did I believe I could not do it alone? I feel a queasy sense of betrayal when this arises.

Yet, such events are mere diversions, designed to reassure myself and my friends that "I'm okay." Well, I am, I guess, but completely without anchor, ballast. I cannot see patients; I cannot possibly sit with their lives when mine is so unmoored. For some, working soon after the death of a partner is soothing, and at first, I think I'll go back to work in a couple of weeks. Friends encourage this. In the end, I do not return for nearly two months.[4] Inside me, there's way too much wonder. Where is he?[5] Send me a message, Bob. There are too many signs of the man who was—still is—my husband and best friend. I cannot imagine sitting with my patients without this intruding.

In the weeks that follow, there are more questions: "Where am I? Who am I? What now?"

The memorial

Thankfully, because I need to dissociate from the real grief, there's other stuff to do. How to mark a life? The memorial. Details: Venue? When? Who should speak? Should I? Nothing feels quite right. I decide to make a slideshow and hire a tech guy to help me. It's agonizingly cathartic: I weep my way through hundreds of photos of Bob's life, choosing those that will narrate its largeness. I find a video of Bob a few years ago, in which he is saying: "Hi everybody, have a good time"; this, a little gift to my sisters when he couldn't come for a visit. Perfect music, some written by Bob's nephew, is set behind the slides. A song, "It Still Isn't Over," from one of the shows he directed[6] sets me off each time we read it. The tech guy is compassionate. Struggling to write my contribution "eulogy," I can only think of adjectives. So that's what I do. Read adjectives.

Referring to death rituals like "memorials," anthropologist Renato Rosaldo (1989) calls them "busy intersections." This feels right to a patient whose husband has recently died[7]: lots of chaotic traffic, several ways to cross. It's also exactly my experience. Everything's hectic, off kilter. Again, the house is bustling with friends, family, people from out of town, family that barely know me or Bob. I am now feeding "guests" and being fed. I tell myself that Bob is watching this and having a great old time. These are his people and mine. This thought is comforting. But now, I'm alone.

Regrets

Regrets creep up and linger. One friend wishes that she and her husband didn't drink so much. A young widow believes she could have done more in her husband's last days: "I sometimes wish I could have told him how much I loved him, talked to him more, ask him things, be with him." The death was a prolonged one and harrowing; she was exhausted.

Sitting in the hospital from early morning to evening for the month while Bob became increasingly frail wore me down, too. I was mostly attentive, but sometimes had my nose in my computer, finding a strange consolation in editing articles about the Holocaust for my academic journal (worse things had happened to other people than what was happening to me and Bob!). There were long periods of monotony, punctuated by dramatic ups and downs. Decisions.[8] Witnessing his suffering. Trying to remain calm, keep my wits about me so I could be his advocate and tell his friends and family what was going on.

My widow friend and I agree we did the best we could, but we are both sad that the ordeal of watching our husbands die sapped us so that we were dissociated when it actually happened. But then, dissociation is common, perhaps necessary. Widows and widowers whose partners die unexpectedly have an added shock, a shock one woman can only describe as "weird." Joan Didion (2005) is called a "cool customer" by a hospital social worker when the doctor announces her spouse's death. Elizabeth Alexander's (2015) hairdresser remarks that "It's the shock, not the grief, baby" (p. 88) that has turned her hair to gray after her young husband suddenly dies.

No emergency contact

Death is a bureaucratic nightmare and there is business to attend to. Most of it is horribly painful. I am marching around robotically, meeting with the estate lawyer and gathering needed information about "the deceased." But, I'm also reaching out. On my way to dinner with a friend a month after Bob's death, I fall on some ice. Not a big deal. But then, my hand is swollen. After several weeks, I have it checked out. Ouch. Surgery was needed that would render my "good" hand useless for a number of months. I go through the motions. Someone must fetch me from the hospital after surgery, not Bob. When asked by the admitting nurse who my "emergency contact" is, I gasp and cannot reply. Who is my emergency contact? I am feeling very sorry for myself.

And then, my cat dies. A dear, undemanding companion, and soft comfort for the two months following Bob's death, he abruptly stops eating. I race him to the vet, Bob's best friend who was with me when Bob died. A tumor is found and surgery recommended. Perhaps I can buy some more time with this cherished soother. He does not survive the surgery; my vet and I weep together. And I wonder what stars are lined up against me. Poor me! Joan Didion (2005) raises the question of "self-pity," which she calls "the most universally reviled of our character defects" (p. 193), and like her, I am appalled at and ashamed of my indulgence. How to appropriately mourn as a widow or widower?[9] Gorer (1955) referred to death in Western society as "pornography," a taboo. There's not much room for the griever: "The bereaved is crushed between the weight of his grief and the weight of social prohibition," writes Aries (1977, p. 583).

So embedded am I in this cultural/social proscription against giving in to self-pity, a battle rages between succumbing to my waves of grief and the hypocrisy of putting on a brave face for the world. In this struggle I am not alone: one widow was criticized by family for not expressing her grief openly (she could not cry); another was told by a friend that she *must* pull herself together.[10]

Now, for me, there are layers of losses: Bob, my damaged hand, and the death of my sweet, soothing cat. Perhaps I have permission to wallow in sadness. Yet, I know that accumulated losses are dangerous: I scare myself by reading about the "broken heart phenomenon" (Stroebe, 1994), which refers to disturbing statistics showing an excess risk of mortality for the bereaved, especially widowed people (see also Kaprio, Koskenvuo, & Rita, 1987; Rees & Lutkins, 1967).[11] Although grateful I didn't do more damage, I'm certain my fall had to do with the strain of caregiving and the loss of Bob. It's a wake-up call to take better care.[12]

Beyond pity

Sorry for myself, yes, but I don't feel lonely. I'm talking to Bob all the time. His ashes are in a black box. They are almost too heavy for me to lift. I can't part with them, although I have promised to scatter them in the park. Now in the apartment, I walk by and fondly pat the box. I anthropomorphize, moving the box away from a chilly window so "he" won't be cold, setting it near some flowers so "he" can enjoy their beauty, putting it on the bed next to me as I sleep to keep me company. Strange behaviors, these. Yet, I know from others who have lost their spouses that I am not alone in them. Oh, the mystery of it all.

WHOOSH! I'm sleeping—at least I think I am, but awakened by a sound, like a matador flicking his cape to provoke the bull's charge. Suddenly, there is Bob. I say, "Oh, so happy to see you!" And he replies, "Are you really?" "Yes," I answer. "How is it?" Bob: "Well, actually, it's not so bad!" I reach out to embrace him, and he disintegrates in my arms. That part is sad, but I love the "visit," and although I don't know if that was truly Bob or my mind, it doesn't matter because there he was. And I smile. (This is just the first of many so-called "visitations" from Bob during the next several months.)

Dreams, "visitations," meaningful signs that feel like messages from the lost partner, and a sense that the partner is present are not uncommon (Bonanno, 2009). It depends on a number of factors—including the quality of the relationship and the resilience or its lack of the widow or widower—whether these phenomena may be healthy responses to a partner's loss or unhealthy lingering attachments to the deceased. Freud (1917e) tended toward the latter interpretation. He wrote that such uncanny sensory experiences were caused by a "hallucinatory wishful psychosis" (p. 243), representing a "turning away from reality," and resulting in melancholia when taken too far. Yet, more recent bereavement scholars (e.g., Klass, Silverman, & Nickman, 1996) and researchers (Bonanno, 2009) challenge this notion, citing the events as possibly rejuvenating—a way of honoring the bond, even helping the bereaved to move past the loss and make peace with it. As for me, the experiences are calming, reminding me of the preciousness of my ties to Bob and even giving me a sense that he still "has my back." In fact, the meetings are so tender as to carry me forward into my "new life," a life that I cannot begin to imagine.

About this "new life"

There are so many ways of missing. It's not just the intimate contact, but the sense of ongoing-ness: the safety in sharing another's experience and opinion, even if it differs from yours. The joy in reviewing mundane and extraordinary experiences of one's day. Being known and knowing. Trusting in someone's love for you. Recognizing the other as a separate person and yet also recognizing the power of the relationship as another entity. And then there are shared relationships of a marriage or close partnership:

Leon (1999) writes:

> The bereaved steps into an interpersonal vacuum ... bereavement serves to undercut critical life support systems of the self. That is, we all depend to some extent on validation of who we are and, for most of us, that is embedded in relationships. (p. 385)

Distinguishing between who to be with and who to not (i.e., who soothes and who does not) is an interesting question. C. S. Lewis (1961) writes: "An odd byproduct of my loss is that I'm aware of being an embarrassment to everyone I meet .... Perhaps the bereaved ought to be isolated in special settlements like lepers" (pp. 10–11).

There are times when I agree. Sometimes, people's reaction feels similar to what people with serious illness encounter: a kind of revulsion, although that's not what they intend. I cannot trust myself to be with anyone else, and certainly not with a group. Often, newer friends feel easier to be with than those who knew Bob or me and Bob as a pair. With couple friends of ours, I am aware of who is missing. What's more, every widow or widower I consult agrees that the dilemma of being alone versus being with others is constantly vacillating. Writes one friend: "When I'm alone, I'm dying for company. And an equal amount of time, when I have company, I just want to be alone." That is, making social plans is dangerous; *not* making them is searingly painful. Some examples from my experience follow.

First, my professional community. It embraces me, but, oddly, I cannot bear to see my colleagues or to attend any events or meetings at my institute. Perhaps, seeing these friends or being there reminds me too much of how much support I received from Bob in my career, and how I sometimes used my career to hide when he and I had rough patches.

And then there are social events: I go to a huge, elegant birthday party of a friend. I have many acquaintances who are part of this friendship. But I can barely stand it. Less than a year before Bob died, I threw him a huge birthday party. We (modestly) and everyone else agreed that it was one of the best parties ever. Perfection. Now, I'm judgmental about this party's food, the shape of the evening, and even the guests. I know it's just out of sadness and anger. I flee.

I keep trying: a musical friend has a gig in a cabaret. She's amazing. Her children and husband are there, celebrating with her. Every sad song brings me to tears—not just tears but heaving wails that I fear interrupt the music. I try to contain myself, not wanting my self-pity to be on display.

Another time, it's a memorial service for an old, dear friend and a musical theater collaborator of Bob's. Before going, I'm worried about melting down, especially since the song I used in Bob's memorial ("It Still Isn't Over") is to be performed. Oddly, however, I sit there, cold as ice. Unmoved. And wanting so very much to have Bob to share my feelings with. I think: he would have directed this event so much better.

Indeed, social interaction is dicey, but there's an alternative: being alone. That's *what* soothes. And we all have different criteria. For me, it is only music, any kind of music, but mostly classical guitar. I play it in my apartment every day; I sleep to it. Others I speak to find solace in television, in reading, in work, in the comfort of pets, in travel, even in shopping. There is no generalization to be made here, and I remember this as I sit with my widow and widower patients, witnessing their navigations of this dark and fraught journey.

Back to work

Notman (2014) reflects that the "one place where I felt like my old self, or close to it" (after losing her partner) "was at work" (p. 84), and Oates

(2011) discovers that she is restored by her writing and teaching after the death of her husband. I hope this will be so for me, but I'm not sure. I'm still raw and concerned about my seemingly endless self-absorption and sense of fragmentation. I reflect on Colson's questions (1995). Will I be able to tolerate my patients' needs? Their fluctuations in levels of regression? Can I, as Abend (1986) asks, "maintain an empathic, non-judgmental stance" (p. 571) toward patients who are exhibiting anger, hostility, or embittered feelings toward their partners? In contrast, will I have the ability to "respond objectively to the analysand's expressions of love or longing" (p. 572) toward his or her partner without becoming consumed with my own envy and grief?

Even with these thoughts, more than two months after Bob's death I know it's time to return to my work.[13] Still not resuming, but visiting my beautiful office, just a block away, I feel out of sorts. It seems so wrong. Bob helped me organize it and built a wonderful bookcase where all my treasured professional literature resides. Yet he is not here, and almost immediately, I start imagining leaving this "haven," a thought previously unthinkable. I tell myself I need to move home to save the rent. The real truth is that I am closing in; my career is my "home," now where Bob was once "home." Leaving the apartment to go to this other space almost seems like a betrayal of Bob and of my relationships with patients, as if I'm suddenly not bringing *myself* to my work. I make the decision to move my office to home. This will take some time and planning. Until I can make the move happen, I remain in my old space. Seeing patients again arouses another surge of insecurity. Countertransference is rampant.[14] I'm sure it is inappropriate, but I feel more intimately involved with these people I see every week than with friends or family. Unlike Singer (1971), I am not surprised at most of my patients' genuine concern and capacity for sympathy and caring.[15] I feel valued, even loved.[16]

Also positive is that most of my patients' struggles and suffering take me out of my own, and my empathy for them is at full volume. That is, except for two, who completely deplete me. I know they need more from me than I can give now, maybe ever. Wrestling with this dilemma, I tell them that I cannot be as present with them as I would like or as they deserve, and refer them to colleagues. They are angry at me for my abandonment and I have pangs of guilt. But, mostly, I am relieved and just pray that I have done right by them and me. In truth, the patients I most look forward to seeing are two recent widows, one younger, the other older than me.[17] So keenly am I aware of my solidarity with them, I make special efforts to keep my eye on boundaries. This hardly works. I find myself crying when they cry, and sometimes speechless in the face of our shared grief.

Despite differences in how we're handling this, that is, my coping and theirs (one, so depressed she can barely come to sessions, and another bravely soldiering on, even beginning an intimate relationship with a close friend of her husband), we have more in common than we have differences. Among the most striking: our intrusive thoughts— one might say, flashbacks—of the actual deaths of our partners, down to minute details. Especially early on, these plague daily, and my patients and I (to my analyst) need a space to verbalize them. The grim images, often with an overwhelming recognition of the immensity of loss are not the stuff of conversation with those who have not had the experience. This is the way it is. Thank goodness, say my widow patients, friends, and I for the sacred space of psychotherapy and psychoanalysis. Thank goodness for these patients; I am in it with them, but also joining them as they explore their moving, constantly evolving grief.[18]

Planting my garden—"sublimatory activity"[19]

I am fortunate to have a terrace where Bob and I planted a beautiful garden each spring. Now, it's the spring of the year of his death and new sprouts are appearing on the bushes, their appearance a sign of rebirth. It is time to add flowers to the budding greenery.

Leon (1999), Niederland (1989), and Pollock (1989) reflect on how mourning can "liberate" creative energies and serve as a healing process.[20] As I choose flowers, plant them, watch them grow, and then tend to my garden, I think it's the most positive and enriching thing I have done since Bob died. Two birds, clearly a couple, share the sun on the terrace parapet. A katydid that I'm convinced is Bob hides among the leaves and calls to his mate in the warm evenings. This is healing. I am still unable to write, but at least I can do this.

Renovation

But there is still more to do, some of it creative and some not. Moving my office to the apartment will require modifications. Soon after Bob's death, I shamefully begin thinking of changes to make in my home: for example, renovating our thirty-year-old kitchen that has no dishwasher and cabinets too high for me to reach. I meet with an architect friend and he and I discuss options. It's astonishing to me that I know so little about design and building, Bob's realm.[21] I call on Bob's friends in the profession: architect, contractor, woodworker. After a number of meetings, the project morphs. Now, I am having the entire apartment painted, a door added to close off the bedroom and my desk area so I can see patients in my living room. Everything feels like a betrayal: to do this, I must rip out Bob's office and trash our beloved kitchen where we cooked and entertained for nearly thirty years. I proceed—in part because it is a massive distraction to my grief and because I have no other idea how to act as if I am still in the world. I find myself grateful for the surreality of this very real project that catapults me into areas I have never visited. Revelation: feelings of empowerment as I tackle the renovation, a job I once would have "surrendered" to Bob (see Notman, 2014).

I'm told the renovation will take a month. I stumble around, living there as it unfolds, with only a microwave and fridge, the smell of paint, and poor lighting. I tangle with the contractor and woodworker. Three months later, it is done. It is now a year since Bob died.

Anniversary

Friends ask me about anger. Both widows and widowers in my practice express it, often vigorously. For a year, I wonder why I'm not actively feeling this—no strong sense of anger at Bob for "abandoning" me or at the world for "taking" him. Instead, I float in what feels like a cloudy haze, raw beyond words, wondering, wondering. Music and art and poetry make me cry. Food loses its taste. Sleep is longed for, but spotty. I see a tendency to romanticize my marriage and idealize Bob, and this strikes me as dangerous, somehow. He was complicated and challenging, and so was our union. I vacillate. I know I am blessed to have had him, and lucky to have been so loved. Nonetheless, as the first anniversary of Bob's death comes closer—and I still cannot write this chapter—rage pierces the boundary of dissociation.

I invite about twenty-five friends for a remembrance of Bob on the anniversary of his death: January 4. These are people who have taken care of me this year. I busy myself with choosing buffet recipes for this big dinner party and buy flowers and candles to decorate my "new" apartment. I ask my friend K to help with the evening. Before she arrives (early), everything is ready. She remarks that I seem calm. I have been planning this for a year.

Then, seemingly from nowhere: K is putting cheese on a platter, and suddenly, I lash out that it looks terrible and take over the job myself. I then ask her to make a sign about the two stews (one vegetarian, the other not) so guests can choose. To me, her sign looks sloppy. I grab the pen, mumble, "I guess I have to do everything myself," and "fix" it as she stands bewildered, wondering who this Ruth is. Guests have been asked to put their coats on the bed. Some load their coats on my desk instead, and I hostilely remove them, grumbling that no one listens to me. Everyone but me and my dear friend K have a great time at this gathering. The next morning, I call K to apologize, but the cat is out of the bag.

I have what Ronaldo Rosado (1989, 1993) calls "grief and a headhunter's rage." Rosado describes a ritual once practiced by male members of the Ilongot tribe in the Philippines who, after the death of a loved one, were compelled to find a victim and to cut off that victim's head. When asked what prompted this dramatic and horrifying action, one man replied that it was "rage, born of grief," and that "severing and tossing away" the head enabled him "to vent and ... throw away the anger of his bereavement (p. 1)." Although this might seem extreme, somehow it makes sense. I can only tell you that the force and power of my rage, now a year after Bob's death, is combustible: I long for a symbolic gesture to banish this persistent anger forever.[22]

Recent widow

I am filling out some forms for insurance. There are boxes to check: married, single, widow/widower. I pause. WIDOW. What a strange word, that! Black widow, the venomous spider, comes to mind. What does it mean? In a stunning poem, Sylvia Plath (1961) riffs: "The word 'widow' consumes itself," she writes. It's a "dead syllable, with its shadow of an echo" (p. 164). It's a "great, vacant estate." Especially strange to me is saying it aloud. "Widow. Recent widow." There's almost some shame in it, as one patient reports: "I've referred to myself as a widow, but only out of dismay." There is not one widow or widower

I know or have read of who hasn't found the label confronting as a new identity. Again, what does widow/widower mean? Maybe it's defined as when "we" becomes "I" and when "our" becomes "my."

Suddenly I'm lonely!

I have survived the first year, the so-called year of "magical thinking," as Joan Didion (2005) coined it. My anger is no longer seeping out at inappropriate times, although I know it's there, just too hot to handle yet bubbling beneath the surface and emerging with triggers. (Thank goodness for dissociation!) The good news is that I love seeing patients in my home and enjoy cooking in my newly renovated kitchen. My friends are less attentive, although this is expected. I also seem to be reaching out less. Mostly as year one ends and year two begins, I imagine I will begin to feel myself again. I look forward to this next phase and think about how and when to scatter Bob's ashes, which I've not been able to do this past year. Perhaps my grief will lift in year two, as I've been told or have read: "It takes a year," they say.

Surprise! As year two begins I am not "moving on" or mourning less, but paralyzed and even sadder. I discover the second year slump is not so unusual. Casement (2000) calls this period "an absence that can often seem relentless;" and an absence that "can ... become a painful 'presence' which never quite goes away" (p. 21). One friend emails me that she (now deeply into year two) is "for some reason, bluer than I've been," and a widow patient, also in the second year, isolates to an alarming degree, leading me to intervene. Another says that she is missing and appreciating her husband more than ever, which causes an upsurge of anger and sadness. Witnessing his protracted illness and death had, she says, dimmed positive memories of their connection for her in the year after his death. Now she can truly mourn.

As for me, I am seized with an overwhelming sense of anxiety, a panic that I can barely contain. Fortunately, it comes and goes, never arising when I am with patients and showing up only after they leave. In time, I recognize a pattern. A workman comes on a Saturday to install some flooring. Prior to his arrival, I find myself completely undone: my heart is pounding and I'm filled with dread. I wonder how I will be when this guy arrives and hope I can calm myself in order to supervise the job. What I notice is that I feel immediately soothed when the stranger appears, although we barely interact. Diagnosis: I am LONELY!

This realization comes with some shame, as "lonely," for me, has a similar connotation as self-pity (see above)—a weakness, I think, in this path of self-discovery. Single for many years before my marriage, I never longed for company. In fact, I often craved solitude after Bob and I married: he occupied much space. Yet now, I find myself in a spiral of missing and emptiness. Bob is truly gone and is not coming back. This is final, unchangeable. He is, I'm sad to say, no longer even "visiting," except vaguely. Yes, I still hold him in my heart, but I need to fill the void. How?

"Loss forces the individual into a painfully passive position," writes Gaines (1997, p. 560). He believes the state is only countered by the creation of continuity, that is, making commitments, planning for the future, but with an "active determination and control in the very area where the loss has deprived [one] of all control (p. 561)." A remobilization is called for and, in time, shows up in my patients, and eventually, in me. A widower moves back to the city where he lived when first courting his wife. One widow patient begins an intimate relationship with a widower friend of hers; another rents a bedroom in her small apartment to a married couple, and says she's thrilled to have roommates again. A third lands an enriching new job; and a friend, also in her "second year" impetuously gets two large dogs. I start meditating and go online. Meditation will help quell the anxiety. So will meeting someone. Perhaps I can feel alive again. Forming a new "object relationship," they call it.

Oh, the absurdity of it all! I choose an online site but have no idea how to write a profile. I scribble something—only the barest of descriptors—and throw on some pictures, one from which I must remove Bob. That feels creepy. I kind of hope no one will "pick" me and I kind of hope I won't see anyone online that I'd pick. My interest is in widowers close to my age, maybe with children.

No dice. I talk to a number of men who fill that bill. Widowers, especially, leave me oddly cold. They seem too sad, too needy, too expecting that I will fill their emptiness, which I cannot do for them, nor can they do for me.[23] Finally, there's someone who appeals, even though he doesn't meet the checklist. We speak by phone and I find myself smiling throughout the conversation. It's a smile that I have missed, a smile of connection, a smile of pleasure. We meet and there's chemistry. He's quirky and creative and interesting, all of which I like. I am stunned that I could have butterflies like a teenager. I feel my body coming back and it's totally frightening. I see him for two months, until I allow myself to know that we do not want the same thing and to accept that each meeting is evoking a sadness in me that only exacerbates my missing of Bob. Is this how it should be? I want to laugh and feel loved, and it's not happening. Yet, it's too late: Now, I've kicked up my longing. I go back online.

Meanwhile, I cannot write this chapter. As deadlines pass—one after the other—I sit frozen at the computer, thinking: "I cannot do this; I cannot capture Bob, I cannot articulate this experience, cannot possibly capture it while I'm in it, cannot imagine myself out of it." It occurs to me that, like other obstacles to finding myself, there is some mysterious corner to turn. Maybe it's this chapter. If I finish it, where will Bob go? Where will I? "Stay awhile, stay awhile," I keen. I don't write.

And then, I meet someone: kind and caring, wise, and loving. I am a handful for him. Little things trigger my grief and my rage. I weep when he tells me he cares for me. I attack him for minor lapses in attentiveness, unquestionably a reaction to my fear that he, too, will leave, which makes me furious. He is patient, understanding. I begin to feel hopeful, excited. A stirring of lovingness. Erotic feelings that mostly blissfully—although sometimes ambivalently—arise. How grand! Perhaps, I can finally really let Bob—partner and best friend—go, while keeping him in my heart.

Onward

So here this chapter ends, although I continue on my arduous, painful, and poignant journey. What have I learned? More about the impermanence of experience, of life. And more about the gifts of life, especially the gift of glimmer in the face of sadness. Maybe, just maybe, with Bob watching over me, I will find myself again. Maybe, just maybe, I'll find a new "emergency contact." We do go on. We don't know how we do it; we just do. Stay tuned.

Notes

1. I am in my sixties and have no children. Although I have treated and spoken to widows and widowers who are younger and do have children, this account is primarily about *my* experience. Of course, each experience is different, and everyone grieves in his or her own unique way.

2. See: Alexander (2015), Coutts (2014), Didion (2005), Jamison (2009), Lewis (1961), Oates (2011), Rehm (2016), and Roiphe (2008), among others.
3. Shiva, the Jewish custom of receiving visitors for a week in remembrance of the deceased, allows the community to share the loss and consoles the bereaved. Although my "gatherings" were not shivas per se, they were certainly comforting.
4. When one chooses to return to work is highly individual. Linda Sherby (2013), for example, resumed her psychotherapy practice only a month or so after the death of her husband.
5. C. S. Lewis (1961), writing about the death of his wife, H., asks: "... in what place is she at the present time ... It's as if she's on a journey without me" (p. 23).
6. Bob was the conceiver/adaptor and director of the award winning musical *Taking My Turn* (1983). The beautiful song "It Still Isn't Over" (music by Gary William Friedman, lyrics by Will Holt) is from that show.
7. I am grateful to my patient, H., who shared this reference with me when describing her experience.
8. I regret that I didn't challenge the doctors' decision to start Bob on dialysis. Although he agreed, it was nothing but frightening and uncomfortable and it certainly did not prolong his life.
9. Doka and Martin (2010) distinguish between two types of grief: intuitive and instrumental. The intuitive type is characterized by waves of powerful emotions and expressions that mirror feelings. The instrumental is an inward, quiet process, combined with physical action. Although intuitive grieving may be more likely associated with widows and instrumental with widowers, there are no universals. In point of fact, I am a mixture of both types of grievers.
10. As an analyst or psychotherapist, it is critical to allow the widow or widower to mourn in his or her own way, without judgment, while simultaneously keeping an eye on the patient's outside functioning. After Bob's death, I used my weekly therapy sessions to openly grieve—often sobbing through the entire fifty minutes. In this way, I was able to bracket my sadness and to accomplish what I needed to accomplish in work and friendships. Some, but not all, of my widow/widower patients also use the therapy hour to attune to mournful feelings, while others report that they are not able to compartmentalize as I was fortunate enough to do.
11. "Death of a spouse" ranks number one on the Holmes–Rahe Stress Inventory (1967), a scale that predicts illness related to stress.

12. My self-vigilance is helpful in working with bereaved patients, especially those who have been long-time caregivers prior to the death of their loved ones. We all need reminders to keep ourselves healthy.
13. I wait this long, although many urge me on: "Work helps," they say knowingly. I think, what/how do they *know*? This is a piece of advice I find especially insensitive in the early days of my mourning.
14. Colson (1995) writes after the death of his wife: "I struggled against an intensified wish for my patients to be aware of my plight, to appreciate my struggle, and to acknowledge the courage required of me to carry on … I felt the need to monitor my wish for my patients to know more than they already did about my circumstances, longing for their support and caring, versus the danger of my recoiling in guilt from their exploration of these fantasies and feelings" (p. 470).
15. All my patients knew that my spouse had died. There was no reason not to disclose it, especially since I suspended my practice. Although I provided coverage while I was absent, no one took advantage of this and all returned. Like Sherby (2013, see below), our loss was always in the consulting room, especially in the early days. Particularly now that I am seeing patients in the space we shared, Bob remains a presence in both the transference and countertransference.
16. Sherby (2013) poignantly describes the meaningfulness of her work with patients after the death of her husband, including those who also suffered loss. In a particularly moving chapter entitled "Endings," she deeply reflects on how the mutually agreed-upon termination of one long-term patient profoundly impacts her.
17. The shared grief of widows and widowers can be quite powerful. Women tend, at least in my experience, to seek each other out individually for support. But widowers, in part because of their conditioning and perhaps because there are fewer of them—according to statistics there are four times as many widows as widowers (*Administration on Aging*, 2011)—may find it more difficult to reach out. I have found that support groups for the bereaved are particularly helpful to men who have lost their partners. It is there that they can feel safe in sharing their sadness with others who are also grieving.
18. In terms of working with bereaved patients, I agree with Casement (2000) who writes: "I don't think there can be a right way for this kind of therapeutic endeavor. We each have to learn to use ourselves in whatever way is natural and honest, and, as far as possible, to remain nondefensive. But we will find that people are different. Therefore, however

many bereaved people we have seen, we still have to learn from each new person afresh what helps and what doesn't help" (p. 24).
19. See Nimroody (2014, p. 320).
20. For example, Leon (1999) writes: "The structure of the creative process promotes a sense of unity, thereby maintaining cohesion, against centrifugal fragmentation ... The finality of death, the boundaries of mortality, are defied by attaining a sense of omnipotence and eternity through the creative product" (p. 388).
21. In addition to being a stage, theater, and television director, Bob was a custom cabinetmaker with a successful NYC business, The Craftsmen of New York.
22. Still working on it!
23. I'm certain there are many spectacular widowers. This was merely my experience in the strange world of internet dating.

CHAPTER SIX

Death of child

Ann G. Smolen

There is a dearth of writings on the topic of the death of a child within the psychoanalytic literature. Psychoanalysis, beginning with Freud (1917e), has delved deeply into the topic of mourning, exploring what is deemed "normal and pathological." The general topic of "loss" has also been extensively studied and written about by many psychoanalytic scholars. Beginning with Freud, psychoanalysis has placed importance on separation and the loss of the object, demonstrating "the extraordinary impact of disorganizing, potentially lethal sequelae of significant loss throughout the lifespan" (Aragno, 2003, p. 433). I can only begin to speculate as to why the death of a child has fundamentally been overlooked within psychoanalysis. In the few articles and chapters available on this subject, the analyst (and non-analyst) author always prefaces his or her thoughts with: *The death of a child is too horrible to comprehend*, or *There are no words*, or *The most painful death is the death of a child*. Perhaps this is one reason so few have embarked on this excruciating yet imperative journey.

Freud's personal journey

Although Freud had made some passing remarks about the outbreak of neurotic symptoms upon bereavement (Freud, 1893) and mourning being a riddle that could not be fully explained in terms of drive economics (Freud, 1916a), it was in a seminal essay, "Mourning and Melancholia" (1917e) that he explicated the affective response to a major loss in detail. Freud emphasized that the emotions invested in significant love objects are "strengthened by a thousand links" (p. 253) with them. And, when such a love object passes away, the "work of mourning" demands a decathexis of it so that one might become "free of it" and find a new object. However, the mourner rebels against the reality of the loss and only reluctantly abandons the original attachment, initially denying the reality of the death. Freud maintained that in normal grief, the person must experience total decathexis from the lost object. He postulated that when mourning does not go well, and the person is unable resolve the anger and disappointment towards the deceased, melancholia ensues. This is because the relationship that existed was a highly ambivalent one and after its loss, the conflicted feelings concerning the deceased object were turned upon the self. In order to "protect" Freud's beloved drive theory, later psychoanalysts focused on Freud's statement that identification is used to resolve ambivalent attachments. Because normal relationships are partly ambivalent, identification accounts for enduring ties even when reality asserts that the object can no longer offer gratification.

A significant shift, however, occurred in Freud's 1917 views. This was mostly in consequence to his encounter with the deaths of three people he deeply loved.[1] His daughter, Sophie, died in 1920. Her four-year-old son, and Freud's favorite grandchild, Heinnele, died in 1923. Freud's mother, Amalia, died in 1930. Really with anguish and "informed from within," Freud softened his stance about mourning getting fully resolved and also about the decathexis-object replacement hypothesis.

In response to a letter from his friend, the renowned Swiss psychiatrist, Ludwig Binswanger, Freud described his own bereavement, writing of the deaths of his daughter and grandson. He wrote: "Your letter has renewed in me a memory-nonsense, it has never been dormant ... Since the death of Heinnele, I don't like the grandchildren any more, but I do not enjoy my own life either" (cited in Schmidl, 1959, p. 43).

In a letter written upon hearing the news of Binswanger's son's death, Freud wrote:

> We know that after such a loss the acute process of mourning will close at some point, but there is no real consolation, no substitution. Whatever may replace the lost [one], even if it could fill the void completely, still it is something different. As a matter of fact, this is the way it should be. It is the only way of continuing the love which one does not want to abandon. (cited in Schmidl, 1959, p. 43)

Freud also told Binswanger "he remained inconsolable after the death of his grandson, who had come to represent for him the future of his children and grandchildren (Shapiro, 1994, p. 559). In a letter to Samuel Freud in September of 1923, Freud wrote about a visit from Heinnele's older brother, Ernst, just a few months after the death: "[I] did not find him a consolation to any amount" (Gay, 1988, p. 422). On the anniversary of Sophie's death and six years after Heinnele's death, Freud once again wrote to Binswanger:

> Although we know that after such a loss the acute stages of mourning will subside, we also know we shall remain inconsolable and will never find a substitute. No matter what may fill the gap, if it be filled completely, it nevertheless remains something else. And actually, this is how it should be; it is the only way of perpetuating that love which we do not want to relinquish. (cited in E. Freud, 1960, p. 386)

Freud's unambiguous private communications of his personal mourning coincide with contemporary belief representing the necessity for connection with the lost object as well as a gradual separation. Thirteen years after Sophie's death, Freud disclosed to a patient that his daughter had died during the influenza epidemic. He showed his patient a tiny locket that he wore attached to his watch chain and said: "She is here" (Shapiro, 1994, p. 30). Sussillo (2005) writes:

> I think this report is meaningful since it suggests that Freud had an essential need for an ongoing affective connection, a visceral bridge to his dead daughter as he carried a concrete reminder of her on

his physical being and spontaneously displayed this memento to a patient more than a decade after his loss. (p. 507)

Ernest Jones (1957), in *The Life and Work of Sigmund Freud*, documented Freud's correspondence with Marie Bonaparte following the death of his grandson: "This one has killed something in me for good" (cited in Jones, 1957, p. 92). A few years later, when Freud was over seventy years old, he told Marie Bonaparte "that he had not been able to get fond of anyone since that misfortune, merely retaining his old attachment; he had found the blow unbearable" (cited in Silverman & Klass, 1996, p. 6). Sussillo (2005) beautifully wrote: "Freud's words evocatively underscore the primitive longing and absolute need for the specific being who was lost and for the meaningful love relationship that nourished, fortified, and sustained the self" (p. 507).

Freud's early theory of mourning burdened psychoanalysis with the troublesome assumption that normal bereavement ends with giving up all emotional bonds to the lost loved one. Moreover, Freud's theory of mourning focused on "the mourner's internal disorganization and gradual restoration of a sense of balance rather than addressing the actual death and the loss of the relationship" (Malawista, Adelman, & Anderson, 2011, p. 205). In light of these two observations, I wonder if Freud has let us down by not revisiting and revising his 1917 views on mourning.

Freud's theory enlarged

Early followers of Freud

Several psychoanalytic writers added to and embellished Freud's theory of mourning. Abraham (1924) enhanced Freud's theory of identification in object loss, stating that in normal mourning, the deceased loved one is "introjected" in order to hold on to the memory and feeling of the person. Abraham made use of his own bereavement experience of his father's death to endorse his theory. Fenichel (1945) used Abraham's concept of "introjection" to describe that the mourner uses introjection to keep the dead loved one close and that this is given up when grieving is accomplished. Deutsch (1937) studied unexpressed grief. Keeping with the quintessential assumptions of Freud's theory, she wrote:

> The process of mourning as a reaction to the real loss of a loved person must be carried to completion. As long as the early libidinal

and aggressive attachment persists, the painful affect continues to flourish and vice versa the attachments are unresolved as long as the affective process of mourning has not been accomplished. (p. 20)

Melanie Klein's oldest son died in a hiking accident in 1934. Through her struggles with her personal loss, she felt that "[T]he task of mourning is to rebuild one's inner world by experiencing the intense anguish of loss that ultimately reawakens loving affect for the lost loved one, thereby reintegrating the original depressive position" (cited in Sussillo, 2005, p. 508). For Klein, mourning was a time of repair during which unleashed destructive fantasies are recaptured and a positive internal relationship with the lost object is reestablished.

Subsequent contributors

Three decades later, Loewald (1962) postulated that it is the relationship to the deceased person that is internalized. He explored the interrelationships between separation, object-renunciation, mourning, and the creation of psychic structure. Loewald set the stage for the beginnings of a transformation in analytic thinking as he disagreed that "identification" plays a vital role in the completion of mourning. Loewald wrote: "The work of mourning is not confined to a gradual relinquishment of the lost object but also encompasses processes of internalizing elements of the relationship with the object to be relinquished" (p. 139).

A few years later, Schafer (1968) elaborated on Loewald's views, stating that what is internalized are "regulatory interactions" (p. 9). Pollock (1961) described bereavement as occurring in two states: acute and chronic. He wrote that the first state consists of experiences of shock and denial. Pollock suggested that the chronic stage of grieving is the same as Freud's theory of the "work of mourning" except that it requires one year to work through as against Freud's (1909d) suggestion that it takes one or two years.

Bowlby (1960, 1961, 1969) made significant contributions to psychoanalytic literature on object loss and attachment. He hypothesized that the child who has lost a parent, through searching and longing behaviors, maintains the relationship with the beloved lost parent. A decade later, Bowlby (1980), wrote that when there is a death in the family, an attachment crisis ensues. He felt that resolution of grief came about by re-stabilizing internal working models. Bowlby and Parkes (1970) postulated that mourning takes place in four stages. The first stage consists of feelings of numbness intermingled with intense distress and anger. This first stage lasts from a few hours to several weeks. Their second stage is one of yearning. This stage can last for many months or even years. The third stage is one of disorganization after searching for and longing for a lost loved one. The fourth stage is when psychological reorganization takes place, which includes a feeling of sadness as well as guilt. E. Furman (1974) focused her work on childhood grief, stressing the importance of the influence of the environment and the developmental stage of the child in understanding the child's subjective understanding of a parent's death.

Volkan (1981, 1984) highlighted the intense and often disturbing feelings of anger associated with the initial stage of grief. Volkan (1984) states:

> This anger serves the ego's need for mastery of immediate shock and panic and indicates that the ego has now begun to interpret and integrate the impact of the loss in time and space. The experience of anger at being abandoned by the one now dead requires a recognition of the actuality of the death, a crucial event in the course of mourning. (p. 324)

Volkan (1984), echoing Freud, stated that the mourner needs time to review and remember her relationship to her deceased loved one. During this time, there is a:

> ... struggle to keep or to reject a close tie; and an initial regressive disorganization that is followed by a new inner organization able to test reality more fully for confirmation that the death, with all its psychological implications, has indeed taken place. (p. 324)

Even though Volkan agreed with the "official" view of Freud (1917e) to a degree, he does acknowledge that we never forget or completely relinquish our investment from our dead loved one. Volkan stated: "We can never purge those who have been close to us from our own history except by psychic acts damaging to our own identity" (p. 325). He further elucidated how he conceptualizes the final stage of mourning: "The process of relinquishing has proceeded like the slow healing of a wound

DEATH OF CHILD   123

(Engel, 1961), and an open lesion has gradually been closed and covered over, though not without leaving a scar" (p. 325).

Perhaps Volkan's most valuable contribution to the theory of mourning is his concept of the "linking object." A "linking object" is an object that represents both the mourner and the dead person. It represents the mourner's ego ideal and superego and offers a symbolic reunion and connection to the lost loved one. Volkan explains that the linking object is not used as it was meant to be used. In other words, it is tucked away in a safe place where the mourner can count on knowing where it is at all times. When the mourner holds or gazes at the linking object, the person experiences a feeling of reunion and connection with the dead person. The linking object functions as an external bridge between the representation of the mourner and his representation of the deceased, just as the introject serves as an internal bridge. Volkan explains that the mourner is in complete control, making use of the linking object as an illusion allowing the mourner to straddle two possibilities: bringing the dead back to life or of killing him. He clarifies that this is different from pathological mourning where the person is fixated on the act of mourning and it affects daily living. We saw how Freud made use of a linking object by keeping a small photograph of Sophie in a locket attached to his watch.

By the end of the "decathexis" era, most psychoanalysts agreed on the following points: (1) mourning is a normal process that must be felt and articulated; (2) conflicts of ambivalence need to be acknowledged; (3) conflicts should become conscious; (4) there should be a resolution of mourning (Aragno, 2003).

Newer models

Until the 1980s, psychoanalysis focused on specific behaviors and how the mourner was functioning in order to affectively evaluate whether the person exhibited pathological mourning. This "tended to overshadow the quality of the recollected and remembered relationship to the deceased as a significant and independent feature of the outcome to mourning and loss" (Rubin, 1996, p. 218). For the most part, psychoanalysts now believe that when the mourner's functioning reaches homeostasis, it is assumed that the death has been accepted as permanent and the internal relationship to the dead loved one has stabilized. When this occurs, mourning is considered accomplished. However, mourning has an addendum. This involves "less intense but emotionally charged memories, associations, and representations of the deceased" (ibid., p. 220), which stay with the person forever.

Social developmental theory of mourning states that a death in a family causes an identity crisis within each individual and the family as a whole. This theory suggests that the "creation of new, stable structures for self-organization requires access to a variety of social and relational resources, including the creation of a new form of relationship with the deceased" (Shapiro, 1996, p. 552). Gaines (1997) considered mourning as an attempt to "create continuity," not decathect from the lost object. Stroebe and Schut (1999) proposed a dual process model of bereavement. Instead of moving through stages of grief, this model suggests that mourners fluctuate between two positions: there are moments when the mourner faces her loss and allows herself to feel and express intense affects; however, there are other times when she puts aside her grief in order to face daily challenges. Within this theory, this oscillation between two very different points is considered normal; problems occur when a person gets stuck in one position or the other.

Generally speaking, contemporary leanings focus on the "meaning" of the adaptive process of reconstruction (Neimeyer, 2001). This newer view of bereavement places a strong emphasis on the role of attachment and the qualities of both the internal and external relationship to the deceased loved one. In addition, "[S]ocial and interpersonal factors now come to the fore and are viewed as feeding right into the psychological process" (Aragno, 2003, p. 444), which in turn depends on a supportive social environment. Most psychoanalysts now feel that the work of mourning is to protect and maintain the intrapsychic relationship to the dead object (Malawista, Adelman, & Anderson, 2001).

When a child dies

When a child dies, an identity confusion and crisis supervenes. The parent's core sense of self becomes "… depleted and deprived of familiar narcissistic comforts and sustenance. Suddenly, the self-with-other identity has been supplanted by a self that is without" (Aragno, 2003, p. 452). In the words of Malawista, Adelman, & Anderson (2011),

> There are no words for this pain. If a husband dies, you are a widow; with the death of a wife, you are a widower; when your parents die,

you are an orphan. There is no word for what you become. It doesn't exist in our vocabulary. It is too horrific to be named. (p. 204)

As stated at the beginning of this contribution, the most painful death is the death of a child. Casement (2000) emphasizes that psychotherapists and psychoanalysts who have not personally experienced such a devastating loss "… can only imagine what that could be like for someone else. And mostly it will still remain beyond our imagination" (p. 21). Mothers and fathers who have suffered the loss of a child have often said that there are no words to describe their pain.

A child's death is a truth that feels surreal. Bereaved parents often feel they are between two worlds, realizing the awful truth of the loss of their child while simultaneously demanding that it not be their reality. Many newly bereaved parents feel as if a part of themselves has been amputated, and a part of their self has died with the child. Parents often feel alienated from their communities and extended families and cannot find comfort in well-meaning yet hurtful comments such as: "He is in a better place," or, "You have your own angel now," and, "You can have more children." Friends and family do not know what to say and feel threatened and scared that it could happen to them, so they stay away and remain silent. Often the exquisitely attuned bereaved parent senses the other's vulnerabilities and finds herself comforting others: "It's okay," and, "I'm strong," "Don't worry about me." A peculiar silence gradually descends upon the event.

> It often seems that neither the child nor the child's death has any social reality. People will not mention the child's name in their presence … it seems to the parents that their lives have stopped while other people's lives go on. The sense of isolation can be bitter. (Klass, 1996, p. 202)

Parents project aspects of self and dreams of the future onto their children. When a child of any age dies, these aspects of self and wishes for the future—a part of the structure of adult personality—are destroyed. When a child dies, there is a rupture that cannot be repaired. A parent's job is to protect his or her child and keep him safe. The parent feels helpless and powerless as her or his efficacy and self-esteem are destroyed. This is one reason why the death of a child is so overpowering and mourning is often prolonged (Rando, 1986; Shapiro, 1994). When a child dies there are grave narcissistic ramifications. The cohesion of the self is shattered. The bereaved parent's sense of self fragments and there might even be a feeling of disorganization on a physical level (E. Furman, 1978; Grubb, 1976; Leon, 1990).

As we enter this realm more deeply, we encounter the following questions:

- Does mourning differ and does the impact of loss differ with the age of a child ... miscarriage, stillborn, infant, toddler, adolescent, adult child?
- Does mourning differ if it is an only child?
- Does mourning differ depending on the gender of the child?
- Does the gender of the child affect the grieving parent of the same gender more?
- Does mourning differ if death is by illness? Accident? Suicide?
- Does mourning differ if a parent sees the child murdered?
- Does mourning differ when one's child does not return from war?

My answer to these complex and unanswerable questions is, while the pain is the same for every parent whose child dies, the issues parents must confront are dissimilar. It is not a contest as to who suffers the worst pain, and we cannot compare the pain one endures from the death of a young child to that of an older child. No matter the age of the child or whether the child dies suddenly or after a prolonged terminal illness, the end result is the same: Those who are left are devastated. When a very young child dies, there is often a yearning and desire to imagine what type of older child and adult he would have become. Parents whose children died in young adulthood "at least knew something of what types of adults our sons and daughters would become in later years" (E. Mitchell, 2004, p. 81).

The prose and poetry of my child's death

I begin my story by telling you about myself. I trained as a ballet dancer from childhood, and was accepted as a scholarship student into the School of American Ballet in New York City at age twelve. I commuted by train from my home in Trenton, New Jersey, to New York City, six days a week until I moved into my own apartment in Manhattan at age sixteen, and I was dancing professionally with New York City Ballet by age seventeen. I left my performing career after dancing with the company for only two years, married, moved to Philadelphia and gave birth to my first child.

My infant son, Alex, was diagnosed with leukemia at nine months of age, and died just before his fourth birthday. The parent of a critically and chronically ill child is thrust into a counterintuitive corner: The very treatment that holds hope and promise of a cure is also the tormentor of her child by causing terrible side effects. I willingly participated in this double-edged treatment, constantly praying for what was not to be. My mothering instincts were perceptive, as Alex would reenact, on me, his bone marrow extractions and spinal taps and chemotherapy that left burns on his skin when the poison leaked out, and I was a very willing participant in his play. He would command that I lie down and he would "doctor" me over and over and over. He would tell me to cry, and I would cry out, and he, in a wisdom that three year olds should never have, would tell me it was all right to cry, because after all it really hurts. Allow me to take a break from this factual narrative and enter the chamber of verse. Here are three poems I wrote while caring for my son who was becoming increasingly ill.

(1)
A Boy and his Cat

In remission, a precarious relief
We bring a kitten into our world of pills,
kisses, finger sticks, hugs, bone marrows,
Tears that refuse to come as I gently urge him to cry
"It's ok to cry" I whisper in his ear as I bend over him
helping the nurse to hold him as they insert their needle into his tiny hip.
A small soft pure white kitten
To hold and play with to cuddle and purr together

A kitten will grow and live
Perhaps together they will grow-up?

"Pickle" he names her
She loves her boy as he plays car using her as the passenger

Pickle watches him intently as he drives his cars around the floor and pounces on top of his balding head as each precious hair falls out once again
He laughs and calls her "silly Pickle!"

Pickle and I are left without our boy
Courageously he dies
Alone I cry out
Only Pickle hears the strange animal sounds that explode from my heart, from my gut
She rushes to me pushing her nose against my tears as if to tell me that she too hurts
New life begins and as I lay curled on my side Pickle presses against the baby growing
as we sleep together missing him

She lives for twenty years
Amazing as if she had to live so long because he couldn't
She dies a terrible death
Her old white body filled with cancer
I am cruel
I don't let her die
He suffered she suffered
A boy and his cat

(2)
He Knew and Tried to Tell Me

One day
As he was dying and we were driving someplace
Alex asked, seemingly from nowhere
"Mommy, are there dogs in heaven?"
I held my breath and calmly answered
"Yes, Alex, there are dogs in heaven"
He needed to know more
"Mommy, are there kittens in heaven?"
My heart felt in a vice
"Yes Alex, kittens also get to go to heaven"
He was not yet finished

He had to let me know
"Mommy do boys go to heaven?"
I swallowed down great sobs,
tears appeared, dropping from my lashes
"Yes Alex" my voice was shaky "Boys go to heaven"
He knew
He knew things almost-four-year-old boys
should not need to know
He knew so much more than me
He was telling me
I refused to listen as those swallowed sobs swelled around my heart

(3)
Dancing

Toward the end
Those last six weeks
He spent his time in bed
I read him his favorite books, we watched TV
I had a wish to entertain
How silly of me as he was working hard to live, to die
A serious conflict, what to do, a most difficult job to comprehend
Live because he was not yet four and so much more to do?
Or die because he had to?

I worked so hard to bring a smile to his face
At times a story in a book would do the trick or his favorite TV character
But it got harder and harder his smiles were few
Our home once filled with the laughter of a little boy went sickly quiet

So at last in those final weeks I danced
The sound of a boy playing with his cars and trucks was gone
The toys left isolated in a corner
I filled our tiny home with Mozart and with Bach
and danced
It was what I knew, it was all that I could do

He must have seen my sorrow as the music filled my soul
He would watch unimpressed
In fact distressed
As I remember now
I wonder if he saw too much

After a short duration
He would yell out "Stop!"
It was all that he could bear
Music playing I would lay next to him in bed
As close as I could get without touching
Touching hurt
How does a mother comfort her young boy without a mother's touch?

Now I fill my house with Mozart mostly
I think that I know why
I dance inside my gut, I dance my sadness, I dance of suffering, I dance of torment
Both mine and his
But most of all within my soul, my self, I dance within these poems the greatest love of all
I dance the terrible anguish that this great love could not save my boy

In the end it was this vast magnificent love
My enormous love for him
The love a mother has for her son
That finally let me say *enough*
And let him die

After Alex died, I had four more children and for the next fifteen years dedicated myself to mothering, thinking of myself as a "professional" mother. I focused all of my time and energy on making sure these children would live and live well … until my youngest daughter forced me to begin to think differently. This child suffered from separation anxiety and could not leave my side, which scared me and infuriated me; after all I was the perfect mother: how could she be so miserable?! I researched and found the best child analyst and my six-year-old daughter began her own analytic journey.

My daughter's analyst changed the course of my future. I will never forget one particular parent session, when she wondered with me what I intended to do with my life now that my youngest child, a son, was nearing kindergarten. I remember feeling shocked. She further explained to me that it might be easier for all four of my children to grow up, separate, and eventually leave if they knew I had another part to my life that was meaningful and important. She also suggested that perhaps getting into my own treatment would be beneficial and help further guide me.

My two analyses

I began my own personal analysis while simultaneously matriculating at Bryn Mawr College as a McBride Scholar, which is a special program for non-traditional-aged students. I was forty years old and really had no idea what I wanted to study, but felt wonderful yet terrified as I sat side by side with brilliant eighteen-year-old young women in stimulating, but difficult classes. I majored in cultural anthropology and for my senior thesis wrote an ethnography titled: *Breaking The Silence: A Phenomenological Analysis of the Art of Ballet as Seen through the Eyes and Bodies of Female Professional Ballet Dancers*, clearly making use of my ballet background. The study of cultural anthropology gave me a glimpse into people's lives while simultaneously I had embarked on my own personal journey of understanding my own inner psyche within my analysis.

During these years, I was in awe of my daughter's treatment, as I watched her grow and develop and become more confident of her own abilities, and I was extremely grateful for my own analytic journey. I came to understand that my training as a professional dancer was beyond comparison, as I had developed an unwavering work ethic. To become a member of a world-renowned ballet company takes talent of course, but it also takes tenacity and determination. All of these traits have aided me in my academic pursuits. However, on the downside, I missed out on a whole phase of my own development, adolescence, and used my first analysis to help grow myself up again.

After graduating from undergraduate, I continued on, obtaining a master's degree in social work, also from Bryn Mawr. My two oldest children had moved out of our home, my oldest daughter pursuing her own professional ballet career, and my son went off to college. I still had two school-aged children at home, so chose to continue my studies nearby in a part-time program. At first I thought, given my ballet background and the subject of my senior thesis, I would be interested in working with eating-disordered women. That particular internship was not available to me. My dean was apologetic and told me there was an opening at a shelter for homeless mothers and children: Surely there I would get to work with women's issues. As a social work intern, I was given a full therapy caseload of very young, severely traumatized homeless children. I quickly realized I was completely under-qualified and actually appalled that I was treating these fragile children. I realized that my social work curriculum and my onsite supervision was not enough, and enrolled in the Child Psychotherapy Training Program at the Psychoanalytic Center of Philadelphia. Through this program, I obtained the necessary theory I was missing, but most important, and also life altering, was my relationship with my PCOP supervisor, Jennifer Bonovitz. Dr. Bonovitz was not only an incredible supervisor, she became my mentor as well. She taught me psychoanalytically informed technique, she taught me how to formulate my cases, how to think analytically, she taught me how to write and bring to life my work with these children, but most of all she taught me how to sit with and bear the unbearable, to bear witness.

As all this was unfolding, I was nearing termination after seven years of my first analysis. I was, of course, quite indebted to my analyst. We had touched on Alex's illness and death, but mostly around anniversaries and birthdays. I had witnessed and participated in my daughter's analysis and knew the pain and anguish of being the parent who felt tremendous guilt. My daughter's analyst never made me feel blamed and helped me assuage my guilt. Both of these treatments, my child's and mine, were catalysts in my next academic and professional move. I wanted to bring this incredible way of working and being with patients to those who could not afford it, so applied and was accepted into both the Child and Adult Psychoanalytic Training Programs. I maintain a personal philosophy of providing analytic treatment to families and individuals who may not otherwise be able to afford it.

Even though I had already completed a full analysis with a training and supervising analyst, as a candidate, I needed to reenter analysis. I went back to my former analyst, but after a year, he became quite ill and had to stop practicing. I needed to find a new analyst.

It was my second analysis that was the most meaningful part of my journey. This analysis, too, lasted seven years. It was in this very personal journey that I was able to go back to my own traumatic experiences and relive the illness and death of my first child, only this time I was able to share it, and he, my analyst, bore witness to my unbearable pain. The following poems capture the essence of my experience during this era of my life.

(4)
What will I have left?

My memories repressed
Unbearable to contemplate
Almost two years since I came to you for help
Help of a different kind
I was protecting my analyst who was impaired
I needed help to leave him
He had become my burden
I was terrified
I was baffled, I wasn't sure
I thought I had worked through so much
But I knew, somehow knew
There was so much more
It happened slowly
I glimpsed my terror
I held my breath, I froze
I told you of my son, I cried
You gently said "We need to do this"
So here I am
The floodgates opened
I am overwhelmed with love
Love for the boy I loved so much and lost
Love for you as you gently guide me
I am overwhelmed with pain as the memories consume me
They come pouring out
in pristine form, unaltered
I have opened up my heart
To my memories of years ago
You hold me safe
As we do this work
It hurts, I sob
You are there
Mixed up with all my love and pain and sadness
But now

The fear that grabs my heart and threatens death
Is what will happen when there are no more memories?
if I use them up?
What will I have left?
The printed poems I hold so dear?
What of the cars and trucks
the tears and kisses
The little boy who so long ago filled my days, my nights
My life?

(5)
A poem for Syd

All those years
I thought I was getting on with it
Quickly the boxes were packed away
And moved from the place of hugs
And tears and medicine and love
I couldn't pack Alex away
No tape could hold those boxes shut
Today I sobbed with you
You saw my grief
Later, after many sad sighs
Sadness also cannot be packed away in attics
Or closets, in pages of photos falling apart from years and years
    of neglect
No little boy all grown to look back over his childhood
    memories
His kitten, the fire hat, his Pop-Pop
Later I smiled and remembered how he used to put Pickle in the
    cat carrier
And drive her all over the apartment
He went onto other play
So good was he at his job
He could play and we played so well and so long
After a walk, naming types of cars (he knew them all), and
    saying hi to the pretzel man (he craved salt), we would arrive
    home dirty

and tired to a soft "meow" Pickle had been left forgotten in a
    corner "parked"
"Alex" I would exclaim in an exasperated tone
"You can't drive Pickle around and forget her!"
And we would laugh together.
All these years
I thought I was getting on with it
I tried, I really did
But only cried in solitude
His life was small his death enormous
I will always have the memories
Good, bad, loving, agonizing, beautiful
Memories refuse to be packed away in boxes, in photos
A sight, a place, the smell of springtime
still provoke my love
No, my love cannot be packed away or cried away
But as I share my pain with you and you take some of it for
    yourself
For I saw and felt your tears
I hurt less, at least I hope to.
"I can't do it" he told me, "I can't live, but I love you"
He played so hard, he played for a lifetime
He was so wise, trying hard to teach his mom
what life is really about
Playing hard and letting go.
I loved him
And he was dying
I loved him desperately
It was a desperate love
For it was all I had to give
There was nothing else, it had to be enough
But it wasn't.
No balls, or trucks or shiny trinkets could delight
and he was gracious
as he gently returned my love.
I strive to somehow weave my grief into my life
But loose strings dangle everywhere and get
tangled and knotted and ugly

I strive to sew my grief into a quilt of Molly, Joey, Wendy, Ben,
my work, my play,
But I can't make it fit
My loss, like his death is too great.
I thought I was getting on with it
But I stumbled over missing him
I fell into holding on too tight
I have become exhausted in the mist of thinking I was getting
    on with it
I fell backward into interminable grief
I have been lost and now found
Found safety and love in sharing my deepest grief with you
I stumble over empty spaces,
spaces that will be empty forever
If only I could touch him one more time
nuzzle my face onto the top of his head
The smell of springtime brings me pain as I remember the boy
    who smelled of fresh cut grass in springtime.

I thought I was getting on with it
Each breath a possibility
I created new life, new love, new work
I could not, would not wallow in death
Instead I died inside and only a portion of me has loved, created,
    lived.
I am healing but the cure is killing me
Can I go on from here? Will you be able to share and help bear
    this pain, is it too much of a burden for you?
I thought I was getting on with it
I saw death
It was hard work and he did it well

For well over a year, I revisited the life, illness, and death of my first child and shared my grief in the form of poems that seemed to pour effortlessly from my soul. During this time, sleep would not come and I would spend long nights alone in my kitchen, playing Mozart and Bach as the memories overcame me. I sent each poem to my analyst. We never spoke about them. Just knowing he had read them and had understood me was all I needed. I wrote hundreds of poems that year that tell Alex's story, our story.

(6)
His last breath

His last breath, I died inside
As I look back
Find myself back in that room
The room where Alex died
I see myself, frantic dying inside
Nobody could see
I must have appeared calm
Inside my head I'm pleading to get it over with
"Please" I implore: "Don't let him suffer"
My voice is from another place
I fall into pieces, become disconnected

His last breath, I died inside
a lethal dose of morphine
It will ensure a quick demise
It seems to take forever, went too fast
They stop the respirator,
disconnect him from that terrible machine
give me back my boy, finally
I have him back his body touching mine

As I lean over to gather him in my arms his eyes flutter open for just a second
But he doesn't really see me
Maybe he did and knew that I was helping him to die
My final act as a mother
His body limp and burning hot
That grotesque tube protruding from his mouth
Naked in my arms
all entwined
Arms hugging holding trying to help him take his last few breaths
All of us touching talking to him
"I love you Alex, you can go now it's ok to die, you can do it" I encouraged him just like when he was taking his first steps

"You can do it, I love you so much, no more leukemia, no more hurts, it's ok, it's ok to die, thank you thank you thank you" I say quickly
It is a tremendous effort to take those last few breathes his biggest job yet
Silence
Dreadful silence fills the room
John steps close to me and listens for a heartbeat
Shakes his head
He has died, it's over
My baby, my little son who fought so hard to live
Courageously he has gathered up all his cars and trucks and little white kitten
And dumps his last heavy load of love
At that moment I change my mind
I scream silently give me back my baby
Put him back on that damn machine
I'll take him with leukemia, no bargains can be made
There are no words
As his tiny burning naked body dies within my arms I feel life leave him
The stain is on my pants
Those plain brown corduroy pants
How similar to birth I marvel to myself
His last little bit of life has leaked onto my leg
Packed away in that box in that room on my third floor
I held him tight in disbelief how could this be, what had I done

I was fierce I would not give up my baby
I refused to give him up
His dying brought out the nasty in me
I don't remember what happened next I think I was left alone
The docs and nurses peering at me from another room
I sat and rocked and moaned
As I held my dead son
There were no more songs, no more words
He played so hard so well, a job well done!
The doubts set in what if I had waited maybe the medicine would have started to work
Maybe he would have lived

DEATH OF CHILD

If only I had not been so selfish
We would have had more time
Another Christmas
Another birthday only weeks away
Those cars that zoom and trucks that shine
hidden in my closet
I can't forgive myself
I loved him desperately
For a desperate love was all I had to give
It wasn't enough
Gallantly, graciously, courageously he dies

I lost time
He was taken from my arms and given to his father
I was taken
to a little room
It must have been the place they take the mothers after their little boys are dead
All a blur, I said something funny about Alex, the silly things he said and did
Taking care of others
Didn't anybody know I had died inside?
Time to leave, how could I leave him there
In this place he hated
He just wanted to go home
If only I had listened
They have him all tucked in so proper
How grotesque he was not a proper kid
The tube protruding from his mouth evidence of my cowardice
I kissed him shocked to feel him cold
So quickly he turned cold
I am horrified

I see myself leave that place
The place he really hated
What will I do
How can I live when I am already dead?

His job well done but I was a stupid girl
I didn't learn what he had to teach

> My suffering begun
> Now twenty-seven years have passed
> I have kept these poems deeply hidden
> I did not dwell in death I could not, would not dwell in death
> I have carried all my fears and sorrows all the guilt for too long
> I thought I was getting on with it
> I am sure my children suffered
>
> Now I know the one thing I forgot as he was dying in my arms
> I forgot to ask him to forgive me
> His greatest gift of all, the lesson to be learned
> To accept my faults, my frailties, my vulnerabilities, my failures
> And forgive

Over a decade has passed since I relived and shared my grief with my analyst. The poems stopped, the memories remain. I carry a sadness inside of me and sometimes, usually in the dark and stillness of night, the hurt returns but as a shadow. My husband and I delight in our blended family of six magnificent children and our four incredible grandchildren bring joy to our hearts.

Final thoughts

I was in awe of my analytic experience where, in the safety of my analyst, poetry appeared. I do not claim to be a poet or have any poetic talent, but this is how I was able to share my grief with my analyst. Leon (1999) states: "The structure of the creative product promotes a sense of unity, thereby maintaining cohesion against centrifugal fragmentation" (p. 388). When my son died, I was a very young "single" mother. I was alone in my grief and knew those around me just wanted me to be okay … so I was, and my grief was kept private. My poems not only told my story, but they served to protect me from the helplessness I felt and provided me with a sense of mastery and worth. When that time of reliving Alex's life and death came to an end, I possessed a book of poems that documented our life together. Leon writes: "Poems can be viewed as transitional objects occupying that space between the poet's inner world and external reality. They are meant to be handled, seen on the page and read out loud" (p. 389). Through my poems, I found a way to hold onto Alex. I found a way to get back the time we had together.

I was very fortunate to have found an analyst who could journey with me to that unbearable place. Casement (2000) writes: "Professionally, I know it is the pain which cannot be shared that remains most unbearable. For no other person can bear it, then how can the bereaved person bear it alone? ... I have learned to stay with what patients bring to me of their pain, and to let their pain reach me" (p. 23). My analyst was able to do this for me.

Those of us who have lost children fear that we, too, will die and often wish to die, yet we survive. Perhaps one of the most painful, yet innocent moments is when a friend or relative says: "I don't know how you had more children and went on living. I love my child so much I would never be able to do that." I hope this contribution has demonstrated that love endures and the bereaved can go on to live productive and very meaningful lives. We can create works of art, develop professional careers, and deeply love our living children and grandchildren.

Note

1. The impact of his younger brother Julius's death when Freud was four years old persisted throughout his life (Rudnytsky, 1988) though seemed to contribute little to his views on mourning.

CHAPTER SEVEN

Death of pet

Christie Platt

On any given spring day, or rainy day, or wintry day, for that matter, if you are out on the street, you cannot fail to notice people who are walking their dogs. Or, it may seem that the dogs are walking their humans. Dogs are sniffing and running ahead, exuding the sense that they are fully engaged in the business of seeing and inhaling what's going on in the world. And you will often see a distracted owner being pulled away from a mobile phone to see just what discovery the hound is making to turn the leash taut. For an instant, maybe more, the preoccupied human is also drawn into the natural world around, the squirrels, the skittering leaves, and the social life of dog meeting dog. Occasionally, you will see a human/dog couple that is completely in sync. They seem to slow down simultaneously to stop at a corner or take note of another dog walking down the street. As you look more closely, the personalities of dog and owner emerge and seem to resemble one another to an almost uncanny degree. While a bulldog may waddle along behind its bumbling owner, a frisky terrier may be bouncing in front of a dapper gentleman wearing a fedora. Dogs come in and out of favor just as clothing styles do. Today, the pug is fashionable but in the 1930s, it was Cairn terriers that delighted the Duke and Duchess of Windsor.

144 BEREAVEMENT

For Sigmund Freud, it was the chow that famously captured his affections, a breed that boasts an august ancestry dating back to the T'ang dynasty in China. Over the centuries, chows served as temple guard dogs and also as the model for the stone guardians that stand outside many Chinese and Tibetan temples. Such lineage must have appealed to Freud's love of antiquities; owning a chow was almost like adding an *objet d'art* to his collection. Was it the chow's natural expression, "essentially scowling, dignified, lordly, discerning, sober and snobbish, one of independence," that also suited him? (American Kennel Club website). By all accounts, Freud's two favorite dogs were his chows, Jofi and Lün.

Freud admired dogs in general, valuing their directness and lack of human guile. Several of his colleagues shared his love of dogs; Dorothy Burlingham gave him his first (short-lived) chow, Lün Yug. The Deutsch's, the family of Freud's personal physician originally, cared for his dog, Lün, when Jofi couldn't tolerate the competition of sharing a house with her. Perhaps his friendship with Princess Marie Bonaparte would have been deep with or without the presence of their respective dogs, Jofi and Topsy, but the role that these dogs played in their lives seems to have been an integral and poignant facet of their friendship. Freud owned Jofi from 1933 to 1937 and Bonaparte had Topsy during that time period although the exact dates are unclear. Both Freud and Bonaparte were suffering from cancer and the length of time left to either of them was uncertain. The civilization as they knew it was eroding as Europe was being systematically ravaged by the Nazis. Although their letters do not speak of it directly, neither of them knew whether they would succumb to death by cancer or by the Gestapo.

Thus, I wanted to begin this chapter with their reflections on dogs. Their correspondence provides us with a glimpse into the ways they were comforted by their dogs during this extremely difficult period of their lives. Bonaparte wrote a book about her chow, Topsy, that Freud translated during his final days in Vienna. In the subsequent sections, I will look at the unique ways dogs have of befriending us and why losing them is so painful. I will also have some thoughts about losing my own dogs, one in childhood and the other as an adult. We tend to think of dog ownership as an unadulterated pleasure, but occasionally one's guardianship of a dog becomes burdensome. I have provided a clinical example of a more complicated bereavement. I will close with some observations about the void that is left when a dog dies.

Sigmund Freud and Marie Bonaparte

Freud's friendship with Marie Bonaparte had many facets. She was his analysand, his friend, as well as a financial benefactor. Their shared love of dogs can only have strengthened the sense of simpatico that existed between them. Freud liked the fact that dogs lack the capacity for feckless deceit that characterizes humans and observed to Bonaparte in a letter:

> Dogs love their friends and bite their enemies, quite unlike people who are incapable of pure love and always have to mix love and hate in their object relations .... It really explains why one can love an animal like Topsy or Jofi with such an extraordinary intensity; affection without ambivalence, and the simplicity of a life free from the almost unbearable conflicts of civilization, the beauty of an existence complete in itself. And yet, despite all divergence in the organic development, there is that feeling of an intimate affinity, of an undisputed solidarity. Often when stroking Jofi, I have caught myself humming a melody, which unmusical as I am, I can't help recognizing as the aria from Don Giovanni. A bond of friendship unites us both. (Freud, cited in Sacks, 2008, p. 501)

In contrast to Freud's gruffer manner, Bonaparte wrote a lyrical and deeply sentimental account of her relationship with her chow, Topsy, who was diagnosed with cancer at roughly the same time that Bonaparte received her own diagnosis. She wrote the book in 1936 and sent Freud excerpts from it as she finished them, thus making the endeavor a sort of extended letter to him. In the book, she reflects on Topsy's illness and mortality as well as her own. Bonaparte struggles with the capricious and uncontrollable nature of time and mortality, wondering who will die first and who will be left behind. She thinks wistfully about how she and Topsy share the same sky, the same forests, and the same house.

> Despite the gulf that separates our races, Topsy, you are still my sister, my terrestrial sister ... At nightfall, tired by our activities of the day, a similar weariness, mounting to our brain from our muscles, our blood, our nerves, forces us each to lay those weary muscles on a bed or low cushion, to close our eyes, and sink into the same blissful slumber. A same death, one evening of ultimate weariness, will lay us in the earth. (p. 64)

It would seem that Topsy's innocence and the threat of her impending death symbolically express Bonaparte's fear that her friends in the world of psychoanalysis and her beautiful, cultured life in Paris may soon be extinguished. In contrast to unfolding world events, she is soothed by her feeling that "… dogs are ignorant of the extent and bitterness of human quarrels, their quarrels being limited and short-lived" (p. 72). She delights in watching her dog gamboling around her beloved garden, and believes that Topsy is oblivious to death.

Bonaparte sends Topsy for treatment at the Curie Institut where her father was once treated, unsuccessfully, for cancer. She never speaks directly about her concerns for Freud's health, but it is likely that when she wrote of her father, she had Freud in her thoughts as well. She was well-informed regarding the latter's health issues. Felix Deutsch, his original physician, had correctly diagnosed Freud's cancer in 1923 but withheld his findings, worried that Freud, who was then grieving the loss of his six-year-old grandson, might have a heart attack. He included six of Freud's closest colleagues, including Ernest Jones, in the secret. When Freud learned of the deception following his first surgery, he was livid. Deutsch resigned. On the recommendation of Princess Marie, a very young Max Schur became Freud's new personal physician. Freud and Schur agreed that the latter would always be honest with his patient. Freud instructed Schur that when the time came, he would not prolong Freud's suffering but would let him go by giving him an extra injection of morphine.

Freud read Bonaparte's manuscript in its entirety. He wrote to her saying, "I love it; it is so movingly genuine and true. It is not an analytic work, of course, but the analyst's thirst for truth and knowledge can be perceived behind this production, too" (cited in Genosko, 1993, p. 13). In fact, he liked it so much that he translated it from the French into German in 1937. Perhaps, he wanted to occupy himself during the long hours that were no longer filled with seeing patients as those who had the wherewithal to consult him had already fled the city. Perhaps it was because his own beloved Jofi died that year. He told his friend, Arnold Sweig, "One cannot easily get over seven years of intimacy" (ibid., 1993, p. 11). Whatever the reasons were, they were, of course, overdetermined and the translation of *Topsy* occupied him for part of the year. His daughter, Anna, assisted him in this endeavor. Whatever respite the dogs provided, the German march across Europe moved inexorably forward towards Austria.

Bonaparte and others were feverishly seeking safe exit for the Freud family. Twice, the house was searched by the Nazis but it was when the Gestapo arrived and took Anna down to headquarters for questioning that Freud became frantic. He spent an interminable afternoon waiting with Max Schur, wondering if Anna would ever return safely. Dr. Schur had provided all members of the Freud family with an individual dose of barbiturate sufficient to end their lives should any of them be captured by the Nazis. He knew that Anna had hers tucked into her clothing that day she was driven away in the event that she should not be released. Upon her return, Freud finally decided that it was imperative that the family leave as soon as arrangements could be made.

While Bonaparte's efforts were coordinated with Dorothy Burlingham, Ernest Jones, and others, her financial contributions were essential to the procurement of the necessary exit papers. In June 1938, most, but not all, of the Freud family managed to leave Austria. There were sixteen people in the Freud entourage, four of whom included Max Schur's family. At the last moment, Schur had to stay behind due to illness. He was able to make it to London later. Bonaparte deeply regretted that she was unable to save the entire family. Several of Freud's sisters perished in the gas chambers.

The Freud family first found a safe haven in Paris where they stayed with Bonaparte for a brief ten days. By then, Freud, "feeling he could not get on without a dog" (Jones, 1957, p. 212) had reacquired Lün, the chow who had aroused so much jealousy in Jofi that she was sent to the Deutsch's for safekeeping. She was now an essential part of the escape party. A black and white photograph, taken in Bonaparte's garden during their stay, shows Bonaparte, Sigmund and Martha Freud as well as the two dogs, Lün and Topsy, serenely sitting in the Paris garden. The viewer is compelled to imagine how each of them must have been feeling at that moment in time.

When the Freud family arrived in London at last, Lün was quarantined by the British government for six months. Freud made extraordinary efforts to visits her at the "animal asylum" in Ladbroke Grove. By then, Freud's health was failing and the thirty surgeries on his jaw had been able to stop neither the pain nor the severity of his cancer. Jumbo, a Pekinese, joined the household to fill in for Lün until she could be reunited with the household, but Jumbo proved to be an inadequate substitute for the dog Freud really wanted. By the time Lün's quarantine had been completed and she was reunited with the household, Freud's jaw had become necrotic, exuding a horrific stench. Lün began to avoid him, refusing to stay in the same room with him, leaving him disconsolate. He stopped seeing patients two months before he asked Max Schur to make good on his promise to allow him to leave this world with dignity and without unnecessary suffering. Schur honored this request and gave him two injections of morphine that allowed him to slip away. He lapsed into a coma and died as peacefully as was possible on September 23, 1939. Three days later, he was cremated and once again Bonaparte was an integral part of the process, furnishing the Grecian urn in which his ashes were placed.

For Freud, as for so many, dogs fill a particular niche in one's life that is like nothing else. So just exactly what is that niche? And when we lose them, as we inevitably will with their shorter life span, how does it affect us? After considering just a bit more about the ineffable role that dogs play in our lives, I will write about my experience of losing my two favorite dogs, one in childhood and one as an adult. I will also give a clinical example of a patient whose bereavement was complicated by the difficulties she encountered in trying to rehabilitate a rescue dog.

Our love affair with dogs

We love our dogs because they possess a spirit of independence, coupled with an enormous capacity to both love and understand us. When I told people that I was writing this chapter, there was a consistent reaction: People's faces became softer and they often sighed or looked off into the distance saying, "It's *so* hard to lose a dog." An acquaintance told me unequivocally, "I lost my best friend. My dog understood me. The minute I walked in the door, she could tell how I was feeling. If I had a hard day, she would come over and put her head in my lap, just what I needed." After his dog died, she would appear in his dreams at moments of acute stress. She would lick his face in the dream and he would be able to find sleep in an otherwise restless night. He made another observation, "I never want to talk about the people in my life who died, but I notice I have no problem talking to anyone about missing my dog." There seems to be an almost universal understanding between dog lovers of the special bond that exists between a dog and its owner(s). The family dog can maintain a loving relationship with every person in the family, even when parents and siblings are fighting with one another. A dog doesn't take sides in such conflicts and will instinctively go from one family member to the next in an effort to restore harmony.

Research confirms that our relationships with dogs can have a salutary effect on our health and our ability to self-regulate. A 1988 study found that when dog owners simply petted their dogs, blood pressures were reduced. When dog owners talked to their dogs, blood pressures were also reduced but not to the same degree as when they were quietly stroking the dog (Vormbrock & Grossberg, 1988, p. 509). In this context, Winnicott's (1960b) attentive yet nonintrusive, "holding mother" comes to mind. It seems a dog can serve as a benign surrogate mother who fosters our capacity to be alone. Our dogs provide us with a unique experience of mutual unconditional love. This seems to promote the development of a soothing, self-regulating function (Sacks, 2008). Their usefulness in therapeutic settings is increasingly recognized. They are brought into hospitals, nursing homes, and even prisons. In 2011, the notoriously demanding Yale Law School introduced a therapy dog pilot program. When students went to the law library, they could reserve a half hour session with Monty, a service dog whose owner was one of the librarians. The program was an overwhelming success and has become a permanent one. Students reported feeling calm and refreshed after spending time with Monty (Aiken & Cadmus, 2011).

Freud's chow, Jofi, is perhaps the first dog to become a permanent fixture in a consulting room. It is Jofi that we see in photographs, sitting regally next to Freud and his desk. By several reports, Jofi was a comfort to Freud, but not to his patients. Hilda Doolittle, the famous poet who wrote a book about her treatment with Freud, was initially disgruntled when Freud told her to simply avoid Jofi as his dog would never take to her. Doolittle immediately took this up as a challenge and crouched down to meet Jofi, who nuzzled her hand (Doolittle, 1956). She later said that she would not have been able to continue if she had not been able to befriend the dog. She remained irritated by the fact that Freud's attention shifted to Jofi at the end of sessions when she seemed to become restless with clock-like regularity (Freud claimed she was accurate within two to three minutes) at the end of sessions (ibid.).

Another psychoanalyst, Roy Grinker, Senior, told his son that Freud used her to make interpretations to him: "If she scratched to be let out, Freud would say, 'Jofi doesn't approve of what you're saying.' And if she wanted back in, he'd say, 'Jofi has decided to give you another chance ...'" (Grinker, 2001, p. 10). Once, when Grinker, Senior, was emoting a great deal, Jofi jumped right on top of him, feet-to-genitals, nose-to-nose. Freud said, "You see, Jofi is so excited that you've been able to discover the source of your anxiety" (ibid., p. 10). The senior Grinker, well trained in wild animal behavior, closed his eyes and did not move a muscle, as one is taught to do with big brown bears, wild boars, and ferocious, charging rhinos. The important thing seemed to be that Jofi's presence comforted Freud.

No wonder many therapeutic programs are finding ingenious methods that capitalize on such comforting presence of dogs. A military veteran of the Iraq War participates in a program in which children who have learning challenges are brought into a dog shelter to read to the dogs. The children seem to relax into a more spontaneous mode that allows them to stumble, hesitate, and mispronounce words without the fear of being shamed. As a volunteer for this project, this veteran was both amused and uplifted by the process; she told me of one child who fretted that she must be a boring reader because her dog kept falling asleep and missing the story.

Painters, poets, and psychoanalysts have all been inspired to write about just what it is that makes a dog such a unique companion. It is the dog's curious mix of independent innocence and its capacity for attachment that seems to allow us to project so many feelings on to them. In part, no dog is a blank screen however. The distinct nature of a dog's personality will inevitably be part of the equation. In part, we feel that dogs know us, recognize us, in essential ways that are only possible because of the wordless nature of their knowledge. When Odysseus returns from the Trojan wars, dressed as a beggar, it is only Argos, his dog, that recognizes him beneath the disguise. We value the unswerving loyalty of which dogs are capable. Every April 8th, dog lovers gather at Tokyo's Shibuya railroad station to honor Hachikō, an Akita who went there to meet his master, Hidesaburō Ueno, a professor of agriculture, at the end of every day for two years, starting in 1924. Unbeknown to Hachikō, his master died, but he went to meet him nonetheless for the next nine years. Winston Churchill had a place set for his poodle, Rufus, in the dining room right next to him. No one was to begin eating until the butler had also served Rufus. David Douglas Duncan, a photographer, introduced Pablo Picasso to his dachshund named Lump. They became so attached to each other during their first visit that Lump stayed at Picasso's Villa Californie, where he remained until the end of Picasso's life. Picasso captured his likeness in a ceramic plate the weekend they met, but Lump was also featured in numerous paintings.

Duncan's photographs capture their friendship but also Lump as muse to the artist (as well as the photographer).

E. B. White, who wrote for *The New Yorker* magazine for many years and is perhaps most famous for writing *Charlotte's Web* (1952), often made whimsically penetrating observations about his dogs. Of his dog, Daisy's, perpetual youthfulness, he wrote (2013), "She never grew up, and she never took pains to discover conclusively the things that might have diminished her curiosity and spoiled her taste. She died sniffing life and enjoying it" (p. 15). White did not find all his dogs to be easy companions, but this did not diminish his affection for them. In fact, it seems that his favorite dog, Fred, was quite an irascible fellow: "His activities and his character constitute an almost uninterrupted annoyance to me, yet he is such an engaging old fool that I am quite attached to him, in a half-regretful way. Life without him would be heaven, but I am afraid it's not what I want" (2013, p. 80).

While our dogs may be faithful companions, we very much appreciate the fact that they will not pander to us. We somehow believe that they are incapable of deception and are expressing their true, unvarnished nature. The expressiveness of a dog's eyes is a testament to such "purity". A dog can plead with you, tilt his head and question you, or tell you he needs a walk and that it will be a good thing for you to take one with him. If you are sad, he can look back at you with sad eyes that seem to know what infinite sorrow is. You don't have to explain yourself to your dog or justify your pain by providing the details of a situation that a human friend might ask you to consider from another perspective. You can just be sad with your dog.

Dogs seem to have an enormous capacity for pleasure. They delight in your return from the smallest excursion, but they would probably have been even more delighted if they had been included in your brief peregrination. Going on a jaunt with your dog will inevitably make you notice things you would have passed by in your otherwise preoccupied manner. He runs, he sniffs, carries a "dictionary of smells" (Akhtar, 2014, p. 16), he comes back to let you know what he has seen and to find out if you see it, too. He is such a good companion. When he ages and slows down and needs to be coaxed to do the things you used to do together, you might not want to notice. Billy Collins, US poet laureate, often writes poems from a dog's perspective. The one titled *A Dog on His Master* (2012) captures the bittersweet dilemma of our divergent life spans.

> As young as I look,
> I am growing older faster than he,
> seven to one
> is the ratio they tend to say.
> Whatever the number,
> I will pass him one day
> and take the lead
> the way I do on our walks in the woods.
> And if this ever manages
> to cross his mind,
> it would be the sweetest
> shadow I have ever cast on snow or grass.

I cannot leave this section without mentioning the epistolaries that dogs write on behalf of their owners, often when the owner wants to express something tender that might be difficult to say directly. Early in his marriage to Katherine White, E. B. White wanted to tell his new wife a bit of just how pleased he was to be married to her, so he sent her a letter from their dog, Daisy, that closed in the following understated manner:

> Well, Mrs. White, I expect I am tiring you with this long letter, but as you often say yourself, a husband and wife should tell each other about the things that are on their mind otherwise you get nowhere, and Mr. White didn't seem to be able to tell you about his happiness, so I thought I would attempt to put in a word. (White, 2013, p. 8)

The Freud family was also fond of communicating by way of birthday poems written by the dogs to the head of household. Anna Freud wrote any number of poems to her father, supposedly "penned" by her Alsatian wolfhound, Wolf, the first dog to join the Freud household. Acquired for Anna in 1925 to protect her on the solitary walks she enjoyed, he was apparently quite rambunctious. Nonetheless, both she and her father grew so fond of him that Anna grumbled in a 1926 letter to Lou Andreas-Salomé that her father had "transferred his whole interest in [her] on to Wolf" (cited in Pellegrini, p. 231).

Wolf became quite the "wordsmith." In a well-researched article entitled, *Of Dogs and Doggerel*, Molnar (1996) translated a number of "his" birthday salutations into English. He posits that these verses gave Anna a way to express tender feelings to her father that might have seemed too oedipally charged to say directly in conversation. He suggests that Wolf's obstreperous behavior paralleled Anna's own difficult behavior and made him the perfect communicator:

> Someone who's been banished from the home
> Is dumbly paying his respects today
> In contrast to his usual noisy way.
> His love for everything that's friendly and edible
> Is not even with swallowed thermometers measurable,
> So out of the nourishing things at the feast retain
> His share of what remains.
> He greets you, despite the transience of every delicacy,
> With unchanging doggy fidelity.
>
> (cited in Molnar, 1996, p. 272)

When Jofi, the chow, became part of the household in 1930, she quickly established herself as Freud's favorite and was therefore in a position to write poems herself. Shortly after her arrival, Freud needed to go to Berlin for medical treatments. It was then Jofi who wrote a letter to him, almost certainly giving voice to Anna's feelings as well. Like Wolf, Jofi confesses her wish to be better behaved, but ends with the heartfelt, "So speaks Jofi, sad at heart—sorry that we are apart" (ibid., p. 276).

My dogs and their deaths

The bittersweet reward of owning a dog almost inevitably involves losing a dog. For children, this may well be their first introduction to death. In his book for children about losing a dog, Fred Rogers (1998), of *Mr Rogers' Neighborhood* television fame, explained death in the following way, "One thing we know about dying is that it isn't like going to sleep. When a pet dies, it isn't alive anymore, so it can't wake up again. A pet that dies stops breathing and moving. It doesn't see or hear anymore. And it doesn't need to eat anymore" (p. 15). Rogers speaks to the feelings of responsibility a child may feel, or an adult for that matter: "People often wish they could have done something to stop their pets from dying … even when there was nothing they could have done. Or they might wish they could find a way to make their pet come alive again—even though that can't happen" (p. 160). In the introduction to his book, he says that losing his own dog as a child taught him that "[I]t was all right to cry when somebody you love dies … and that loss takes time to understand" (p. i). And finally, "Happy times and sad times are part of everyone's life. When a pet dies, we can grow to know that the love we shared is still alive in us and always will be" (p. 27). These profound words sum up much of what needs to happen when we mourn the loss of our pet. Perhaps one can paraphrase Tolstoy's observation that all happy families are alike while all unhappy families are unhappy in their own way by saying that the deep feelings of pleasure we obtain in their lives through our dogs has a universal quality, while our grief in their loss is a grief unique to each of us.

Although there have been several dogs who were part of the households I lived in, only two fully captured my heart. Should one attribute anything more than coincidence to the fact that they were both named Willie? Was it perhaps an unconscious communication 'twixt me and my daughter that we both gave the puppies we got for our ninth birthdays the same name? Our reasons were completely different, but nonetheless our dogs shared the identical name.

When I was young I lived in the country. The house had once been the foreman's for a farm that had been dismantled. It sat on the edge of an apple orchard, a meadow, and woods with clusters of bluebells. My mother didn't much like the few neighbors we had, so she strongly discouraged the children who lived nearby from playing with me.

I was a sickly, asthmatic kid who had frequent bouts of bronchitis. Like so many lonely kids, I read. My favorite books were often about mistreated animals that were separated from their owners. Collies seemed to be the dog of choice for romantic canine stories. Jack London's (1903) *Call of the Wild* recounted the story of Buck, a St. Bernard/Scotch collie mix, who was stolen to become a sled dog and eventually liberates himself and becomes a noble creature of the wild. Albert Payson Terhune (1919, 1922), a rough collie breeder, recounted endless stories about his dogs, all of whom had inner lives and thoughts. Eric Knight's (1940) *Lassie Come Home* is the story of a poor Welsh mining family who sell their son's dog to a wealthy Scotsman to make ends meet. The boy is devastated but Lassie escapes and finds her way back to him through every kind of travail, forsaking her new wealthy owner for love of the boy. These dogs were loyal with stout hearts and I yearned for such a companion.

Enter Willie

I pleaded, bargained, and promised to be good for the rest of my life if I, too, could have a dog, not just any dog, but a collie. To my utter astonishment, my parents agreed. On the day of the ninth birthday, I brought my Brownie Starflex camera to capture the moment when we went to meet the gangly, vanilla and butterscotch colored puppy that would become mine. In the picture, I am wearing seersucker shorts and am as scrawny as the pup. My mother is wearing a red bandana-patterned pup tent of a maternity shirt, as was the fashion in those days, and her dark glasses. My father stands to the side, watching thoughtfully. I remember being a little disappointed that Willie didn't have the thick mane I associated with rough collies, but the breeder assured me that his would come with time.

It seemed utterly magical to me that this wonderful creature could belong to me. He was steady and patient and was increasingly possessed of that regal bearing so particular to collies. The more he grew in stature, the more his dignity shone through. As his owner, I felt ennobled by my association with him. When he was a young puppy, I spent hours interpreting the world to him, explaining things to him that I thought he needed to know. We went everywhere together, just as I had hoped. When I sat in the crook of a willow tree reading a book on a summer's day, he made a nest in the grass beneath me.

My youngest brother arrived in the world shortly after Willie came to live with us. Something was wrong with his leg and he had a tiny baby cast to make it straight. My mother was overwhelmed with his care and had little time for me or anyone else. She lost patience for any additional tasks and scolded me for my failure to feed and brush Willie regularly. When his thick coat grew in, I found that it collected hundreds of tiny burrs that got tangled up in his fur. They were so difficult to remove that he would cry during my novice grooming sessions with him. I hated to hurt him and would apologize to him and bury my face in his neck feeling clumsy and inadequate. I hated my ineptness but I couldn't seem to brush him without causing him pain. I wasn't able to be as responsible to him as I'd promised to be. I compared my pitiful efforts to the boy in *Lassie Come Home*; I was certain that he would have been able comb out his collie.

While Willie seemed to become more majestic with time, my new baby brother was failing to thrive. Doctors were consulted. I wanted to help him grow and would try to teach him things as I had taught my dog, but my mother kept him in the nursery, where his twisted leg and slow ways were not in view. Mostly, I assumed that he would eventually catch up and join the rest of the family. I was wrong. I knew that my parents were worried that my brother wasn't advancing from crawling to walking, but I didn't understand what the implications of this failure might be. I'd been coaxing him to crawl to me and even though my efforts didn't result in total success, he seemed excited to try. One morning, my mother told me in a serious, scary voice that she and my father were taking him to a doctor who would tell them whether or not my brother could stay in our house. He might have to live in a place for the mentally handicapped, at least for a while. I had no idea that being unable to crawl could have such dire consequences. All that day, I prayed and promised God that I would talk to my brother all the time; I would teach him to read; I would do anything in the world for him if he could just stay home with us. Simultaneously, I had a curious feeling of importance that something so awful was happening in my life that day. I wasn't supposed to tell anyone about it and secrets can make you feel important. But when my mother called and said that he would be removed from our house as soon as they could find a place for him to go, I felt dizzy and my stomach turned over.

By the time it was summer, my brother was gone. He had been moved to a facility with a live-in nursery for children with a wide range of disabilities. We visited him once in the autumn, but my parents had been advised that it would be too hard on the family to keep seeing him, so we did not visit him again until many years later. At the time, I did not know that he would never return to our home again. I also could not have imagined that years later, I would become his guardian and that he would make visits to *my* home where he would revel in his role as an uncle to my children.

At the time, I was grief-stricken about my brother's departure. I cried about what a terrible person I was. Not only was I a failure taking care of my dog; I was now faced with the fact that I hadn't helped my brother learn enough to stay with us. I felt sure that I could have done something, if only I had just tried hard enough. Over time, Willie's presence continued to provide comfort. He could always be found on the cool green front hall floor where he kept watch over our comings and goings. I often went to sit beside him, or to put my arms around him, just to anchor myself with His Steadiness.

By the time I was twelve, I wanted to spend time with friends and get out of the house when I could. Willie would greet me at the door and I would pat him and go up to my room to do homework or talk on the phone. I felt a twinge at times, thinking he'd been waiting for me all day and now I was rushing upstairs. I'd promise to spend more time with him the following day. One sparkling fall morning, I came back from spending the night at a friend's house to find the front hall empty, no Willie Strange. I went looking around the house for him, calling his name. I found my parents instead. They had the same look they'd had when my brother left. My Willie was gone. They had gone to the veterinarian, who put him to sleep because he was sick. They thought I would be less upset if they just took care of it and told me afterward. Just the way they thought it would be easier to send my brother away swiftly and efficiently, as if we could all forget him more easily if he were out of sight. But it didn't work out that way. I was left with the terrible sense that because I failed to comprehend how seriously fragile each of them was, I had let both of them down in critical ways. I lived with the terrible uncertainty of not knowing whether either one of them knew how much I had cared.

Losing Willie was devastating. A dog doesn't care whether you are popular or whether you got an A in math or whether your hair is a disaster. Your dog will take you as you are and help you do the same about yourself. I wasn't spared sad feelings because he was whisked away in the night. Instead, I felt enormous sadness and guilt that I hadn't prepared him for what was coming and especially that I hadn't had a last chance to hug him and cry and say goodbye.

It was that peculiar time in adolescence when I felt uncertain of my place in the world. I changed schools twice during the years following Willie's death; my parents sold their house in the country and we moved into town. I was trying to figure out how to keep my old friends and how to make new ones in a school with a very different culture from the one I had previously attended. How I would have been comforted by Willie's unswerving affection had he still been around. But he was gone and, in some sense, my childhood innocence seemed to have vanished as well.

Forty years later

When my daughter was turning nine, just as I had been nine, she had an ache in her heart to have a dog, too, but she wanted one that would be small enough to sit in her lap. Like me, she promised to feed him, walk him, do everything for him if she could please have a dog. And so, one fine day, we went out to a farm and looked at adorable little puppies that were a Yorkshire terrier/miniature poodle mix. She picked out the smallest puppy, who seemed friendly and joyful.

When we picked him up six weeks later, it was immediately apparent that he was possessed of a most sweet disposition. He liked everyone, didn't nip at people, and jumped up and down with pleasure when he was given attention. Astonishingly he didn't bark all the time the way little dogs are wont to do, so I dubbed him the "Little Dog with the Big Dog disposition." We had another dog at that time who was lovely as well, but I didn't fall in love with him the way I did with my daughter's dog. He got named Willie. He had this eagerness to connect with you that took over his entire body; he became a four-legged bouncing pogo stick when he greeted you.

I remembered a morning in San Francisco when I had seen a woman walking her cairn terrier and she was laughing with amusement at the way he was investigating the street. I had thought at the time that I wished I could have a dog who entertained me the same way. So Willie became part of sleepovers, Girl Scout meetings, and all parts of family life. When my daughter went away to college, I spent more time with him and I grew to love him more and more. When she came home, he slept in her room with her and curled up on the couch with her; that made me happy, too.

Because he was so full of life, I was slow to acknowledge that he was getting older and that he couldn't levitate quite so high when he jumped. When he dragged on walks, I attributed it to boredom with the same walks. Indeed, when we took him up to the mountains in the summertime, he would accompany us on seven or eight mile hikes and then come back to the city and balk on his leash. But truth to tell, as one can be with one's elders, I felt unreasonably upset with him for getting old, as if he'd given in to it unnecessarily. Why did he have to get those nasty little bumps on his back? Why must he suddenly be such a finicky eater? Why was he having accidents all over our apartment? I wanted both of us to be forever young and frisky, gently gliding into an old age that went on indefinitely.

When he went, it was if he were suddenly tired. He couldn't bounce anymore and no longer came to greet me at the door when I came home from work. He lifted his head but he couldn't really muster enthusiasm for the ritual. His walks became almost impossible, although there were occasional vestiges of his jaunty gait. On one of those early summer mornings, when the leaves on the trees were freshly green, he was convulsed by an enormous seizure. During the night before it happened, I kept waking up to see if he was still alive. He had seemed so frail in the preceding days. When I left for the office, I was afraid that I might come home to find him gone. All morning, I heard the following refrain in my head, "His ticker just gave out," which isn't a phrase I'd ever used before. He had the seizure while he was with my husband that morning. He called me and we met at the animal hospital. The veterinarian said to us, "You have a very sick dog." We knew. She advised us that she maybe could give him a little more time, but his quality of life was finished. And, he'd had a good long life, fifteen years, during most of which he was blessed with remarkable health. We spent a little time with him alone, his body listless and his eyes lifeless. She returned and talked us through the three injections would let him slip away for the last time. We walked blinking out into the sunlight, without him.

I had been so caught in Willie's seizures and agony to think of anything but relieving him of his misery. When we walked outside into the sunset, blinking our salty eyes, it was still too early to call my daughter, who lived on the other side of the country in a different time zone. She had visited frequently and had seen how weak Willie was becoming but she could not bear to talk of how old he was getting to be and how weak. We wanted to tell her as soon as possible but no matter how much she knew about his condition, we were conscious that the news would feel abrupt. We called her and spoke to her, sharing our tears. He wasn't part of her daily life anymore, but she had grown up with him. She had given him endless numbers of nicknames, dressed him up in silly outfits, and probably held on to him in private moments the way I had held on to my childhood Willie.

Every little piece of my day at home is different now. That moment of walking into the house is now filled with the absence of sound. I used to hear the sound of his dog tags jingling as he jumped off the couch to come bouncing down the hall to say hello. He seemed to be some part of me, literally, as if my love had somehow generated his buoyant gait and vice versa. I felt like we knew each other—maybe I should say I felt like he knew me. But still I was left to wonder, as I had with my childhood dog Willie, "Did he have any idea how much I loved him?"

*Making life and death decisions and the
resulting conflicted bereavement*

We have the ability to adopt a dog, train a dog, care for a dog, and finally to make decisions about when to end her life. This is rarely an easy decision. If we are deeply attached to a dog, we may take extreme measures to prolong her life with medical interventions such as excessive surgeries or medications. Our feelings are inevitably complicated by our own attitudes towards death.

Marie Bonaparte's book captures the ways that facing the death of a dog can be intertwined with feelings about one's own mortality. *Topsy* is both an ode to her dog, but also a meditation on the finitude of life. She describes the delight she feels sitting in her garden watching her chow frolicking about in the flowers with an energy that she no longer has. For her, it is most comforting when her dog settles down beside her with no wish to be anywhere else. She writes with great beauty about her unequivocal love for her dog at the same time that she is pondering if and when she might have to euthanize Topsy, should her cancer worsen.

It is an entirely different matter to hold a dog's life in one's hands if one feels ambivalently about the dog. Even otherwise, the decision to "put a dog down" can be fraught with conflict. Many people have confessed to me that they kept their dogs alive far beyond their pet's ability to experience any quality of life whatsoever. "We knew it was selfish," they told me, "but we could not bear to let her go."

The following story is about one patient's agonized struggle to decide whether her rescue dog was too dangerous to keep alive. Unlike Bonaparte, she became increasingly conflicted about her dog, Ingrid, who complicated her life with her uncontrollable aggression.

A clinical vignette

Mrs. S. was a professional woman in her early thirties. Highly intelligent and sensitive, she had been in treatment in another city to deal with a recurrent depression that sprang, in part, from her demanding expectations of herself. Although she recognized her dysphoric moods, she told me that she tended to be very matter-of-fact about things and wished that she could be more in touch with her feelings.

She had been married for a short while and was discovering the extent to which her husband suffered from anxiety. Although she tried to be patient and understanding with Mr. S., his indecisiveness tested her reserves and she would feel frustration and hopelessness about his passivity. As both a child and an adult, she had served as a quasi-therapist for her family of origin. She was conflicted about this role, recognizing that she enjoyed the feelings of power and authority it conferred on her within her family. On the other hand, her efforts to help others in her family had generalized into a helping position with everyone in her life. She recognized that this stance had come to serve as a defense that enabled her to avoid delving too deeply into her own psyche.

Mrs. S. thought she was ready to start a family, but she worried that if her husband could not deal with his anxiety, she might end up feeling like the only adult in the family that they would create together. She would be doomed to recreating the same family situation that she knew kept her constricted.

With this in mind, she and her husband decided to take a trial run and see how they managed with the lesser commitment of adopting a dog. They decided upon a sleek and muscular rescue dog, a Rottweiler who they named Ingrid. The dog's history was unknown, save for the fact that she had been in the shelter for ten months. The more she and her husband knew Ingrid, the greater their certainty that she had been seriously mistreated and had suffered extensive trauma, the exact nature of which they would never know. It was increasingly evident that Ingrid was fundamentally terrified of people and that she managed her fear with formidable aggressiveness. Ingrid was, more often than not, an affectionate presence when she was at home with the two of them. However, if she heard an unfamiliar sound or sensed someone coming up to the house, she was instantly transformed into a terrifying Cerberus who barked and growled viciously. When these episodes occurred, both Mrs. S. and her husband were frightened as well. As soon as Ingrid sensed that the danger was gone, she settled back into being the sweet dog that she could be.

Mrs. S. was hopeful that with love, steady discipline, and a calm environment Ingrid's fear would gradually dissolve. Mrs. S. worked in a high stress job where her calmness in the face of charged emotions was greatly valued. However, her evenhanded manner could diffuse neither her husband's perpetual state of agitation nor soothe her highstrung dog.

As the months went by, Mrs. S. found her life increasingly constricted by Ingrid's needs. It became impossible to invite people to her house because even when Ingrid was confined to another room, she would bark and growl incessantly. Days were arranged so that Mrs. S. could minimize the likelihood of chance encounters with neighbors. When they did run into other people or dogs, Ingrid would lunge towards them and Mrs. S. would feel ashamed of her inability to control her dog. People stared at her as they do at mothers who have a screaming child in the supermarket as if to say, "What do you think she does to that child that it behaves that way?" She consulted dog books and conferred with a myriad of dog training experts, but the problems with Ingrid seemed to be worsening. At the same time, she was unsuccessfully trying to bolster her husband's self-confidence and feeling exhausted by all of it. It was as if her reserves were being sucked dry by the both of them, yet she failed to adequately nourish either. This left her feeling depleted but also frustrated and angry that she couldn't supply what it seemed each of them needed.

When spring came, Mrs. S. suddenly became more positive, for no apparent reason other than the appearance of daffodils and cherry blossoms. She reported enjoying her husband more and was pleased that he had been decisive on a number of household decisions. The outcomes were far less important to her than the fact that he had been able to make them. Together, they began to think about moving to a neighborhood that would be more conducive to having a family, but Mrs. S. refrained from saying that she was thinking about getting pregnant. I was certain that she didn't want to discuss this because she couldn't justify her new perspective rationally. After all the complaints she had leveled about her husband, I suspected that she would be ashamed about her change of heart.

She went away for the summer and when she returned, she announced that she and her husband had moved to a house that they liked a great deal. Also, she was pregnant and would be having a baby in six months' time. She expressed no ambivalence about having the baby; rather she displayed a cheery affect when talking about her pregnancy and the move. Indeed, the move was positive in every way, except that Ingrid was falling apart in her new home. The new neighborhood smells and people set her off into paroxysms of fear and intensified her aggressive behaviors. Mrs. S. worried about how she could possibly have a baby in the same house with Ingrid.

With her husband's begrudging agreement, she began to look for a new home for the dog. She scoured the internet and talked to countless people in hopes of finding a place where Ingrid could be safe. She became an expert in "no kill" shelter options. She felt guilty and despondent about her unsuccessful efforts to find a place where Ingrid could be safe and feel self and she began to contemplate putting Ingrid down. Her sessions were filled with tears and self-recriminations. Her husband's commitment to moving Ingrid out of their home vacillated. When they did, he would accuse Mrs. S. of not trying hard enough, of not loving the dog enough, and in his darkest moments, of being a murderer.

Mrs. S. became desperately afraid that her sadness would affect her unborn child; she redoubled her efforts to find a solution but none came. How could she know if she had done enough to save Ingrid? Her baby was to be born in six weeks and she was exhausted. Time was running out and no one was willing to take Ingrid. They could return her to the shelter where they had gotten her where she would be re-traumatized and almost certainly be terminated or she and her husband could take her to a veterinarian who would also put her to sleep. Mrs. S. did not want Ingrid to suffer any more than was necessary. She recognized that she would have to make the judgment call because her husband couldn't.

It was at this point that she told me she needed someone to just say to her, "Enough is enough!" Several years before I began seeing Mrs. S., my family had a dog whose personality changed, most probably because of a brain lesion. Like Ingrid, he was sweet and affectionate when alone with us, but when he heard the sound of dogs walking by or the postman arriving, he hurled himself at the front door, almost foaming at the mouth. He had bitten the postman, the neighbor's gardener, and even me. I feared what would happen if he got out of the house one day and attacked one of our neighbors or one of their children when he was in one of these states. I had looked for new homes and other alternatives, but after a similarly agonizing struggle, had made the decision to put him down. All of us were devastated by the decision but my guilt was softened by the kindness of our veterinarian who said, "This must have been so hard on you. You must have been worried all the time." I had been, more so than anyone else in my family and because of that I had been the most adamant about our need to protect ourselves and others from the potential of him seriously hurting someone.

During the months that Mrs. S. struggled with her decision, I kept examining my own feelings, of course, hoping that I would not allow my own experience to interfere with her decision. One day, she looked at me and asked, "Do you have children? What would you do?" Although I am not at all in the habit of disclosing personal details about my life,

I told her that I did have children. I told her that when she had her baby, I was certain she would not want to risk anything happening to her child because of the dog, that she would never forgive herself. Mrs. S. was visibly relieved by this bright line judgment call.

She was able to make an appointment to put Ingrid to sleep. Once she did so, her grief opened up and this allowed her to experience the love she felt for Ingrid during the final days preceding her euthanasia. The more she was able to feel her attachment to Ingrid, the more aware she was of all the things she would miss about her. For the most part, she was confident about her decision. The night before the appointment, she called me to say how hard this was and to reassure herself that she was doing the right thing. In the end, when the time came, she didn't let her dog suffer unnecessarily either. She recognized that Ingrid suffered greatly in her inability to adapt to her world.

Several weeks later, Mrs. S. went on to have a beautiful healthy baby. While she missed Ingrid terribly, she could not imagine how the dog would have been with her son. She was saddened but also glad to be free of the constant stress she had been experiencing and which would have increased exponentially had Ingrid remained in the house.

About a year later, she bought a puppy from a breeder who she could raise herself. This proved to be a happy and healing experience for her, reassuring her that she could be a good mother to both her baby and her dog. The dark decision-making period is a somewhat distant memory. Perhaps all her fears about her marriage and her ability to successfully nurture a family were displaced onto the very real problem of what to do about Ingrid. Sometimes she looks back at that period and laughs ruefully, remembering how she had once told me that she wished she could have more feelings. Ingrid inspired more love, guilt, and regret than Mrs. S. could ever have imagined. Her grief remains complicated, yet she is also certain that she did what she could for her dog and that the well-being of her child is paramount for her.

Conclusion

E. B. White wrote that he never visited the grave of anyone he knew, save that of his impossible dachshund, Fred. He buried him down the hill from his house in a beautiful spot where White was happy to sit contemplatively. Seven years after Fred died, he wrote after one of these visits:

> I do not experience grief or pay tribute to the dead. But I feel a Sadness at ALL last things, too, which is probably a purely selfish, or turned in emotion—sorrow not at my dog's death but at my own, which hasn't even occurred yet but which saddens me just to think about in such pleasant surroundings. (White, 2013, p. 134)

White suggests that the spirit of Fred allows him to bear some of his most difficult reveries with a feeling of equanimity. At the same time, it is true that we don't fall in love with every dog we meet and not every dog falls in love with us, but when it happens, we are raised up by it. When such a dog dies, we are left not only with his absence but are continually reminded of the generosity of his spirit and his forbearance.

Two questions, nonetheless, haunt us. The first is what to do with the dog's remains? To be sure, there is no easy answer. Some dogs are buried, others cremated. One woman told me that she and her husband went to the cemetery where her mother was buried and when no one was looking, dug into the topsoil so that they could deposit the mother's dog's ashes on top of her grave. A powerful testimony to retaining relationships with pets after their burial is evident in the case of the psychoanalyst, Dominic Mazza. Born and raised in the suburban community of Scranton, Pennsylvania, Mazza entered psychoanalytic training in the cosmopolitan Washington, DC. Throughout his fifteen-year stay there, he had a sense of being an immigrant. When he decided to move back to Scranton, he dug up the grave of his dog, a Doberman named Damien, and reinterred the remains in the backyard of his house in Scranton (personal communication, cited in Akhtar, 1999, p. 37).

We took my daughter's dog Willie's ashes up to the woods in New Hampshire, where he had been free to trot around without his leash, chasing squirrels to his heart's content. I want to think of him resting in a place where he was unfettered and where we could visit him, remembering his jaunty high-stepping.

The second question has to do with getting a new dog after losing a dog. Some people plan in advance, getting a dog to replace the older one while he is alive; the older dog becomes a wise mentor for the younger one while the puppy reinvigorates the elder. But one must have the time and energy to devote to a puppy, full of energy and in need of frequent walks. While one might yearn for a new dog, it might not be fair to be an absent parent to the newborn animal.

In my experience, when a dog is put to sleep, it happens quickly and peacefully. All the tension melts away as the dog looks at you, closes its eyes, and imperceptibly stops breathing. There is a quiet serenity that fills the room as it becomes evident that your dog's spirit is gone. While there is sadness, there is also the hope that your dog has also been spared further pain. In the end, it turns out that losing the particular love we felt for a dog is a deeply private affair of the heart that can't quite be put into words. After all, our relationship with our dog was never about ideas; it was always about love.

EPILOGUE

CHAPTER EIGHT

Death: the last chapter

Gurmeet S. Kanwal

In the story of the *Katha Upanishad*,[1] the main protagonist is a child by the name of Nachiketa. Nachiketa is granted three boons by Yama, the god of Death. The final boon that Nachiketa chooses is to ask Yama to explain the nature of Death. Yama entreats the young boy to ask for something else. Nachiketa persists in his query. Yama tries to lure Nachiketa away from his question by offering him every possible material possession, every worldly pleasure, every kind of power. Nachiketa rejects them all and demands that his question be addressed. The rest of the *Katha Upanishad* is the dialogue that ensues between Yama and the young child Nachiketa, as Yama tries to bestow on him the deep knowledge about Death, Soul, and Immortality. In this way, the *Katha Upanishad* reminds us of the profundity, and agelessness, of humanity's preoccupation with the problem of Death. Not simply at a metaphysical level, but also the psychological problem of death, dying, and the suffering associated with loss, that is, bereavement.

Not all deaths are equal. Some feel natural, and some unnatural or untimely. Some have a very personal and local character, others may be very public. Some deaths are so shameful that one cannot dare to talk about them and all the feelings the bereaved suffers must be suffered alone. We call that "disenfranchised grief" (Doka, 1989). Think of the AIDS epidemic and deaths by suicide. Some deaths induce such rage that grieving and mourning become impossible until the anger can be resolved in some way. Deaths due to medical malpractice, for example, can evoke that feeling, as can death by murder. The bereaved may seek revenge to modify the rage in the form of lawsuits, or physical vengeance (Kernberg, 2010). This kind of coping mechanism is alluded to, albeit in a different context, by Livingston (Chapter Five, this volume). Livingston mentions anthropologist Rosaldo's account of the Ilongot tribe (northern Luzon, Philippines) where a bereaved man might behead someone (with no connection to the deceased) and throw the head away, as a means of resolving his anger about the loss. Pollock (1976) provides an excellent review of various forms of suicide and homicide that can become a part of bereavement in cultures around the world. Death of an individual, or a single pet, may elicit a very different kind of bereavement than situations where death is massive and catastrophic, like in earthquakes and tsunamis. Natural or man-made disasters (e.g., bombing of an entire city with thousands of resultant casualties) involve a unique mixture of individual as well as communal bereavement, each consoling as well as amplifying the other. Deraniyagala (2013), who lost her husband, her two kids, as well as both her parents in the 2004 tsunami, describes in her stunningly painful book, *Wave*, how hard it can be to recover from catastrophic loss and how deeply it can dislodge one's very sense of identity: "When it comes to pancakes, my mind goes blank. Try as I might, I can't remember how to make a pancake. I am thrown by this, I who made pancakes so often. Am I so estranged from who I was?". (p. 179).

Not all encounters with death, however, evoke suffering, or require bereavement. My earliest memory of a person dying (although I must have encountered the concept of death much earlier) is recorded in my mind in this way: I am standing in a long line of kids as we all move past an open casket in some part of my Catholic school in India. As the single file of uniformed, well-behaved kids moves past the casket, I look at the face of the dead person, and I feel a wave of some strange emotion that might have been a mixture of fear, awe, shock, and disbelief sweep over me. I turn to my friend, who is behind me in the line, and say in a hushed but intense tone, "It's 'The Terror,' it's 'The Terror!'" "The Terror" was how we referred to this very strict teacher we had that year in our school. It was either in fourth or fifth grade, I can't quite recall. But that moment of looking at that face and saying those words

DEATH: THE LAST CHAPTER 171

has never left my mind. It is frozen, like the petrified fossil of an animal killed and preserved while running. Only in this case, it is a thought and a vision fixed in a layer of memory right when it was happening. Why we were exposed to this casket during a school day in this manner is a mystery wrapped up in all sorts of local, cultural, and generational complexities. I certainly did not feel bereaved by that death. But I did experience something that must have been traumatizing in some way. I also remember feeling some kind of justice in the fact that a much-feared teacher had been felled by fate.

One question not often addressed in psychoanalytic literature is the role of encountering death in normal human development. I am referring here to death encountered in conversations, in books, in movies, in theater (e.g., *The Lion King*, 1994), in children's stories and rhymes (e.g., "Humpty Dumpty"), in language idioms (e.g., "dead as a doornail"), and death of animals (not one's own pet), or death as observed in the culture in general (e.g., children visiting the Taj Mahal in India and being told that the monument is a tomb). In other words, death encountered by children, while not associated with a personal sense of loss, can still be puzzling and even traumatic. In Erikson's (1950) developmental stages, we don't encounter the significance of coming to terms with death until the eighth stage, "integrity *vs.* despair." But what about coming to terms with death in a non-bereavement related context, in childhood? Is it important? Does it have a lasting effect? Does the absence of such contact impact development negatively, or positively? Development is about continuity in time. Death is about discontinuity. As such, death is always a challenge to development. This, however, does not automatically imply that awareness of death has to become an obstacle to development, although it certainly can. According to Piaget's (1936) developmental scheme, object permanence is established towards the end of the sensori-motor stage (birth to two years). However, others have demonstrated that evidence of object permanence can be seen much earlier (Baillargeon & DeVos, 1991; Bower, 1974). Bowlby (1980) concludes in his seminal work on attachment, "There seem good grounds for attributing a germinal capacity for mourning to young children at least from sixteen months onwards" (p. 437). However, that does not help us understand the emotional-developmental impact of the gradual (healthy) dawning of the comprehension of death. Pollock (1971) perhaps hints at positive aspects of the role of encountering death when he states, "Mourning is an adaptation to change and permits planning for the future. The acceptance of time is the acceptance of change and therefore of death, but it is also the acceptance of multiplicity, growth, and further development" (p. 445). But that is still in the context of loss. One can ask: what is the impact of the way one is exposed to (non-bereavement-evoking) death in childhood on the adult's capacity to tolerate bereavement? Perhaps it would be a good idea for clinicians to be trained from early on, to ask this question of all patients: When is the first time you remember becoming aware of death?

Death is universal, but the ways of handling death and its aftermath vary from culture to culture and from time to time within any culture. Growing up in India, an unusually multicultural country, I saw many different ways of disposing of the dead. There were the "towers of silence" used by the Zoroastrians. The body of the dead is left in these "towers," to be eaten by scavenging vultures.[2] There were Muslim and Christian cemeteries, and Hindu cremation grounds. One could encounter funeral pyres burning on cremation grounds in the heart of a metropolitan city, or see them on the steps (*ghats*) leading down to the water of the Ganges river. Occasionally one might see funeral processions going through the streets with the body lying on a stretcher, under a cloth, lifted up on the shoulders of family members, with the accompanying mourners chanting and singing. Death is much more intimate and accessible in India than it is in the United States. Here, we die invisibly and quietly, in hospitals and hospices. The dead body is whisked away before it disturbs anyone too much, and funeral homes make sure that the dead look just like the living. Not only has dying become so separated from living, but the very moment of death has become technologically, rather than humanistically, defined. Philippe Aries (1974), in describing these changes in our attitudes towards death from the Middle Ages to modern times, writes, "Death has been dissected, cut to bits by a series of little steps which finally makes it impossible to know which step was the real death" (p. 88). What do these changes in our attitudes towards death and dying mean in terms of individual psychology? What do they tell us about the culture of bereavement? Or bereavement in different cultures?

Even as the focus of psychoanalytic work is always the experience of the unique individual, the focus of psychoanalytic theory is to discover for us the common denominators underlying human experience. This sets up a tension between the need to give adequate recognition to the variations across cultures and the need for a reductionist understanding of drives, representations, relations, and dynamics. Without including the richness of culture, one loses the melody, and risks mishearings and misunderstandings. Without depending on the depth of the universals, one loses the harmony, and risks becoming adrift in variations. For example, one can ask: What does the loss of an individual mean in a culture where the "I" is more of a "we" (as in Roland's 1987 explication of the "we-self" in Indian culture); or what complicates bereavement in a "shame-culture" *vs.* a "guilt-culture" (Benedict, 1967)? Several contributors have described, in this book, the theoretical additions and shifts in psychoanalytic literature regarding mourning, since Freud. Hagman (1995b) provides a review and a critique of Freud's theory of mourning, including taking into account cultural variations in bereavement. He writes, "Although painful longing, sadness and grief are common characteristics of mourning, it appears that the type of dejection described by Freud and standardised in the psychoanalytic definition is not a necessary feature of normal mourning" (p. 919). In my opinion, a deeper accounting of culture as it affects defensive mechanisms and relational representations, or interpersonal dynamisms, in the context of bereavement, has yet to occur.

Many stories, few theories

One well known story in Buddhism is that of a woman, Kisa Gautami, coming to a monk in great distress because her only son has just died. She is completely inconsolable and desperate to find some way to bring him back to life. The monk suggests that she go talk to the Buddha. She goes to the Buddha with her dead child in her arms, beseeching him to revive her son. The Buddha tells her that there is only one way out of her suffering. She must go around the village and bring back four or five mustard seeds given to her by a household where there has never been a death. Thinking this was the way to restore life to her son's dead body, Kisa Gautami goes from house to house looking for one untouched by bereavement. At the end of the day, she returns to the Buddha, having failed to find even one such household. By that time, her suffering has been transformed to compassion, as she realizes that no one is spared grief, and that every human being must confront the reality of death. It is interesting to note two things about the Buddha's intervention. First, that he does not simply tell Kisa Gautami that everyone has to suffer. Instead he lets her gain that wisdom through action and interaction, and over the course of a long day. Second, the Buddha's intervention also necessitates that Kisa Gautami go around the village and connect with every household, rather than sit in solitude, wrapped in her grief.

The contributors to this book have each taken the courageous step of revisiting their own grief as they tell us their stories of losing a mother, father, sibling, spouse, child, or pet. In doing so, they do for the rest of us what the Buddha did for Kisa Gautami. They remind us that however we might think of ourselves as being separated from our patients, we, too, live lives and confront death, and grieve and mourn our loved ones. In this respect, we are all in the same boat. None is spared. And that it is only by keeping our own experiences of encountering death, bereavement, and mourning alive in our minds that we can hope to participate in the healing of others.

Each contributing author has a different story, but each is reaching into the existing theories to find language for her or his feelings. There are many stories, ours as well as our patients'. In so many ways, each bereavement situation feels unique. Bereavement dynamics can be determined by: (1) age of the bereaved; (2) gender of the bereaved; (3) race, culture, ethnicity of the bereaved; (4) nature of the relationship with the deceased (i.e., mother, father, spouse, etc.); (5) gender relationship to the deceased (i.e., son-mother, son-father, mother-daughter, etc.); (6) the age of the deceased; (7) whether the loss occurred suddenly or gradually; (8) whether the person or pet died of natural or unnatural causes; (9) whether the relationship with the deceased was good or troubled, and of course (10) the personality structure of the bereaved.

There is no way to capture the many varieties of human bereavement in one book. And yet the theories we have, to understand the experience of bereavement, are few. Which is what theories are meant to be—a way to identify common denominators, fundamental origins, and overarching themes. They may not always feel enough to cover the topographically varied landscape of our bereavement, but they provide us, and help us provide our patients, with some reasonable maps to chart our way through the morass of feelings we encounter. As one reads the accounts in this book, one is struck by the commonalities as well as the differences. Some of the main ones are highlighted here.

Of sounds and silence

When Malawista (Chapter Two) lost her mother, she was a child only about nine years old. Wolman (Chapter Three) was only six when his best friend died. While Lowy writes mainly about the loss of his sister in adulthood, he, too, was only six when his family had to leave Austria under the shadow of the Nazi regime, and at ten he had to travel to the United States, separated from his parents, and in charge of his seven-year-old sister. Platt (Chapter Seven) lost her beloved dog at the age of twelve, but she had "lost" her younger brother some time prior to that. These childhood losses all seem to illuminate the particularly profound impact of silence on the experience of bereavement. What is said, and what is, or cannot be, spoken about seem to become very important at such times.

Ornstein (2010) writes, "The silence among Holocaust survivors that followed the destruction of World War II was a necessary silence: it was needed for recovery so that eventually … the enormity of their losses could be faced and accepted" (p. 644). While the enormity of the losses of several of the authors here may have needed a certain kind of silence, we also see the way in which silence can complicate bereavement. Wolman thought, "Death was an event so acutely embarrassing or shameful that nobody wanted to talk about it." Later in life, after losing his father, Wolman found that it was listening to the mourners' Kaddish that helped break his own emotional silence. Platt describes the awfulness of her parents' "silence" around both the loss of her brother and the death of her dog, Willie. Malawista could only break her silence in the presence of her dog, with no one else around. She also talks about how the silence of members of the community—"school, friends, and neighbors"—can be in the service of their denial, "However, children have a powerful need to verbalize their feelings." Livingston writes "I'm talking to Bob all the time." Smolen (Chapter Six) was only able to break her silence in the form of poetry. Akhtar (2000) calls poetry, "cultural ointment against mental pain" (p. 229). He describes how poetry can help to mobilize defenses and bring about mentalization of "the non-verbal substrate of the psyche."

The role of speaking as well as sharing in silence is obviously important from a therapeutic perspective. Ours is a listening and talking cure. When it comes to bereavement, the nuances of our patients' need for silence as well as for things to be spoken about are what we try to be attuned towards. On a technical level, Bromberg (2001) makes the important distinction in his theory of trauma and dissociation, between "being seen "into"" and "a dialectic between seeing and being seen." What Bromberg is suggesting is that patients may not simply need to talk out their thoughts or feelings, with the analyst "understanding" them and making interpretations, but that it is in the dialectic, the intersubjective matrix, of what is said by each, and not said, and what is seen by each in the other, that a therapeutic process can take place. To the extent that silence may represent being alone, and speaking represents a relational context, the capacity to be able to speak (to someone) about one's grief can be an important signal of the progression of the mourning process. In some cultures professional mourners are hired to get the bereaved to cry, or to experience the expression of grief vicariously. Kundalia (2015) chronicles the use of such professional mourners (*rudaalis*) in Rajasthan, India. She quotes one of the subjects interviewed as saying, "High caste women do not cry in front of commoners. Even if their husbands die, they need to preserve their dignity. These low caste women, *rudaalis*, do the job for them" (Ch. 2, para. 23). Perhaps sometimes it is the job of the therapist to function as a kind of *rudaali* for the patient!

Bereavement and responsibility

Whenever someone dies, there is always the question of responsibility, either in fantasy or reality. We see this playing out, implicitly or explicitly, in many of the accounts in this book. Who, or what, is to be held responsible for the death? If the responsible party is a person, could it be the bereaved herself? Kernberg (2010) describes a patient's inconsolable sense of responsibility,

> One woman, describing the sudden death of her husband of twenty-two years, with whom she had had a very fulfilling relationship in terms of their sexual life, their mutual expectations and interactions in daily life, and their orientation toward values, social life, intellectual and ideological aspirations, described the sense of concern after his unexpected death following shortly after a routine medical examination in which he had been given a clean bill of health. Had she been contributing to causing his death from a heart attack because she had been too demanding, originating stress in his life? (p. 605)

The more reasons the bereaved has had to feel anger and other negative feelings in the relationship, the harder it might be to shake off some sense of responsibility, and hence guilt. As Freud (1917e) first clarified, that can set the stage for complicated grief and melancholia.

The issue of responsibility for death also automatically raises the image of murder and myths. Aries (1974) points out that the Latin word *funus* "can be translated as either the dead body, the funeral ceremony, or murder" (p. 14). Thus, medieval Latin seems to hold a psychological secret reemphasized by Freud in the twentieth century. Wolman delves into this as he discusses the death of his own father. He comes to the conclusion that, "[T]he role of the mythical crime is there to remind us that the loss of the father can never be fully repaired or atoned for." Later, he describes how it is at the moment of praising God in the course of the mourners' Kaddish that he begins to cry and feels "freed to express my grief". Is it that praising God (the "father") enough times, functions as a reparative act, assuaging the guilt of having entertained patricidal feelings, and thus clearing the path to mourning? One is, however, left to wonder how the dynamics might be different if the "primal horde" (Freud, 1912–13) of progeny was all daughters rather than sons? Would they be dealing with the same unconscious fantasies, and have the same difficulty with atonement? Lowy (Chapter Four), in discussing the dynamics of sibling loss, points to the impact of sibling rivalry. Siblings generally have a relational context where rivalry, envy, competition are often much more acceptable and conscious than in other familial relationships like with parents or children. How this impacts bereavement is worthy of attention. Lowy also reminds us of Freud's own ambivalence towards some of his siblings and how that might have impacted their survival at the time of leaving Vienna.

On the other end of the spectrum is the context of the death of a child. Responsibility becomes almost, and literally, unthinkable there. How can one be responsible for giving life, and then confront a feeling of responsibility for the end of that life? Smolen states, "A mother's job is to protect her child and keep him safe. The parent feels helpless and powerless as her efficacy and self-esteem are destroyed." In describing the loss of her own son, she is overcome with a wave of doubt and guilt, "… if I had waited, maybe the medicine would have started to work." Every time there is a death, one has to grapple with placing responsibility. How one handles that delicate emotion can have a huge impact on the outcome of mourning. Platt struggles with this both with regard to her brother who was institutionalized and her dog who died—"… because I failed to comprehend how seriously fragile each of them was, I had let both of them down in critical ways." Malawista describes a patient who was stuck with the sense of being responsible for her father's death, thinking as a child that it was caused by her having hit her sister. Malawista also wonders about her own and her siblings' vulnerability as children to feel responsible for the death of their mother. One can wonder how this dynamic is influenced by the age of each child. Livingston describes her husband saying in the ICU, "You have to let me go." As hard as that is in terms of loss, there is also the implied dimension of responsibility. How can one bear the responsibility of letting go of the person one loves so dearly? A patient who was extremely close with her sister found it impossible to recover from her death due to breast cancer. Even though every proper treatment had been tried, she could not shake off the feeling that perhaps there could have been something else she (the patient) should have been able to do. Her grief was so deep, and bereavement so complicated, that over the following four years she gradually began to develop memory problems and ultimately was diagnosed with dementia, while still in her late sixties. There was no family history of dementia. I was convinced that the patient simply could not go on living with the memory of her loss, and her own sense of responsibility. It was like watching a "failure to thrive" in the setting of bereavement.

Things we turn to

In a way, our theories are like other things we turn to for solace, direction, or coping. There are many such things, both abstract and concrete, animate and inanimate, human and nonhuman. Smolen refers to Volkan's (1984) idea of a "linking object," an object that represents both the mourner and the deceased. Volkan (1984) puts these in four categories: (i) objects used by the deceased; (ii) objects that were used specifically for some sensory experience by the deceased; (iii) symbolic or realistic representations of the dead person's appearance, and (iv) gifts from or to the mourner. In keeping with this notion, Wolman describes his experience of the ritual of Kaddish as what helped him emote through the loss of his father. Livingston also describes the importance of "death rituals" in her process of coping. Smolen's ritual became writing poetry and dancing. Malawista describes how in the depth of her shock and grief as a child, she turned to her dog to help her articulate her feelings and make sense of the incomprehensible loss of her mother. "Don't you understand what happened? … Don't you understand? Mommy died," says Malawista to her dog as a child bereft and in shock. Her dog is the first "person" to whom she can say something about this. Livingston also describes the role of her cat, "soft comfort for the two months after Bob's death". And when the cat dies only two months after her husband, it is a double whammy. Reading these accounts, one can see the deep psychic significance that pets can have for humans—the reason why we have chosen to include a chapter on death of a pet in this book. Platt's account of the loss of her dogs mingled with that of the loss of her brother when he is institutionalized as a child, reminds us that in the relational world, animals and humans can seamlessly occupy similar spaces. They can be "linking objects," substitution objects, replacement objects, transitional objects, and even objects that might be needed to endure the anger and hate of the bereaved. One patient described her recently acquired, very difficult to manage, puppies as reminding her so much of her deceased father, who had been very abusive and demanding, that she had to return them to the breeder. It is worth noting here that mourning and pets are linked in the reverse direction also. That is, not only do humans mourn for their pets, but it is well documented that pets mourn for humans (Pollock, 1961), and animals mourn for other animals (Shanor & Kanwal, 2009). For Lowy, the most significant bridge across his bereavement was the availability of the deceased sister's surviving family. Perhaps in that way, the deceased person's family members can also be seen as another example of "linking objects" that represent both the deceased and the bereaved.

How we carry on

Smolen describes how desperately she needed to find meaning in her existence after the loss of her child. She went back to school, and finally found her way into becoming a psychoanalyst and helping others. She found new paths in poetry, and in life, including in the act of having more children. What a creative "Fuck you" to Death! She reminds us of something very essential about the human spirit, and in fact about the spirit inherent in life itself—the role of the procreative capacity in dealing with bereavement, loss, and grief. Malawista found a new opening in a "chance" encounter with a kind neighbor who could take on the role of a maternal presence. She asserts that, "A maternal presence was not only yearned for, but was required." Malawista's discovery of a kindly maternal neighbor can be seen as a coping mechanism seen commonly in children, which she describes as the attempt to re-find the lost parent.

These reunion fantasies are in fact often embedded in, and sanctioned by, many cultural traditions and beliefs, in some cultures more than in others. For example, in Indian culture, with its acceptance of the notion of reincarnation, re-finding a dead person can take on both fantasy as well as concrete forms. People will sometimes identify a dead person as having been reborn in someone else's body and proceed to have a relationship with the person on that basis. This is not a phenomenon limited to non-Western cultures. An article in *The New York Times* (Wilson, 2015) reported a psychic who kept taking money from a client to reunite him with an ex-girlfriend. When it was discovered that the ex-girlfriend had died, the psychic took more money promising that the ex-girlfriend had been reincarnated in another body and that the psychic would help him establish a relationship with this new woman. One of my adult Indian patients will often refer to his deceased father, who died when the patient was in his forties, as watching over him every time something good happens in his life. Wrapped in that fantasy experience is of course a degree of idealization of a parent, particularly seen in a culture where idealizing parents is a requirement (Kanwal, 2015). Does this imply that he had not been able to mourn successfully? I would suggest that in fact, such a holding on of an ancestral presence is a healthy and normal part of mourning in the particular cultural context.

Wolman describes, in his account, how he started playing tennis again after the death of his father—a game he had abandoned earlier due to his father's critical stance. His father's death made it possible to recover his own connection with a desire he had suppressed. That which he had pursued in order to be loved had become a source of rejection and angry feelings. Now, he was able to find a way to hold on to something good while acknowledging the difficult, by abstracting the symbol of the name (or game!) from the concreteness of the deceased person. As he states in comparing this to the message of the Kaddish, "We can praise his name while being profoundly befuddled by his ineffable being." I had a similar personal experience.

After my father died (the event that spurred the conception of this book), I found myself drawn to the cultural rituals surrounding his last rites as a way to process my feelings in action. Even when I was not talking about the event or my feelings, I was working through them by participating in the rites. Only later would I have the capacity to comprehend what it was that I might have been processing. The morning of his memorial service, where I was going to speak, I woke up very early from a dream, startled that I had just realized how my love for words was shared between us. It was a simple fact that could have been available for me to think about any other time in my life. Nothing should have been unconscious about it. Yet, it never occurred to me, in that way, till that moment! Like Wolman, it helped me to reconcile the good with the bad. What had not been able to be found between us while he was alive was found in a dream after his death. As Kernberg (2010) emphasizes, "The identification with the lost person, particularly with traits that one admired and missed, is a source of strength and, indeed, fosters the experience of a sense of overcoming the mourning process" (p. 608). His observation points to the significant shift in theories of mourning since Freud's (1917e) "Mourning and Melancholia". Identification with the lost object is no longer an obstacle to finishing the task of mourning. One is not expected to achieve some impossibly complete decathexis. Instead, it is seen as a "source of strength." This creates the space to understand why ancestor worship, which exists in many cultures, can be seen as a movement forward in the process of mourning.

Both Wolman and Platt also point out how one death can evoke the grief and mourning of others that have gone before—reawakening sorrow, but also providing another opportunity to work something out. Wolman's narrative about his father's death becomes intricately linked with the loss of a friend in childhood; Platt's loss of one dog brings up memories of a previous dog who also shared the same name. In my experience, part of the work of helping someone during bereavement consists of examining earlier losses, and unresolved issues related to those, that may have been triggered by the current death. It can also provide a way of talking about the feelings related to loss in a context that may be easier than in the context of a very recent death.

Livingston, as she continues to struggle to emerge out of a life-shattering event, describes how the same things that have the potential of helping one carry on, are also at a certain phase the things one very much wants to run away from—professional colleagues, social events, familiar music, and work. The medicine is bitter, and hard to swallow. It can only be useful when the time is right. Then she finds gardening: "As I choose flowers, plant them, watch them grow, and then tend to my garden, I think it's the most positive and enriching thing I have done since Bob died." Kernberg (2010), writing after his own experience of losing his wife of fifty-two years, states,

> In fact, the traumatic loss of a spouse under such circumstances is relatively under-emphasized in the literature on mourning, where the mourning of parental figures, of one's children, the losses that children experience upon the death of parents are focused upon much more frequently. And yet clinical observations indicate the enormously traumatic aspects of the mourning of a life partner of many years. (p. 610)

Aragno (2003) describes it in more poetic terms,

> Mourning the death of a beloved life partner has been likened to the slow healing of a severe wound. Regardless of how smooth or stormy the relationship, the loss of the soul mate is like an amputation: one feels the phantom limb as a great gash in the soul that cannot stop bleeding. Interpersonal ligaments that bind such bonds of infinite intimacy are woven through and through the deep tissue of daily habit, crystallizing into a self-with-other identity rooted in shared hopes and memories, unspoken understanding, comforting conversations, common interests, and the sheer joy of mutual presence. Their sudden absence, like a massive volcanic eruption, produces seismic reverberations that penetrate every sphere and crevice of internal and external experience. (p. 449)

Lowy's loss, on the other hand, while unexpected and premature, did not stop him from going on being, as with Malawista (as a child) or Smolen, or Livingston, or Wolman's loss of his friend in childhood, partly perhaps because it occurred at a different phase in life. It was also perhaps influenced by the experience of having fled the Holocaust. Awareness of having barely escaped such a terrible fate (that many others known to the person did not) lends its own complexity as well as profundity to the bereavement. Perhaps there is an unusual measure of gratitude in having had a life with his sister he could just as easily have not had so many years ago. Having his sister's family there, symbolizing the success of Lowy's mission to protect his sister from the consequences of the Holocaust was important also. It demonstrates that how we carry on may depend on the particular stage in life when we incur the bereavement, as well as what our preexisting expectations might have been. Expectational frameworks, of course, are one of the ways in which culture gets to determine the course of bereavement.

From a theoretical standpoint, the contributors seem to agree on one major feature of bereavement dynamics—that the "resolution" of mourning is not well described by the idea that one has to give up ("decathect") the lost object in order to carry on. Freud (1926d) says,

> Mourning occurs under the influence of reality testing; for the latter function demands categorically from the bereaved person that he should separate himself from the object, since it no longer exists. Mourning is entrusted with the task of carrying out this retreat from the object in all those situations in which it was the recipient of a high degree of cathexis. (p. 172)

Smolen sees this idea that, "[N]ormal bereavement ends with giving up all emotional bonds to the lost loved one," as being one of the two problems with Freud's early theory of mourning. As a contrast to Freud's position, Volkan (1984) writes, "Obviously, a mourner never altogether forgets the dead person who was so highly valued in life and never totally withdraws his investment in his representation" (p. 326). No doubt, there is some kind of letting go, but perhaps letting go is not the same as giving up. Livingston writes, "Perhaps, I can finally really let Bob—partner and best friend—go, while keeping him in my heart." As Kernberg (2010) writes,

> To mourn a lost loved object and yet to be able to love again ... without abandoning the love for the lost object, nor truncating the mourning process itself is an important and yet neglected aspect of normal mourning. It runs counter to the traditional assumption of a mechanical flow of "libidinal energy" that is withdrawn from the object and redirected, but remains essentially constant. (p. 613)

Decathexis of the lost object and identification with the lost object seem to go hand in hand, simultaneously as well as sequentially, at all different phases of mourning, pathologically as well as normally. The decathexis does not need to be a full detachment, just good enough to keep moving on. As Smolen points out, Freud seemed to shift and contradict himself at various times. Smolen's recounting of Freud's as well as other theoreticians' own losses is very helpful in getting a deeper perspective on the theoretical issues. Lowy also adds to this by reminding us of Freud's relationship to his siblings, particularly his possibly ambivalent feelings towards the sisters who never made it out of Vienna. Perhaps Freud's own incomplete mourning may have made it hard to complete his theoretical evolution on mourning. In his paper, "On Transcience," (1916a) he writes,

> But have those other possessions, which we have now lost, really ceased to have any worth for us because they have proved so perishable and so unresistant? To many of us this seems to be so, but once more wrongly, in my view. I believe that those who think thus, and seem ready to make a permanent renunciation because what was precious has proved not to be lasting, are simply in a state of mourning for what is lost. Mourning, as we know, however painful it may be, comes to a spontaneous end. When it has renounced everything that has been lost, then it has consumed itself, and our libido is once more free (in so far as we are still young and active) to replace the lost objects by fresh ones equally or still more precious. (p. 307)

One can wonder if Freud's enthusiasm in arguing that transience need not be an obstacle to enjoyment is fueled by his own need to deny the impact of death, in his own life and all around, as he writes during the course of World War I.

While there have been contributions from many different theoretical backgrounds—classical Freudian, object relations, ego psychology, Kleinian, attachment theory, and cognitive psychology—to an understanding of the psychological experience following the death of a loved one, to date there has not been, as far as I can tell, any truly interpersonal/Sullivanian formulation of mourning.

The interpersonal perspective on bereavement

Harry Stack Sullivan (1892–1949), the originator of the interpersonal school of psychoanalysis, never wrote about bereavement or mourning. When it comes to mourning, even interpersonal analysts fall back on classical, object relational, or attachment terminology due to this historical gap. Sullivan does, however, provide certain notions that can be used to understand mourning in an interpersonal framework. For Sullivan the compelling force behind how relationships are managed is the establishment and maintenance of a sense of "security" and self-esteem. "Security operations" (Sullivan, 1953, p. 191) are thus all those interpersonal behaviors that are meant to achieve this goal, and minimize interpersonal anxiety. From here, one can begin to formulate an understanding of the impact of the death of a person with whom one has established some level of intimacy. Seen from this perspective, what is lost is not "the object," but rather the established and integrated relational dynamisms that have been necessary for maintaining the stability of the self-system, by virtue of engendering security and enhancing self-esteem.

When the interpersonal context, engineered between the deceased and the bereaved previously, is lost, it can lead to varying degrees of disintegration (for varying durations of time, sometimes even permanently) of previously integrated dynamisms, thus destabilizing the self-system and possibly even personality. Some individuals may then respond with what Sullivan calls "disjunctive motivation"[3]—avoiding affiliation with other individuals, or failing to have anything other than anxiety producing interactions. To what degree the destabilization occurs will depend on developmental determinants, specifics of the loss, as well as the availability of support systems. For example, if the self-system of the individual has a predominance of "bad-me" personifications (ibid., p. 161) (or a proneness to "malevolent transformations" in interpersonal relations—p. 213), then it will be much harder for the person to achieve a secure adaptation following the loss. A positive outcome to the process of mourning would require the eventual emergence of more "conjunctive motivations" that lead the individual to explore new avenues of reestablishing a more real and adaptive stabilization.

One question needing to be addressed in formulating the mourning process in interpersonal terms is: Where does "internalization of the lost object" fit in? This is connected to the issue of internal psychic structures in interpersonal theory (see Stern, 1994). One way to understand this is to consider the idea that a bereaved person feels a need to recreate the kind of personification that was being supported through interactions with the deceased. Since the person does not exist anymore, the bereaved individual's attempts constitute what I would term a "phantom personification".[4] This is similar to a brain that has a map of a lost limb, trying to recreate for itself "a phantom limb". I would argue that this sort of mechanism is more aligned with neurobiological reality (Ramachandran & Blakeslee, 1998) than the notion of "internalization of the lost object". To summarize, the significant differences from the classical framework are that:

- Instead of the emphasis on "lost object," the emphasis is on destabilization of previously integrated interpersonal experiences, called "dynamisms" constituting the "self-system"
- Instead of formulating a mechanism of "internalization of the lost object," a Sullivanian framework would suggest that the bereaved person attempts to restabilize his or her self-system through the construction of what I am calling a "phantom personification"
- Instead of the emphasis on a process resulting in the eventual finding of new objects, the emphasis is on restabilizing the self-system by adjustments or new integrations so that a sense of security and self-esteem can become reestablished in a way that is functional and sustainable.

In Sullivan's formulation, anxiety begins as an unmanageable state (Sullivan, 1953, p. 43). All the colors of interpersonal life, from infancy on, are different ways to manage this unmanageable anxiety. As far as unmanageable anxieties go, the anxiety of death is certainly one that humanity has been trying to manage from time immemorial! One way we continue to do so is by trying to articulate our experiences of bereavement in many different kinds of theories, words, songs, stories, poems, paintings, and sculptures. Apart from the mental pain of loss, every death also reflects back to us an undeniable reality of our own death. Unlike Narcissus looking in the water and falling in love with his own image, when we look into the face of death, we are woken out of our narcissistic trance, and forced to accommodate to our mortality, in a way only death can make us. Palgi and Abramovitch (1984), in their review of death across cultures, write, "Death awareness is a natural sequel to the development of self-awareness" (p. 385). I would suggest that the opposite is also true. That death awareness has a way of inducing self-awareness.

The bereaved brain

Without memory, there would be nothing to mourn. At the most fundamental level, memory is the persistence of traces of a stimulus beyond the extinction of the stimulus itself. It is nervous tissue that has evolved to be best at this function. It is life's first attempt to get beyond simply "living in the moment." In fact, if life remained fixated on the Buddhist "living in the moment" sentiment, none of us would be here today! Life would exist for the moment, but also only for a moment. Life and death would be forever separated by nothing but a moment. Now they have come to be separated by what we call a "lifetime": the time for which we live before we die. Embedded in the notion of a lifetime is the notion of death. But we try not to notice that too often. In the course of evolution, we have become so involved with memory and its persistence, with holding on and possessing for as long as possible, with feeling bereaved and grieved when things or people disappear, that we now need to be reminded, nudged, and cajoled, and preached to, to get back a little closer to living in the moment, for the sake of our sanity.

This capacity for retaining an impression of what impacts us has evolved so far that our brain can sometimes utterly fail to recognize when the stimulus has been extinguished. It can keep on experiencing the stimulus (not just remembering it) way beyond its end in reality. One clinical phenomenon illustrating this is phantom limbs and phantom pains. Ramachandran and Blakeslee's (1998) classic book, *Phantoms in the Brain*, details the neurobiology and clinical presentations of this phenomenon. Since then, many authors (e.g., Murphy, 1957; Parkes, 1975; Ramzy & Wallerstein, 1958; Zarnegar, 2015) have referred to this in both scientific and metaphorical ways in connection to grief and bereavement. In this sense, one can consider bereavement to be a side effect of memory!

There is also accumulating evidence for the physical reality of bereavement in our brains. A functional MRI study (Gündel, O'Connor, Littrell, Fort, & Lane, 2003) demonstrated specific areas of the brain that become activated when recently bereaved individuals are presented with textual and visual triggers.

> Three brain regions were independently activated by the picture and word factors: posterior cingulate cortex, medial/superior frontal gyrus, and cerebellum. The two factors also activated distinct regions: for the picture factor, they were the cuneus, superior lingual gyrus, insula, dorsal anterior cingulate cortex, inferior temporal gyrus, and fusiform gyrus; and for the word factor, they were the precuneus, precentral gyrus, midbrain, and vermis. The interaction of the two factors showed significant activation in the cerebellar vermis. (p. 1946)

The authors suggest that this kind of data can help us understand the unique subjective quality of grief. From another perspective, we also know that bereavement can cause acute and fatal physiological changes in the form of the "broken heart syndrome" (Stroebe, 1994), also known as "stress cardiomyopathy." These data are another way at looking at some common denominators of the experience of bereavement.

Pollock (1961), recognizing the need to attend to deaths of various kinds, wrote,

> Secondly, we must recognize the significance of who or what is lost. The death of a parent in childhood differs from the death of a parent in adulthood. The death of the mother during the oedipal stage of a girl may have a different effect from what it has for an oedipal boy. The death of a sibling in childhood differs from the death of one's own child. The death of a spouse may be more significant than the loss of a political election in which there may be great involvement. It is difficult to generalize in this field, but further precision and delineation are necessary in our study of different types of losses and of the different objects that can be lost. (p. 353)

The contributors in this book have generously used their own experiences to highlight some of these different types of losses, while also giving us valuable clinical insights. While Wolman has referred to his childhood loss of a friend, and the way that was intimately connected with his feelings about his father, one important kind of death missing from this book is the death of a friend.[5] Friends occupy a very special kind of place in our lives. In the tripartite conception of healthy living defined by work, play, and love, friends can be seen as occupying the arena of play, and a relational significance that falls somewhere between a lover and a sibling. Sullivan (1953) felt that the development of "chumship" in the preadolescent phase was a very important event. He saw this kind of intimacy as being crucial to healthy development, and an important opportunity for the child to experience "consensual validation of personal worth" (p. 251). Thus, when a friend dies, particularly, a friend of longstanding, this can be a great loss. Friends, like life partners, are most often peers, and thus the death of a friend can often signal anxieties about one's own mortality, which can further complicate the bereavement. Like other deaths, the stage of life at which one loses a friend will, of course, determine many aspects of one's experience and recovery. The loss of a pet can, in some ways, also contain elements of the loss of a friend. The phrase, "man's best friend," referring to dogs, comes to mind.

Concluding remarks

In this book, we have considered some of the many specific deaths encountered by people in life. There is no intention here to suggest any kind of hierarchy of suffering. What is important to realize is that while there are common denominators to how bereavement might proceed from a psychological perspective, there are also contextual specificities, individual variations, cultural particularities, as well as temporal shifts in how we react to, cope with, and recover from, the death of a loved one. Our intention has been to focus not simply on loss, but on loss by death, and not simply on pathology, but on growth from experience. The following quote is taken from the introduction, written by Rabbi Earl A. Grollman, to the book, *Disenfranchised Grief*, by Ken Doka (1989).

> It occurred more than two decades ago, but I will never forget the incident. I had been asked to counsel both faculty and pupils because of a car accident that killed three high school students. I noticed that the school psychologist appeared especially crestfallen and in need of special attention. I still recall his words when we were alone. He said, "I feel terrible because of the tragedy. But to be brutally candid, my pain is mostly because my dog was just run over and died." He paused. "What kind of person can I be if I grieve more for an animal than a human being?" So often, I am asked: "What is the greatest loss—the death of a child, a parent, a spouse, a sibling, or what?" Thanks to Dr. Kenneth J. Doka, I now have the answer to "What's the worst loss?" It's when it happens to you, whatever the circumstances or relationship. In other words, each loss must be recognized and validated. (p. xi)

As many of the contributors, as well as many of the theoreticians they refer to, seem to emphasize, one thing we have learnt is that mourning is often a journey that proceeds in fits and starts, with tangents and detours, through well-known trails and unexpected openings. Each bereaved individual follows a very personal and unique calendar, often not even visible to the mourner herself.

Notes

1. The *Upanishads* (circa fifth century BCE) are ancient Indian philosophical treatises associated with the *Vedas*. While there are four main *Vedas*, there are more than 200 *Upanishads*, of which about twelve are considered the principal (*Mukhya*) ones. The *Katha Upanishad* is one of the principal *Upanishads* and is associated with the *Yajur Veda*.
2. For an interesting related issue see Michele Stephen's (1998) Kleinian analysis of "second burial" rituals.
3. Those impulses which oppose "the manifestation of any integrative tendency in the work of creating and maintaining an interpersonal situation" (Sullivan, 1953, p. 95). These are opposed by "conjunctive motivations": "Those impulses which integrate situations in which needs can be satisfied and security enhanced" (ibid., p. 351).
4. For lack of space, it is not possible to delve into a full description of this concept here, which will be elaborated in a forthcoming paper.
5. This omission is ironically in tandem with the overall neglect of the topic of friendship in psychoanalysis. Rangell's (1963) paper on it stood alone for over a quarter century before the contributions of Rubin (1986), Grotstein (1989), Schulman (2009), and Akhtar (2011a, pp. 81–102) made their appearance. The last-mentioned contribution also brought forth Melanie Klein's (1940) overlooked but astute observations regarding a developmental substrate and the phenomenology of friendship.

REFERENCES

Abend, S. M. (1986). Countertransference, empathy, and the analytic ideal: the impact of life stresses on analytic capability. *Psychoanalytic Quarterly*, 55: 563–575.
Aberbach, D. (1987). Grief and mysticism. *International Review of Psycho-Analysis*, 14: 509–526.
Abraham, K. (1924). A short study of the development of the libido, viewed in the light of mental disorders. In: R. Frankel (Ed.), *Essential Papers on Object Loss* (pp. 72–93). New York: New York University Press, 1994.
Ackerman, P. H. (1975). Narcissistic personality disorder in an identical twin. *International Journal of Psychoanalytic Psychotherapy*, 4: 389–409.
Adelman, A., & Malawista, K. (2013). *The Therapist in Mourning: From the Faraway Nearby*. New York: Columbia University Press.
Administration on Aging (2011). A profile of older Americans: 2011. Washington, DC: Administration on Aging, US Department of Health and Human Services.
Aiken, J., & Cadmus, F. (2011). Who let the dog out?: Implementing a successful therapy dog program in the academic law library. *Yale School Legal Repository*, 21: 11–18.
Ainslie, R. (1997). *The Psychology of Twinship*. Northvale, NJ: Jason Aronson.

Akhtar, S. (1999). *Immigration and Identity: Turmoil, Treatment, and Transformation*. Northvale, NJ: Jason Aronson.
Akhtar, S. (2000). Mental pain and the cultural ointment of poetry. *International Journal of Psychoanalysis*, 81: 229–243.
Akhtar, S. (Ed.) (2001). *Three Faces of Mourning: Melancholia, Manic Defense, and Moving On*. Northvale, NJ: Jason Aronson.
Akhtar, S. (2009). *The Damaged Core: Origins, Dynamics, Manifestations, and Treatment*. Lanham, MD: Jason Aronson.
Akhtar, S. (2010). Freud's *Todesangst* and Ghalib's *Ishrat-e-Qatra*: two perspectives on death. In: S. Akhtar (Ed.), *The Wound of Mortality: Fear, Denial, and Acceptance of Death* (pp. 1–20). Lanham, MD: Jason Aronson.
Akhtar, S. (2011a). *Matters of Life and Death: Psychoanalytic Reflections*. London: Karnac.
Akhtar, S. (2011b). Orphans. In: *Matter of Life and Death: Psychoanalytic Reflections* (pp. 147–180). London: Karnac.
Akhtar, S. (2013). *Psychoanalytic Listening: Methods, Limits, and Innovations*. London: Karnac.
Akhtar, S. (2014). *After Landing*. Charlottesville, VA: Pitchstone Publishing.
Akhtar, S., & Kramer, S. (1999). *Brothers and Sisters: Developmental, Dynamic, and Technical Aspects of the Sibling Relationship*. Northvale, NJ: Jason Aronson.
Akhtar, S., & Smolar, A. (1998). Visiting the father's grave. *Psychoanalytic Quarterly*, 67: 474–483.
Alexander, E. (2015). *The Light of the World*. New York: Grand Central Publishing.
Altman, L. (1977). Some vicissitudes of love. *Journal of the American Psychoanalytic Association*, 25: 35–52.
American Kennel Club. http://www.akc.org/dog-breeds/chow-chow/care.
American Psychiatric Association (2013). *Diagnostic and Statistical Manual of Mental Disorders: Fifth Edition* (DSM-5). Arlington, VA: American Psychiatric Association.
Anderson, C. (1949). Aspects of pathological grief and mourning. *International Journal of Psychoanalysis*, 30: 48–55.
Anisfeld, L., & Richards, A. D. (2000). The replacement child: variations on a theme in history and psychoanalysis. *Psychoanalytic Study of the Child*, 55: 301–318.
Anzieu, D. (1975). *Freud's Self-Analysis*. London: Hogarth, 1986.
Aragno, A. (2003). Transforming mourning: a new psychoanalytic perspective on the bereavement process. *Psychoanalysis and Contemporary Thought*, 26: 427–462.
Aries, P. (1974). *Western Attitudes towards Death: From the Middle Ages to the Present*. Baltimore, MD: Johns Hopkins University Press.

Aries, P. (1977). *The Hour of Our Death*. H. Weaver (Trans.). New York: Alfred A. Knopf, 1981.
Baillargeon, R., & DeVos, J. (1991). Object permanence in young infants: further evidence. *Child Development, 62*: 1227–1246.
Barthelme, D. (2014). *The Dead Father*. New York: Farrar, Straus, and Giroux.
Benedict, R. (1967). *The Chrysanthemum and the Sword: Patterns of Japanese Culture*. Boston, MA: Houghton Mifflin Harcourt.
Benjamin, J. (2004). Beyond doer and done to: an intersubjective view of thirdness. *Psychoanalytic Quarterly, 73*: 5–46.
Berman, L. E. (1978). Sibling loss as an organizer of unconscious guilt: a case study. *Psychoanalytic Quarterly, 47*: 568–587.
Bion, W. R. (1963). *Elements of Psychoanalysis*. London: Karnac.
Blanton, S. (1976). The hidden faces of money. In: E. Borneman (Ed.), *The Psychoanalysis of Money* (pp. 253–270). New York: Urizen.
Bonanno, G. A. (2009). *The Other Side of Sadness: What the New Science of Bereavement Tells Us about Life after Loss*. New York: Basic Books.
Bonaparte, M. (1936). *Topsy: The Story of a Golden-Haired Chow*. London: Transaction Publishers, 1994.
Bouchard, J. J., Lykken, D. J., McGue, M., Segal, N. L., & Tellegen, A. (1990). Sources of human psychological differences: the Minnesota Study of Twins Reared Apart. *Science, 250*: 223–228.
Bourget, D., & Gagné, P. (2006). Fratricide: a forensic psychiatric perspective. *Journal of the American Academy of Psychiatry and Law, 34*: 529–533.
Bower, T. G. R. (1974). *Development in Infancy*. San Francisco, CA: W. H. Freeman.
Bowlby, J. (1960). Grief and mourning in infancy and early childhood. *Psychoanalytic Study of the Child, 15*: 9–52.
Bowlby, J. (1961). Processes of mourning. *International Journal of Psychoanalysis, 42*: 317–340.
Bowlby, J. (1969). *Attachment and Loss, Vol. 1: Attachment*. New York: Basic Books.
Bowlby, J. (1980). *Attachment and Loss, Vol. 3: Sadness and Depression*. New York: Basic Books.
Bowlby, J., & Parkes, C. (1970). Separation and loss within the family. In: E. J. Anthony & C. Koupirnik (Eds.), *The Child and His Family, Vol. 1* (pp. 197–216). New York: John Wiley & Sons.
Brenner, C. (1974). Some observations on depression, on nosology, on affects, and on mourning. *Journal of Geriatric Psychiatry, 7*: 6–20.
Bromberg, P. M. (2001). *Standing in the Spaces: Essays on Clinical Process, Trauma and Dissociation*. Hillsdale, NJ: Analytic Press.
Burlingham, D. (1952). *Twins: A Study of Three Pairs of Identical Twins*. London: Imago.

Cain, A. C., & Cain, B. S. (1964). On replacing a child. *Journal of the American Academy of Child Psychiatry, 3*: 443–456.
Cain, A. C., Fast, I., & Erickson, M. E. (1964). Children's disturbed reactions to the death of a sibling. *American Journal of Orthopsychiatry, 34*: 741–752.
Carrington, A. (Ed.) (2015). *Money as Emotional Currency: Psychoanalytic Ideas*. London: Karnac.
Casement, P. J. (2000). Mourning and failure to mourn. *Fort Da, 6*: 20–32.
Cheever, J. (1999). *Goodbye, My Brother*. New York: Vintage, 2010.
Cohen, L. (2014). How Sigmund Freud wanted to die. *Atlantic Monthly*, September 23.
Colarusso, C. A. (1997). Separation-individuation processes in middle adulthood: the fourth individuation. In: S. Akhtar & S. Kramer (Eds.), *The Seasons of Life: Separation-Individuation Perspectives* (pp. 73–93). Northvale, NJ: Jason Aronson.
Colarusso, C. A. (1998). A developmental line of time sense in late adulthood and throughout the life cycle. *Psychoanalytic Study of the Child, 53*: 113–140.
Colarusso, C. A. (1999). The development of time sense in middle adulthood. *Psychoanalytic Quarterly, 68*: 52–83.
Collins, B. (2012). *A Dog on His Master*. Facebook, July 5.
Colson, D. B. (1995). An analyst's multiple losses: countertransference and other reactions. *Contemporary Psychoanalysis, 31*: 459–477.
Conway, J. K. (1989). *The Road from Coorain*. New York: Alfred A. Knopf.
Cournos, F. (2001). Mourning and adaptation following the death of a parent in childhood. *Journal of the American Academy of Psychoanalysis, 29*: 137–145.
Coutts, M. (2014). *The Iceberg*. New York: Black Cat Publishing.
Crehan, G. (2004). *The Surviving Sibling: The Effects of Sibling Death in Childhood*. London: Routledge.
Cuijpers, P., Sijbrandij, M., Koole, S. L., Andersson, G., Beekman, A. T., & Reynolds, C. F. 3rd. (2014). Adding psychotherapy to antidepressant medication in depression and anxiety disorders: a meta-analysis. *World Psychiatry, 13*: 56–67.
Deraniyagala, S. (2013). *Wave*. New York: Vintage.
Deutsch, H. (1937). Absence of grief. *Psychoanalytic Quarterly, 6*: 12–22.
Didion, J. (2005). *The Year of Magical Thinking*. New York: Alfred A. Knopf.
Doka, J. K. (1989). *Disenfranchised Grief: Recognizing Hidden Sorrow*. Lexington, MA: Lexington.
Doka, J. K., & Martin, T. L. (2010). *Grieving beyond Gender: Understanding the Ways Men and Women Mourn (2nd edn.)*. New York: Routledge.
Doolittle, H. D. (1956). *A Tribute to Freud*. New York: New Directions.
Edwards, J. (2010). *The Sibling Relationship*. New York: Jason Aronson.

Engel, G. L. (1961). Is grief a disease?: a challenge for medical research. *Psychosomatic Medicine, 23*: 18–22.

Engel, G. L. (1975). The death of a twin: mourning and anniversary reactions—fragments of ten years of self-analysis. *International Journal of Psychoanalysis, 56*: 23–40.

Erikson, E. H. (1950). *Childhood and Society*. New York: W. W. Norton.

Etezady, H. (2010). Demise and illusion. In: S. Akhtar (Ed.), *The Wound of Mortality: Fear, Denial, and Acceptance of Death* (pp. 155–170). Lanham, MD: Jason Aronson.

Fanos, J. H. (1996). *Sibling Loss*. Mahwah, NJ: Lawrence Erlbaum Associates.

Fanos, J. H., & Nickerson, B. G. (1991). Long term effects of sibling death during adolescence. *Journal of Adolescent Research, 6*: 70–82.

Faulkner, W. (1936). *Absalom, Absalom*. New York: Random House.

Fenichel, O. (1945). *The Psychoanalytic Theory of Neurosis*. New York: W. W. Norton.

Fichtner, G. (Ed.) (2003). *The Freud-Binswanger Correspondence: 1908–1938*. London: Open Gate Press.

Fiorini, L. G., Bokanowski, T., & Lewkowicz, S. (Eds.) (2007). *On Freud's "Mourning and Melancholia"*. London: Karnac.

Foster, B. (1987). Suicide and the impact on the therapist. In: J. L. Sacksteder, D. P. Schwartz, & W. Akabane (Eds.), *Attachment and the Therapeutic Process: Essays in Honor of Otto Alan Will, Jr.* (pp. 197–204). Madison, CT: International Universities Press.

Frankiel, R. V. (Ed.) (1994). *Essential Papers on Object Loss*. New York: New York University Press.

Freud, A., & Burlingham, D. (1944). *Infants without Families*. New York: International Universities Press.

Freud, E. (1960). *Letters of Sigmund Freud*. New York: Dover.

Freud, S. (1893). Draft G: Melancholia. *S. E., 1*: 200–206. London: Hogarth.

Freud, S. (1896). Draft K: The neuroses of defence. *S. E., 1*: 220–229. London: Hogarth.

Freud, S. (1899a). Screen memories. *S. E., 3*: 301–323. London: Hogarth.

Freud, S. (1900a). *The Interpretation of Dreams*. *S. E., 4–5*: 1–626. London: Hogarth.

Freud, S. (1908b). Character and anal erotism. *S. E., 9*: 167–176. London: Hogarth.

Freud, S. (1909d). Notes upon a case of obsessional neurosis. *S. E., 10*: 153–249. London: Hogarth.

Freud, S. (1910d). The future prospects of psycho-analytic therapy. *S. E., 11*: 139–151. London: Hogarth.

Freud, S. (1912–1913). *Totem and Taboo*. *S. E., 13*: 1–161. London: Hogarth.

Freud, S. (1914c). On narcissism: an introduction. *S. E., 14*: 67–103. London: Hogarth.
Freud, S. (1916a). On transience. *S. E., 14*: 303–307. London: Hogarth.
Freud, S. (1917e). Mourning and melancholia. *S. E., 14*: 237–260. London: Hogarth.
Freud, S. (1921c). *Group Psychology and the Analysis of the Ego. S. E., 18*: 65–143. London: Hogarth.
Freud, S. (1923b). *The Ego and the Id. S. E., 19*: 3–68. London: Hogarth.
Freud, S. (1926d). *Inhibitions, Symptoms and Anxiety. S. E., 20*: 70–174. London: Hogarth.
Freud, S. (1927e). Fetishism. *S. E., 21*: 149–157. London: Hogarth.
Freud, S. (1930a). *Civilization and Its Discontents. S. E., 21*: 59–145. London: Hogarth.
Friedman, G. W. (1983). It still isn't over. In: *Taking My Turn*—musical drama by R. Livingston & G. W. Friedman, lyrics by W. Holt. New York: Samuel French.
Frosch, J. (2014). From grievance to grief: narcissism and the inability to mourn. *Canadian Journal of Psychoanalysis, 22*: 259–275.
Furman, E. (Ed.) (1974). *A Child's Parent Dies: Studies in Childhood Bereavement*. New Haven, CT: Yale University Press.
Furman, E. (1978). The death of the newborn: care of the parents. *Birth and Family Journal, 5*: 214–218.
Furman, E. (1986). On trauma—when is the death of a parent traumatic? *Psychoanalytic Study of the Child, 41*: 191–208.
Furman, R. A. (1964). Death and the young child—some preliminary considerations. *Psychoanalytic Study of the Child, 19*: 321–333.
Furman, R. A. (1968). Additional remarks on mourning and the young child. In: R. V. Frankiel (Ed.), *Essential Papers on Object Loss*. New York: New York University Press, 1994.
Gaines, R. (1997). Detachment and continuity. *Contemporary Psychoanalysis, 33*: 549–571.
Gay, P. (1988). *Freud: A Life for Our Time*. New York: W. W. Norton.
Genosko, G. (1993). Freud's bestiary: how does psychoanalysis treat animals? *Psychoanalytic Review, 80*: 603–632.
Godfather, Part II, The (1974). Directed and produced by F. F. Coppola.
Gorer, G. (1955). The pornography of death. *Encounter*, October: 49–52.
Greenspan, S. I. (1977). The oedipal-preoedipal dilemma: a reformulation in the light of object relations theory. *International Review of Psycho-Analysis, 4*: 381–391.
Grinker, R., Jr. (2001). My father's analysis with Sigmund Freud. *Annual of Psychoanalysis, 29*: 35–47.

Grollman, E. (1989). Introduction. In: K. Doka (Ed.), *Disenfranchised Grief: Recognizing Hidden Sorrow* (pp. xii–xiv). Lexington, MA: Lexington.

Grotstein, J. (1989). Of human bondage and of human bonding: the role of friendship in intimacy. *Contemporary Psychotherapy Review, 5*: 5–32.

Grubb, C. A. (1976). Body image concerns of a multipara in the situation of intrauterine fetal death. *Maternal–Child Nursing Journal, 5*: 93–116.

Gündel, H., O'Connor, M.-F., Littrell, L., Fort, C., & Lane, R. D. (2003). Functional neuroanatomy of grief: An fMRI study. *American Journal of Psychiatry, 160*(11): 1946–1953.

Guzder, J. (2010). Symbolic death, East and West. In: S. Akhtar (Ed.), *The Wound of Mortality: Fear, Denial, and Acceptance of Death* (pp. 51–70). Lanham, MD: Jason Aronson.

Hagman, G. (1995a). Bereavement and neurosis. *Journal of the American Psychoanalytic Association, 23*: 635–653.

Hagman, G. (1995b). Mourning: a review and reconsideration. *International Journal of Psychoanalysis, 76*: 909–925.

Harris, M. (2015). *The End of Absence: Reclaiming What We've Lost in a World of Constant Connection.* New York: Penguin.

Harris, T. (1999). *Hannibal.* New York: Bantam Dell.

Hartman, S. (2012). Cybermourning: grief in flux from object loss to collective immortality. *Psychoanalytic Inquiry, 32*: 454–467.

Hilgard, J. (1953). Anniversary reactions in parents precipitated by children. *Psychiatry, 16*: 73–80.

Hitchcock, J. (1984). The sinking feeling. *Psychoanalytic Study of the Child, 39*: 321–329.

Hoffman, L., Johnson, E., Foster, M., & Wright, J. (2010). What happens when you die: three-four year olds chatting about death. In: S. Akhtar (Ed.), *The Wound of Mortality: Fear, Denial, and Acceptance of Death* (pp. 21–36). Lanham, MD: Jason Aronson.

Holmes, T. H., & Rahe, R. H. (1967). The social readjustment rating scale. *Journal of Psychosomatic Research, 11*: 213–218.

Irving, J. (1989). *A Prayer for Owen Meany.* Toronto, Canada: Vintage Press.

Jacobson, E. (1965). The return of the lost parent. In: R. V. Frankiel (Ed.), *Essential Papers on Object Loss* (pp. 233–290). New York: New York University Press, 1989.

Jamison, K. R. (2009). *Nothing Was the Same: A Memoir.* New York: Vintage.

Jones, E. (1953). *Sigmund Freud: Life and Work, Volume I.* London: Penguin, 1964.

Jones, E. (1955). *The Life and Work of Sigmund Freud, Vol. II.* New York: Basic Books.

Jones, E. (1957). *The Life and Work of Sigmund Freud, Vol. III*. New York: Basic Books.
Kanwal, G. (2015). Indian culture and the experience of psychoanalytic treatment. *Psychoanalytic Review, 102*: 843–872.
Kaprio, J., Koskenvuo, M., & Rita, H. (1987). Mortality after bereavement: a prospective study of 95,647 widowed persons. *American Journal of Public Health, 7*: 283–287.
Karyotaki, E., Smit, Y., Holdt-Henningsen, K., Huibers, M. J., Robays, J., de Beurs, D., & Cuijpers, P. (2016). Combining pharmacotherapy and psychotherapy or monotherapy for major depression? A meta-analysis on the long-term effects. *Journal of Affective Disorders, 19*: 144–152.
Keefe, P. R. (2015). The avenger. *The New Yorker*, September 18: 40–53.
Kernberg, O. F. (2010). Some observations on the process of mourning. *International Journal of Psychoanalysis, 91*: 601–619.
Kerouac, J. (1963). *Visions of Gerard*. New York: Farrar, Straus and Giroux.
Kieffer, C. (2008). On siblings: mutual regulation and mutual recognition. *Annual of Psychoanalysis, 34*: 161–173.
Killingmo, B. (1989). Conflict and deficit: implications for technique. *International Journal of Psychoanalysis, 70*: 65–79.
Klass, D. (1996). The deceased child in the psychic and social worlds of bereaved parents during the resolution of grief. In: D. Klass, P. R. Silverman, & S. L. Nickman (Eds.), *Continuing Bonds: New Understandings of Grief* (pp. 199–215). Philadelphia, PA: Taylor & Francis.
Klass, D., Silverman, P. R., & Nickman, S. L. (1996). *Continuing Bonds: New Understandings of Grief*. Philadelphia, PA: Taylor & Francis.
Klein, M. (1929). Personification in the play of children. *International Journal of Psychoanalysis, 19*: 193–214.
Klein, M. (1940). Mourning and its relation to manic depressive states. In: *Love, Guilt and Reparation and Other Works—1921–1945* (pp. 344–369). New York: Free Press, 1975.
Klein, M. (1957). *Envy and Gratitude and Other Works—1946–1963*. New York: Free Press, 1975.
Knight, E. M. (1940). *Lassie Come-Home*. New York: Square Fish, 2007.
Krueger, D. W. (1986). A self-psychological view of money. In: D. W. Krueger (Ed.), *The Last Taboo: Money as Symbol and Reality in Psychotherapy and Psychoanalysis* (pp. 24–32). New York: Brunner/Mazel.
Kubler-Ross, E. (1969). *On Death and Dying*. London: Routledge.
Kundalia, N. D. (2015). *The Lost Generation: Chronicling India's Dying Professions*. Haryana, India: Random House. (Kindle file, retrieved from Amazon.com.)

Leavy, S. A. (2011). The last of life: Psychological reflections on old age and death. *Psychoanalytic Quarterly, 80*: 699–715.
Leon, I. (1990). *When a Baby Dies: Psychotherapy for Pregnancy and Newborn Loss*. New Haven, CT: Yale University Press.
Leon, I. (1999). Bereavement and repair of the self: poetic confrontations with death. *Psychoanalytic Review, 86*: 383–401.
Lewin, V. (2014). *The Twin in the Transference*. London: Karnac.
Lewis, C. S. (1961). *A Grief Observed*. New York: HarperCollins, 1976.
Lindemann, E. (1944). Symptomatology and management of acute grief. *American Journal of Psychiatry, 101*: 141–148.
Lion King, The (1994). Walt Disney production.
Loewald, H. (1962). Internalization, separation, mourning and the superego. In: *Papers on Psychoanalysis* (pp. 257–276). New Haven, CT: Yale University Press, 1980.
London, J. (1903). *Call of the Wild*. New York: Macmillan.
Macdonald, H. (2014). *H is for Hawk*. New York: Grove Press.
Malawista, K. L., Adelman, A. J., & Anderson, C. L. (2011). *Wearing My Tutu to Analysis: Learning Psychodynamic Concepts from Life*. New York: Columbia University Press.
Martinson, I. M., & Campos, R. G. (1991). Adolescent bereavement: long-term responses to a sibling's death from cancer. *Journal of Adolescent Research, 6*: 54–69.
Masur, C. (2001). Can women mourn their mother? In: S. Akhtar (Ed.), *Three Faces of Mourning: Melancholia, Manic Defense, and Moving On* (pp. 33–45). Lanham, MD: Jason Aronson.
Melgar, M. C. (2007). Mourning and creativity. In: L. G. Fiorini, T. Bokanowski, & S. Lewkowicz (Eds.), *On Freud's "Mourning and Melancholia"* (pp. 110–122). London: Karnac.
Meyers, H. (2001). Does mourning become Electra? Oedipal and separation-individuation issues in a woman's loss of her mother. In: S. Akhtar (Ed.), *Three Faces of Mourning: Melancholia, Manic Defense, and Moving On* (pp. 13–32). Lanham, MD: Jason Aronson.
Mitchell, E. (2004). *Beyond Tears: Living after Losing a Child*. New York: St. Martin's Griffin.
Mitchell, J. (2003). *Siblings, Sex and Violence*. Cambridge: Polity Press.
Molnar, M. (1996). Of dogs and doggerel. *American Imago, 53*: 269–280.
Moradi, T. (2010). Eastern intersubjectivity: relational homes for frailty and death. In: S. Akhtar (Ed.), *The Wound of Mortality: Fear, Denial, and Acceptance of Death* (pp. 135–154). Lanham, MD: Jason Aronson.
Murphy, W. F. (1957). Some clinical aspects of the body ego. *Psychoanalytic Review, 44*: 462–477.

Nagera, H. (1970). Children's reactions to the death of important objects. *Psychoanalytic Study of the Child, 25*: 369–392.
Nagpal, A. (2011). A Hindu reading of Freud's "Beyond the Pleasure Principle". In: S. Akhtar & M. K. O'Neil (Eds.), *On Freud's "Beyond the Pleasure Principle"* (pp. 230–249). London: Karnac.
Nagy, M. (1948). The child's theories concerning death. *Journal of Genetic Psychology, 73*: 3–27.
Neimeyer, R. A. (2001). *Meaning Reconstruction and the Experience of Loss*. Washington, DC: American Psychological Association.
Neubauer, P. (1983). The importance of the sibling experience. *Psychoanalytic Study of the Child, 38*: 325–336.
Niederland, W. (1968). Clinical observations on the "survivor syndrome". *International Journal of Psychoanalysis, 49*: 313–315.
Niederland, W. (1989). Trauma, loss, restoration, and creativity. In: D. R. Dietrich & P. C. Shabad (Eds.), *The Problem of Loss and Mourning* (pp. 61–83). Madison, CT: International Universities Press.
Nimroody, T. (2014). Mourning, identity, creativity. *Journal of the American Psychoanalytic Association, 62*: 313–321.
Notman, M. T. (2014). Reflections on widowhood and its effects on the self. *Psychodynamic Psychiatry, 42*: 65–88.
Oates, J. C. (2011). *A Widow's Story*. New York: HarperCollins.
Oltjenbruns, K. A. (1991). Positive outcomes of adolescent experience with grief. *Journal of Adolescent Research, 6*: 43–53.
Ordinary People (1980). Produced by Paramount Pictures; directed by R. Redford.
Ornstein, A. (2010). The missing tombstone: reflections on mourning and creativity. *Journal of the American Psychoanalytic Association, 58*: 631–648.
Palgi, P., & Abramovitch, H. (1984). Death: a cross-cultural perspective. *Annual Review of Anthropology, 13*: 385–417.
Parens, H. (1988). Siblings in early childhood: some direct observational findings. *Psychoanalytic Inquiry, 8*: 31–50.
Parens, H. (2001). An obstacle to the child's coping with object loss. In: S. Akhtar (Ed.), *Three Faces of Mourning: Melancholia, Manic Defense, and Moving On* (pp. 157–183). Lanham, MD: Jason Aronson.
Parens, H. (2010). Children's understanding of death. In: S. Akhtar (Ed.), *The Wound of Mortality: Fear, Denial, and Acceptance of Death* (pp. 37–50). Lanham, MD: Jason Aronson.
Parkes, C. (1972). *Bereavement: Studies of Grief in Adult Life*. New York: International Universities Press.
Parkes, C. (1975). Psycho-social transitions: comparison between reactions to loss of a limb and loss of a spouse. *British Journal of Psychiatry, 127*: 204–210.

Pelento, M. L. (2007). Mourning for "missing" people. In: L. G. Fiorini, T. Bokanowski, & S. Lewkowicz (Eds.), *On Freud's "Mourning and Melancholia"* (pp. 56–70). London: Karnac.
Pellegrini, A. (2009). The dogs of war and the dogs at home: thresholds of loss. *American Imago, 66*: 231–251.
Piaget, J. (1936). *Origins of Intelligence in the Child*. London: Routledge & Kegan Paul.
Plath, S. (1961). Widow. In: T. Hughes (Ed.), *Collected Poems: Sylvia Plath* (pp. 164–165). New York: Harper & Row, 1981.
Poland, W. (2000). The analyst's witnessing and otherness. *Journal of the American Psychoanalytic Assocation, 48*: 17–34.
Pollock, G. H. (1961). Mourning and adaptation. *International Journal of Psychoanalysis, 42*: 341–361.
Pollock, G. H. (1962). Childhood parent and sibling loss in adult patients. *Archives of General Psychiatry, 7*: 295–306.
Pollock, G. H. (1966). Mourning and childhood loss: their possible significance in the Josef Breuer-Bertha Pappenheim relationship. *Bulletin of Associated Psychoanalytic Medicine, 5*: 51–54.
Pollock, G. H. (1968). The possible significance of childhood object loss in the Josef Breuer-Berth Pappenheim (Anna O.)—Sigmund Freud relationship. *Journal of the American Psychoanalytic Association, 16*: 711–739.
Pollock, G. H. (1970). Anniversary reactions, trauma, and mourning. *Psychoanalytic Quarterly, 39*: 347–371.
Pollock, G. H. (1971). On time, death, and immortality. *Psychoanalytic Quarterly, 40*: 435–446.
Pollock, G. H. (1972). On mourning and anniversaries: the relationship of culturally constituted defensive systems to intra-psychic adaptive process. *Israel Annals of Psychiatry, 10*: 9–40.
Pollock, G. H. (1976). Manifestations of abnormal mourning: homicide and suicide following the death of another. *Annals of Psychoanalysis, 4*: 225–249.
Pollock, G. H. (1978a). Process and affect: mourning and grief. *International Journal of Psychoanalysis, 59*: 255–276.
Pollock, G. H. (1978b). On siblings: childhood sibling loss and creativity. *Annals of Psychoanalysis, 14*: 5–34.
Pollock, G. H. (1989). The mourning process, the creative process, and the creation. In: D. R. Dietrich & P. C. Shabad (Eds.), *The Problem of Loss and Mourning* (pp. 27–59). Madison, CT: International Universities Press.
Provence, S., & Solnit, A. (1983). Development-promoting aspects of the sibling experience. *Psychoanalytic Study of the Child, 38*: 337–351.
Ramachandran, V. S., & Blakeslee, S. (1998). *Phantoms in the Brain*. New York: William Morrow.

Ramzy, I., & Wallerstein, R. S. (1958). Pain, fear, and anxiety: a study of their interrelationships. *Psychoanalytic Study of the Child, 13*: 147–189.
Rando, T. (1986). *Parental Loss of a Child*. Champaign, IL: Research Press.
Rangell, L. (1963). On friendship. *Journal of the American Psychoanalytic Association, 11*: 3–54.
Rapaport, D. (1960). The structure of psychoanalytic theory. *Psychological Issues, 6*: 39–72.
Rees, W. D., & Lutkins, S. G. (1967). Mortality of bereavement. *British Medical Journal, 4*: 13–16.
Rehm, D. (2016). *On My Own*. New York: Alfred A. Knopf.
Reik, T. (1948). *Listening with the Third Ear*. New York: Farrar, Straus and Giroux, 1983.
Roach, M. (2003). *Stiff: The Curious Lives of Human Cadavers*. New York: W. W. Norton.
Rogers, F. (1998) *When a Pet Dies*. New York: Putnam & Gosset.
Roiphe, A. (2008). *Epilogue: A Memoir*. New York: HarperCollins.
Roland, A. (1987). The familial self, the individualized self, and the transcendent self: psychoanalytic reflections on India and America. *Psychoanalytic Review, 74*: 237–250.
Rosaldo, R. (1989). Introduction: grief and a headhunter's rage. In: *Culture and Truth: The Remaking of Social Analysis* (pp. 1–25). Boston, MA: Beacon Press, 1993.
Rosaldo, R. (1993). *Culture and Truth: The Remaking of Social Analysis*. Boston, MA: Beacon Press.
Rubin, L. B. (1986). On men and friendship. *Psychoanalytic Review, 73*: 165–181.
Rubin, S. S. (1996). The wounded family: bereaved parents and the impact of adult child loss. In: D. Klass, P. R. Silverman, & S. L. Nickman (Eds.), *Continuing Bonds: New Understandings of Grief* (pp. 217–232). Washington, DC: Taylor & Francis.
Rudnytsky, P. L. (1988). Redefining the revenant—guilt and sibling loss in Guntrip and Freud. *Psychoanalytic Study of the Child, 43*: 423–432.
Sacks, A. M. (1998). Bereavement: a special disorder of object loss: a comparison of two cases. *Psychoanalytic Psychology, 15*: 215–229.
Sacks, A. M. (2008). The therapeutic use of pets in private practice. *British Journal of Psychotherapy, 24*: 501–521.
Schafer, R. (1968). *Aspects of Internalization*. Madison, CT: International Universities Press.
Schlesinger, H. (2001). Technical problems in analysing the mourning patient. In: S. Akhtar (Ed.), *Three Faces of Mourning: Melancholia, Manic Defense, and Moving On* (pp. 115–140). Northvale, NJ: Jason Aronson.

Schmidl, F. (1959). Sigmund Freud and Ludwig Binswanger. *Psychoanalytic Quarterly*, 28: 40–58.
Schulman, R. (2009). Commentary on friendship. In: S. Akhtar (Ed.), *Good Feelings: Psychoanalytic Reflections on Positive Attitudes and Emotions* (pp. 267–274). London: Karnac.
Segal, N. L. (2012). *Born Together—Reared Apart: the Landmark Minnesota Twin Study*. Cambridge, MA: Harvard University Press.
Settlage, C. (2001). Defenses evoked by early childhood loss: their impact on life-span development. In: S. Akhtar (Ed.), *Three Faces of Mourning: Melancholia, Manic Defense, and Moving On* (pp. 47–94). Northvale, NJ: Jason Aronson.
Shakespeare, W. (1603). *The Tragedy of Hamlet, Prince of Denmark*. New York: Signet, 1998.
Shanor, K., & Kanwal, J. (2009). *Bats Sing, Mice Giggle: Revealing the Secret Lives of Animals*. London: Icon.
Shapiro, E. (1994). *Grief as a Family Process: A Developmental Approach to Clinical Practice*. New York: Guilford Press.
Sharpe, S. A., & Rosenblatt, A. D. (1994). Oedipal sibling triangles. *Journal of the American Psychoanalytic Association*, 42: 491–523.
Sherby, L. B. (2013). *Love and Loss in Life and in Treatment*. New York: Routledge.
Shneidman, E. (2008). *A Commonsense Book of Death*. Lanham, MD: Rowman & Littlefield.
Silverman, P., & Klass, D. (1996). Examining the dominant model-introduction: what's the problem? In: D. Klass, P. Silverman, & S. Nickman (Eds.), *Continuing Bonds: New Understandings of Grief* (pp. 3–27). Washington, DC: Taylor & Francis.
Silverman, P., & Worden, J. (1993). Children's reactions to the death of a parent. In: M. Stroebe, W. Stroebe, & R. Hansson (Eds.), *Bereavement: A Source Book of Research and Intervention* (pp. 41–59). New York: Cambridge University Press.
Singer, E. (1971). The patient aids the analyst: some clinical and theoretical observations. In: B. Landis & E. S. Tauber (Eds.), *The Name of Life: Essays in Honor of Erich Fromm* (pp. 56–58). New York: Holt, Rinehart and Winston.
Smilansky, S. (1987). *On Death: Helping Children Understand and Cope*. New York: Peter Lang.
Smilevski, G. (2012). *Freud's Sister: A Novel*. New York: Penguin.
Solnit, A. (1983). The sibling experience. *Psychoanalytic Study of the Child*, 38: 281–284.
Sophocles (441 BC). *Antigone*. Clayton, DE: Prestwick House, 1998.

Spitz, R. (1946). Anaclitic depression: an inquiry into the genesis of psychiatric conditions in early childhood. *Psychoanalytic Study of the Child, 2*: 313–342.

Stephen, M. (1998). Consuming the dead: a Kleinian perspective on death rituals cross-culturally. *International Journal of Psychoanalysis, 79*: 1173–1194.

Stern, D. B. (1994). Conceptions of structure in interpersonal psychoanalysis—a reading of the literature. *Contemporary Psychoanalysis, 30*: 255–300.

Stroebe, H., & Schut, H. (1999). The dual process model of coping with bereavement: rational and descriptive. *Death Studies, 23*: 197–224.

Stroebe, M. S. (1994). The broken heart phenomenon: an examination of the mortality of bereavement. *Journal of Community and Applied Social Psychology, 4*: 47–61.

Sullivan, H. S. (1953). *The Interpersonal Theory of Psychiatry*. New York: W. W. Norton.

Sussillo, M. V. (2005). Beyond the grave—adolescent parental loss: Letting go and holding on. *Psychoanalytic Dialogues, 15*: 499–527.

Szalita, A. (1968). Reanalysis. *Contemporary Psychoanalysis, 4*: 83–102.

Terhune, A. (1919). *Lad: A Dog*. New York: Dutton.

Terhune, A. (1922). *Further Adventures of Lad*. New York: Grosset & Dunlap.

Volkan, V. D. (1972). The linking objects of pathological mourners. *Archives of General Psychiatry, 27*: 215–221.

Volkan, V. D. (1981). *Linking Objects and Linking Phenomena: A Study of the Forms, Symptoms, Metapsychology, and Therapy of Complicated Mourning*. New York: International Universities Press.

Volkan, V. D. (1984). Complicated mourning. *The Annual of Psychoanalysis, 12*: 323–348.

Volkan, V. D. (2007). Not letting go: from individual perennial mourners to societies with entitlement ideologies. In: L. G. Fiorini, T. Bokanowski, & S. Lewkowicz (Eds.), *On Freud's "Mourning and Melancholia"* (pp. 90–109). London: Karnac.

Volkan, V. D., Ast, G., & Greer, W. F. (1997). *Siblings in the Unconscious and Psycho-pathology*. Madison, CT: International Universities Press.

Volkan, V. D., Cilluffo, A. F., & Sarvay, T. L. (1975). Re-grief therapy and the function of the linking object as a key to stimulate emotionality. In: P. T. Olsen (Ed.), *Emotional Flooding* (pp. 179–224). New York: Human Sciences Press.

Vormbrock, J. K., & Grossberg, J. M. (1988). Cardiovascular effects of human-pet interactions. *Journal of Behavioral Medicine, 5*: 509–517.

Weiss, E. (1934). Bodily pain and mental pain. *International Journal of Psychoanalysis, 15*: 1–13.

Wheelis, A. (1966). *The Illusionless Man*. New York: Harper Colophon.
White, E. B. (1952). *Charlotte's Web*. New York: Harper Brothers.
White, M. (Ed.) (2013). *E. B. White on Dogs*. Gardiner, ME: Tilbury House Publishers.
Wilson, M. (2015). A Manhattan fortuneteller cost him fortune after fortune. *The New York Times*, June 5. Retrieved from http://www.nytimes.com/2015/06/06/nyregion, April 4, 2016.
Winnicott, D. W. (1960a). Ego distortion in terms of true and false self. In: *Maturational Processes and the Facilitating Environment* (pp. 140–152). New York: International Universities Press, 1965.
Winnicott, D. W. (1960b). The theory of parent–infant relationship. *International Journal of Psychoanalysis*, 41: 585–595.
Wolfenstein, M. (1966). How is mourning possible? *Psychoanalytic Study of the Child*, 21: 93–123.
Wolfenstein, M. (1969). Loss, rage, and repetition. *Psychoanalytic Study of the Child*, 24: 432–460.
Wolfenstein, M. (1973). The image of the lost parent. *Psychoanalytic Study of the Child*, 28: 433–456.
Wolman, T. (2015). Primal greed, developmental greed, and terminal greed. In: S. Akhtar (Ed.), *Greed: Developmental, Cultural and Clinical Realms* (pp. 43–69). London: Karnac.
Woodward, J. (2010). *The Lone Twin: Understanding Twin Bereavement and Loss*. London: Karnac.
Zarnegar, G. (2015). Amputated selfhood and phantom selves: musings and reflections on heretofore unformulated experience. *International Journal of Psychoanalytic Self Psychology*, 10: 261–274.

INDEX

Abend, S. M., 106
Aberbach, D., 8
Abraham, K., 120
Abramovitch, H., 186
Ackerman, P. H., 92
Adelman, A. J., 120, 124
adult mourning, 21, 38 see also:
 mother loss
Aiken, J., 149
Ainslie, R., 84, 91
Akhtar, S., 17–18, 22, 24, 26, 28, 40–41,
 46, 52, 69, 83, 85, 151, 190
Alexander, E., 113
Altman, L., 24
American Psychiatric Association
 see Diagnostic and Statistical
 Manual of Mental Disorders 5
Anderson, C. L., 15, 120, 124
Andersson, G., 18
Anisfeld, L., 90
anniversary reactions, 7–8, 92, 108–109,
 119
Anzieu, D., 65

Aragno, A., 123–124, 182
Aries, P., 102, 172, 177
Ast, G., 84, 90

Baillargeon, R., 171
Barthelme, D., 81
Beekman, A. T., 18
Benedict, R., 173
Benjamin, J., 98
bereaved individual, 14–15 see also:
 bereavement
bereavement, xviii, 3, 27–28, 169
 see also: grieving process;
 treatment implications
 bereaved brain, 186–189
 bereaved individual, 14–15
 broken heart syndrome, 188
 children's capacity to mourn,
  20–24
 dynamics determination, 174
 essence of, 3
 established pathological mourning,
  13–15

207

208 INDEX

evidence for physical reality in brains, 187
Freud's views, 4–5
gender differences, 24–26
Ilongot tribe, 170
inoptimally addressed realms, 20
internalization of lost object, 185–186
interpersonal perspective on, 184–186
maladies, 15
melancholia, 11–13
memory, 186
mental pain, 12
mourning, 183
normal reaction to, 4
pathological outcomes, 11
phantom personification, 185
and responsibility, 176–178
role of culture, 26–27
security operations, 185
subsequent contributions, 5–9
totemic feast, 26
work of mourning, 4, 9
Berman, L. E., 90
Binswanger, Ludwig, 5
Bion, W. R., 26
Blakeslee, S., 185
Blanton, S., 77
body disposal methods, 27
Bokanowski, T., 8
Bonanno, G. A., 103–104
Bonaparte, M., 87, 120
and dogs, 144
friendship with Freud, 145
Bouchard, J. J., 92
Bourget, D., 86
Bower, T. G. R., 171
Bowlby, J., 20–21, 37, 42, 121–122
Brenner, C., 7
broken heart phenomenon, 103 *see also*: death of spouse
broken heart syndrome, 188 *see also*: bereavement
Bromberg, P. M., 175

Buck, 154 *see also*: death of pet
Burlingham, D., 20, 91–92
and Freud, S., 144, 147

Cadmus, F., 149
Cain, A. C., 88, 90
Cain, B. S., 90
Campos, R. G., 89
Carrington, A., 77
Casement, P. J., 110, 115, 125, 140
Cheever, J., 86
child's death, 117, 140–141 *see also*: Freud, S.
  author's personal analysis, 131–140
  author's prose and poetry, 126–131
  mourning, 122
  when a child dies, 124–126
child's protective defenses, 47 *see also*: father loss; mother loss
childhood parental loss, 18 *see also*: father loss; mother loss
childish jealousy, 87 *see also*: sibling loss
children's capacity to mourn, 20–24 *see also*: bereavement; father loss; mother loss
Chow, 144 *see also*: death of pet
Cilluffo, A. F., 17
Colarusso, C. A., 71–72
collies, 154 *see also*: death of pet
Collins, B., 151
Colson, D. B., 114
competitiveness, 70
conjunctive motivations, 185, 190
Conway, J. K., 90
Cournos, F., 23, 47
Coutts, M., 99, 113
Crehan, G., 88
Cuijpers, P., 18

de Beurs, D., 18
death, 102, 169, 189 *see also*: father loss; mother loss; sibling loss
  acceptance of time, 172
  awareness and self-awareness, 186
  bereaved brain, 186–189

INDEX

bereavement and responsibility, 176–178
disenfranchised grief, 169
how we carry on, 179–184
interpersonal perspective on bereavement, 184–186
object permanence, 171
reunion fantasies, 180
role of encountering death, 171
of sounds and silence, 174–176
stories and theories, 173–174
theory of trauma and dissociation, 175
things we turn to, 178–179
ways of handling death and aftermath, 172
death of pet, 143, 164–166
author's dogs and their deaths, 153–159
Buck, 154
chow, 144
clinical vignette, 160–164
collies, 154
dog and owner, 143
Freud and Bonaparte, 145–148
making life and death decisions and conflicted bereavement, 159–160
our love affair with dogs, 148–153
therapy dog pilot program, 149
death of spouse, 97, 112
anniversary, 108–109
back to work, 105–107
being lonely, 110–112
beyond pity, 103–104
broken heart phenomenon, 103
grief and headhunter's rage, 109
hallucinatory wishful psychosis, 103
magical thinking, 110
memorial, 100–101
moment before and moment after, 99–100
new life, 104–105
no emergency contact, 102–103

regrets, 101–102
renovation, 107–108
sublimatory activity, 107
sudden and expected deaths, 98–99
visitations, 103
widow, 109–110
deferred obedience, 59 *see also*: father loss
depression *see* melancholia
depressive position, 59
Deraniyagala, S., 170
Deutsch, H., 15, 120
DeVos, J., 171
Diagnostic and Statistical Manual of Mental Disorders 5 (DSM-5), 12
Didion, J., 45, 110, 113
disenfranchised grief, 169 *see also*: death
Doka, J. K., 113, 169, 189
Doolittle, H. D., 149
drive theory, 118
DSM-5 *see Diagnostic and Statistical Manual of Mental Disorders 5*

Edwards, J., 83
Engel, G. L., 8, 92, 123
Erickson, M. E., 88
Erikson, E. H., 171
established pathological mourning, 13–15 *see also*: bereavement
treatment, 16–17
Etezady, H., 26

Fairbairn, W. R. D., 87
Fanos, J. H., 83, 88–89
Fast, I., 88
father loss, 57, 79–81 *see also*: mother loss
in adulthood, 80
competitiveness, 70
contemporary views on, 69–73
deferred obedience, 59–60
depressive position, 59
developmental functions for grandfather-hood, 72

Freud and, 65–69
gender differences in processing of, 80–81
honor thy father, 63–65
incest taboo, 60
killing and murder, 62
life and death of author's father, 73–79
malaise of civilization, 69
primal greed, 58
and primal horde, 58–63
Torah fifth commandment, 63
triadic formula, 61–62
Faulkner, W., 86
Fenichel, O., 120
Fichtner, G., 5
Fiorini, L. G., 8
Fort, C., 187
Foster, B., 8
Foster, M., 22
Frankiel, R. V., 38
Freud, A., 20
Freud, E., 119
Freud, S., 4, 12, 20, 26, 58–59, 77, 87
see also: child's death
adult mourning, 38
drive theory, 118
early followers of, 120–121
favorite dogs, 144
friendship with Marie Bonaparte, 145
about grief, 4
and loss of father, 65–69
malaise of civilization, 69
mourning, 183
newer models of his theory, 123–124
personal journey, 118–120
sibling rivalry, 84
subsequent contributors to, 121–123
theory enlarged, 120
views, 4–5
Friedman, G. W., 113
Frosch, J., 15
funus, 177

Furman, E., 20–21, 37, 51–52, 55, 122, 126
Furman, R., 37, 39

Gagné, P., 86
Gaines, R., 111, 124
Gay, P., 87, 119
Genosko, G., 146
Gorer, G., 102
grandfather-hood developmental functions, 72 *see also*: father loss
Greenspan, S. I., 9
Greer, W. F., 84, 90
grief, xviii *see also*: bereavement
and headhunter's rage, 109 *see also*: death of spouse
normal, 16
symptoms of, 7
types of, 113
grieving process *see also*: bereavement
bereaved's premorbid personality, 9–10
bereaved's relationship with deceased, 10
consequences of death, 11
factors complicating, 9
nature of death, 11
survivor's guilt, 10
work of mourning, 9
Grinker, R., Jr., 149
Grollman, E., 189
Grossberg, J. M., 149
Grotstein, J., 190
Grubb, C. A., 126
Gündel, H., 187
Guntrip, H., 87
Guzder, J., 26

Hagman, G., 7, 15, 173
hallucinatory wishful psychosis, 103 *see also*: death of spouse
Harris, M., 29
Harris, T., 86
Hartman, S., 26
Hilgard, J., 7
Hitchcock, J., 28

INDEX   211

Hoffman, L., 22
holding environment, 52
Holdt-Henningsen, K., 18
Holmes, T. H., 113
Holmes–Rahe Stress Inventory, 113
Huibers, M. J., 18

Ilongot tribe, 170 *see also*: bereavement
internalization of lost object, 185–186
    see also: bereavement
Irving, J., 38

Jacobson, E., 44
Jamison, K. R., 113
Johnson, E., 22
Jones, E., 120

Kanefield, 40
Kanwal, G., 180
Kanwal, J., 179
Kaprio, J., 103
Karyotaki, E., 18
Katha Upanishad, 190
Keefe, P. R., 90
Kernberg, O. F., 170, 176, 181–182
    mourning, 183
Kerouac, J., 90
Kieffer, C., 90
Killingmo, B., 17
Klass, D., 104, 120, 125
Klein, M., 7, 9, 28, 41, 53, 59, 121, 190
Knight, E. M., 154
Koole, S. L., 18
Koskenvuo, M., 103
Kramer, S., 83, 85
Krueger, D. W., 77
Kubler-Ross, E., 83
Kundalia, N. D., 176

Lane, R. D., 187
Leavy, S. A., 98
Leon, I., 8, 104, 107, 115, 126, 140
Lewin, V., 9
Lewis, C. S., 104, 113
Lewkowicz, S., 8
Lindemann, E., 5

linking object, 122, 178
Littrell, L., 187
Livingston, 170
Loewald, H., 121
London, J., 154
Lutkins, S. G., 103
Lykken, D. J., 92

magical thinking, 110 *see also*: death
    of spouse
maladies, 15
Malawista, K. L., 40, 120, 124
manic defense, 41 *see also*: mother loss
man-made disasters, 170
Martin, T. L., 113
Martinson, I. M., 89
Masur, C., 25
McGue, M., 92
meanings of money, 77
meddling, 19
melancholia, 4, 11–13 *see also*:
    bereavement
    management, 17–18
Melgar, M. C., 8
memory, 186 *see also*: bereavement
mental pain, 4, 12–13, 22, 28, 52, 175,
    186
Meyers, H., 8, 25
middle distance, 45
Mitchell, E., 84, 126
Mitchell, J., 83
Molnar, M., 152
Moradi, T., 26
mother loss, 33, 54–55 *see also*:
    childhood parental loss;
    children's capacity to mourn;
    father loss
    adult mourning, 21, 38
    being in fantasy, 44–45
    case study, 33–39, 42–51
    child's protective defenses, 47
    common response to catastrophic
        loss, 46–47
    continual losing and re-finding of
        missing part, 38
    continual sense of disequilibrium, 44

going forward, 51–53
holding environment, 52
initial reactions to loss, 39–42
lack of emotion, 39
love to neutralize destructive
   aggression, 52–53
manic defense, 41
middle distance, 45
seeking other maternal figures, 51
treatment, 53–54
mourning, xviii, 4, 122, 183 *see also*:
   bereavement
   impact of gender upon, 24
   -liberation process, 6
   outcomes, 7
Murphy, W. F., 187

Nagera, H., 20
Nagpal, A., 26
Nagy, M., 22
Neimeyer, R. A., 124
Neubauer, P., 84
Nickerson, B. G., 89
Nickman, S. L., 104
Niederland, W., 10, 107
Nimroody, T., 115
normal grief, 3, 5, 7, 9, 11, 13, 16, 118
Notman, M. T., 98

Oates, J. C., 113
object permanence, 171
O'Connor, M.-F., 187
Oltjenbruns, K. A., 89
Ornstein, A., 175

Palgi, P., 186
Parens, H., 54, 84
Parkes, C., 7, 21, 122, 187
Pelento, M. L., 8
Pellegrini, A., 152
personal stories of bereavement, xvii
phantom personification, 185 *see also*:
   bereavement
Piaget, J., 171
Plath, S.
   poem on widow, 109
   self-restoration, 8

Platt, C., 181
poems, 140 *see also*: child's death;
   Plath, S.
Poland, W., 17
Pollock, G. H., 6–7, 23, 88, 107, 121,
   170, 179, 188
preoedipal character organization, 10
primal greed, 58
Provence, S., 84

Rahe, R. H., 113
Ramachandran, V. S., 185
Ramzy, I., 187
Rando, T., 125
Rangell, L., 190
Rapaport, D., 27
Rees, W. D., 103
re-grief therapy, 17
Rehm, D., 113
Reik, T., 17
reparation, 28
replacement child, 90 *see also*:
   sibling loss
reunion fantasies, 180 *see also*: death
Reynolds, C. F., 18
Richards, A. D., 90
Rita, H., 103
Roach, M., 29
Robays, J., 18
Rogers, F., 153
Roiphe, A., 113
Roland, A., 173
Rosaldo, R., 101, 109
Rosenblatt, A. D., 84, 88
Rubin, L. B., 190
Rubin, S. S., 123
Rudnytsky, P. L., 87, 141

Sacks, A. M., 9, 149
Sarvay, T. L., 17
Schafer, R., 121
Schlesinger, H., 19
Schmidl, F., 118–119
Schulman, R., 190
Schut, H., 124
security operations, 185
Segal, N. L., 92

Settlage, C., 22
Shanor, K., 179
Shapiro, E., 119, 124–125
sharing sorrow, xvii
Sharpe, S. A., 84, 88
Sherby, L. B., 114
shiva, 100, 113 *see also*: death of spouse
Shneidman, E., 27
sibling loss, 83
  adult sibling loss, 90–91
  author's personal reflections, 93–96
  bereavement process, 88
  in childhood, 86–90
  childish jealousy, 87
  loss of twin, 91–93
  neglect of sibling relationships, 85
  nuances of sibling relationship, 84–86
  post-traumatic stress syndrome, 88
  replacement child, 90
  sibling rivalry, 84, 86
Sijbrandij, M., 18
Silverman, P., 24, 44, 104, 120
Singer, E., 106
Smilansky, S., 38
Smilevski, G., 87
Smit, Y., 18
Smolar, A., 69
Smolen, 178
social developmental theory
     of mourning, 124
Solnit, A., 84
spectrum of emotional reactions
     see bereavement
Spitz, R., 20
Stephen, M., 190
Stern, D. B., 185
stress cardiomyopathy, 188
Stroebe, H., 124
Stroebe, M. S., 103, 188
Sullivan, H. S., 184, 190
  formulation, 185–186 *see also*:
     bereavement
survivor's guilt, 10 *see also*: grieving
     process
Sussillo, M. V., 120
Szalita, A., 85

Tellegen, A., 92
Terhune, A., 154
theory of trauma and dissociation, 175
     see also: death
therapy dog pilot program, 149 *see also*:
     death of pet
totemic feast, 26
treatment implications, 16 *see also*:
     bereavement
  depression management, 17–18
  established pathological mourning
     treatment, 16–17
  handling childhood parental loss
     impact, 18
  meddling, 19
  re-grief therapy, 17
  responding to normal grief, 16
  tackling occurrence of grief, 18–20
triadic formula, 61–62

Upanishads, 190

visitations, 103 *see also*: death of spouse
Volkan, V. D., 8, 13–14, 17, 83–84, 90, 122, 178
  linking object, 122
  mourning, 183
Vormbrock, J. K., 149

Wallerstein, R. S., 187
Weiss, E., 13
Wheelis, A., 28
White, E. B., 152
White, M., 152
widow, 109–110 *see also*: death of
     spouse
Wilson, M., 180
Winnicott, D. W., 38, 52, 87, 149
Wolfenstein, M., 20–21, 37
Wolman, T., 58, 175, 180
Woodward, J., 93
Worden, J., 24, 44
work of mourning, 4, 6, 9, 38, 69, 72–73, 118, 121, 124
Wright, J., 22

Zarnegar, G., 187